C# Class Design Handbook:
Coding Effective Classes

Richard Conway
Teun Duynstee
Ben Hyrman
Roger Rowland
James Speer of Charteris plc

Apress™

C# Class Design Handbook:
Coding Effective Classes

ISBN (pbk): 1-59059-257-3

Printed and bound in the United States of America 2345678910

Distributed to the book trade in the United States by Springer-Verlag New York, Inc., 175 Fifth Avenue, New York, NY, 10010 and outside the United States by Springer-Verlag GmbH & Co. KG, Tiergartenstr. 17, 69112 Heidelberg, Germany.

In the United States: phone 1-800-SPRINGER, email orders@springer-ny.com, or visit http://www.springer-ny.com. Outside the United States: fax +49 6221 345229, email orders@springer.de, or visit http://www.springer.de.

For information on translations, please contact Apress directly at 2560 Ninth Street, Suite 219, Berkeley, CA 94710. Phone 510-549-5930, fax 510-549-5939, email info@apress.com, or visit http://www.apress.com.

The information in this book is distributed on an "as is" basis, without warranty. Although every precaution has been taken in the preparation of this work, neither the author(s) nor Apress shall have any liability to any person or entity with respect to any loss or damage caused or alleged to be caused directly or indirectly by the information contained in this work.

The source code for this book is available to readers at http://www.apress.com in the Downloads section.

Some material was first published in a different form in *Visual Basic .NET Class Design Handbook* (1-86100-708-6), May 2002.

Credits

About the Authors

Richard Conway

Richard Conway started programming BASIC with the ZX81 at an early age later graduating to using BASIC and 6502 assembly language, COMAL, and Pascal for the BBC B and Archimedes RISC machines. He is an independent software consultant who lives and works in London. He has been using Microsoft technologies for many years and has architected and built enterprise systems for the likes of IBM, Merrill Lynch, and Reuters. He has focused his development on Windows DNA including various tools and languages such as COM+, VB, XML, C++, J++, BizTalk, and more recently, Data Warehousing. He has been actively involved in EAP trials with Microsoft for .NET My Services and the .NET Compact Framework. He has spent the last two and a half years since the release of the technical preview (of VS.NET) programming proof-of-concept and enterprise system projects in C#. His special area of interest is Network Security and Cryptography. Richard is a contributor to both *C# Today* and *ASP Today*. He is currently involved in a product development and consultancy alliance – http://www.vertexion.co.uk – specializing in data warehousing and security products.

He can be contacted at richard.conway@vertexon.co.uk.

Teun Duynstee

Teun Duynstee lives in the Netherlands. He works with Macaw as a lead software developer and loves programming, his girlfriend Marjolein, and Arnie the cat.

Ben Hyrman

Ben works as a Program Architect for Best Buy, in tropical Minneapolis, Minnesota. Ben enjoys the balmy Minnesota weather with his loving wife, Dawn, and an overactive mutt of a dog, Bandit. When they're not busy with work or off on road trips, Ben and Dawn enjoy painting their house and arguing over database design patterns.

I would like to thank Damon Allison for being my sounding board for all of my crazy ideas. I'd also like to thank Richard Scott, because he's British and he asked me to. Lastly, I'd like to thank Wrox for this excellent opportunity.

Roger Rowland

Roger Rowland is a freelance IT Consultant based in the UK. He has 25 years of software development experience on a variety of platforms, and is a regular contributor to the Wrox *C# Today* web site. He currently specializes in Microsoft technologies including VC++, VB, C#, SQL, and ASP. Roger is a member of the Institution of Analysts and Programmers, a professional member of the British Computer Society, and a member of the IEEE Computer Society. He holds a Masters Degree in computing and is currently undertaking a part-time PhD at the University of East Anglia researching into medical imaging and computer assisted surgery. Research techniques include 3D graphics and volume rendering using OpenGL, and he has published a number of academic papers. Married, with two children and always incredibly busy, Roger may nevertheless be contacted at roger.rowland@rmrsystems.co.uk.

James Speer of Charteris plc

James has been a software developer since 1987, beginning his career programming in BCPL and C++. He currently specializes in distributed .NET component development, particularly - C#, .NET Remoting, Serviced Components and MSMQ. James is currently employed by Charteris plc (www.charteris.com) as a Senior Developer and can be reached at james.speer@charteris.com.

Thanks to Mom and Dad for the Acorn Electron and June for lending me your Vic 20.

C#

Class Design

Handbook

Table of
Contents

Table of Contents

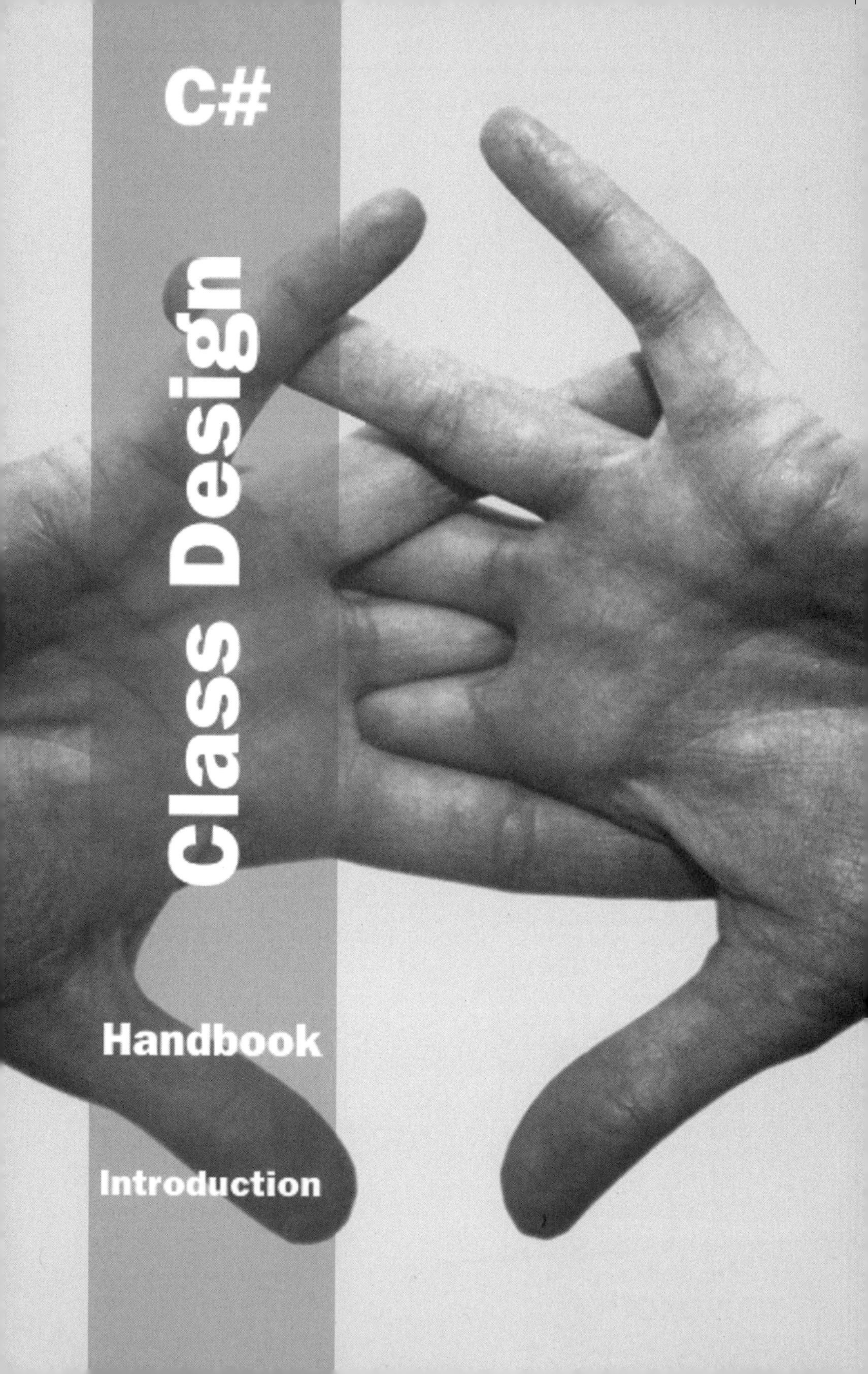
C#
Class Design
Handbook
Introduction

Introduction

C# is a language that follows in a grand tradition of programming language design; it draws its influences from C++ and Java, and even Delphi and Visual Basic – a rich inheritance, which provides it with much that is familiar to many developers, but also much that is alien or unexpected.

Programmers unfamiliar with object-oriented, C-family, 'curly-bracket' languages, perhaps coming to C# from a background with Visual Basic 6 or ASP VBScript, often find the scope of the object-oriented features in C# daunting. Those coming from other object-oriented platforms – C++ or Java for example – find some of C#'s additional facilities surprising or confusing, while other, seemingly familiar syntaxes can behave in curiously different ways.

This book takes the lid off C#'s object-oriented model, and examines how we use C# as a language for creating classes (and, indeed, other kinds of types). Since everything we code in C# is a type, all our logic belongs to methods of types, and the state of our program at any moment is tied up in the values stored in the fields of instances of types in memory. A good understanding of how to create those types is therefore fundamental to good C# programming.

We'll explore what options C# gives us in declaring types and type members in our code, and the impact our decisions will have on code that uses our types. We'll see how we can code differently when our types are for public use, and when types are for use within our own code. We'll look at what we can do to ensure our types are only used in ways we design for, and how we can expose functionality from our types in a consistent, logical, predictable, and user-friendly manner, for other code to exploit.

Who Is This Book For?

This book is for C# developers who want to explore the full capabilities of the .NET platform. If you want to define your own data types, build your own class hierarchies, and build classes with robust interfaces, then you need a deep understanding of the mechanisms C# provides for defining classes. That is the subject of this book.

This book assumes you're already coding with C#, you're already familiar with the basic syntax, and you're regularly writing code that works. You should be familiar with your chosen development tools and know how to compile and run C# code.

You should be aware of .NET's basic object-orientation mechanisms – for example, that objects are instances of classes, how objects are instantiated, and how methods and properties on an object are accessed. We'll recap on the meaning and syntax of most of C#'s class construction keywords as we discuss them, however.

What Does This Book Cover?

Every time we write code in C#, we're coding a class – it's unavoidable. This book addresses the decisions we make as programmers in this environment, by placing them in the context of what they really are: decisions about class design. So, when we write a method and choose whether to make it `static`, whether it is to be `public` or `private`, what parameters it should take, and so on, this book helps us look at those decisions in the context of how they impact on the design of a class.

This book takes a step back from the code we write every day and asks, "What is it really doing?" It asks you not to consider each C# keyword or syntax construction just in terms of its effect, but to consider how it accomplishes that effect. In the course of this book, we'll see how all our code is compiled into .NET types; how we define type members; how type members are inherited; how types are aggregated into assemblies; how we can control the creation of instances of types; and many more aspects of effective class coding.

What Doesn't It Cover?

This isn't a book about object-oriented analysis and design, UML modeling, or design patterns – although we'll encounter all of these along the way, for detailed tutorials in these tools you should look elsewhere. It doesn't address the question of how to take a business problem, and decide which classes you should code to solve it. Instead, it focuses on the questions of implementation: how you can code a class that provides a particular kind of behavior.

It also isn't a fundamental introduction to object-orientation, although any C#
programmer should already be familiar with the idea of having an instance of an
object, and calling methods on it and accessing properties, even if not with the process
of defining your own types. If you're comfortable using objects, then this book will not
assume more than you know.

What Will You Learn?

The book takes a top-down look at what exactly makes up a class in .NET. We begin
by describing what a type is, and how classes relate to the .NET type framework. Then
we examine what makes up types: type members. We devote the majority of the book
to looking at the different mechanisms C# provides for defining type members
(methods, constructors, properties, operators, and events), and finally examine how
types go together to make up assemblies.

Chapter by chapter, here's what to expect:

❑ **Chapter 1 – Defining Types**

This chapter explains what exactly a type is, what role types play in .NET,
and what kinds of types exist. We also examine the different types we can
declare in C# and how they map to .NET types.

❑ **Chapter 2 – Type Members**

In the second chapter, we examine type members: what they are, how we
can define them, and how we can modify them using C# keywords. We
also examine the type members inherited by every type from the .NET root
class, System.Object.

❑ **Chapter 3 – Methods**

Methods are the workhorse of .NET applications; they contain all our
program logic. This chapter examines the behavior common to all methods,
and how simple methods are defined in C#. We look at how parameters
are passed to methods, and how methods return values, or throw
exceptions, to communicate back to the code that called them.

❑ **Chapter 4 – Properties and Operators**

Properties (both scalar and indexed) are a mechanism allowing us to create
specialized methods for accessing data belonging to our type. Operators are
specialized methods that allow consumers of our types to combine them
using convenient operator-based syntax. This chapter examines how
properties are implemented, how indexed properties work, and the
creation and use of operators.

❑ **Chapter 5 – Constructors and the Object Lifecycle**

Constructors are special methods that are called to initialize new instances of a type. In this chapter, we see how these special methods are coded, and how we can use them to control what code can create instances of a type. We'll also examine object cloning, conversion operators, and some common coding techniques for controlling the creation of instances of our classes.

❑ **Chapter 6 – Events and Delegates**

The most complex type member in C# is the Event, and the most complex of C#'s types is the delegate. Events are based on delegates, and the combination of the two can be quite daunting for programmers. This chapter explains how delegates work, and then how .NET provides its event infrastructure through delegate fields and specialized methods.

❑ **Chapter 7 – Inheritance and Polymorphism**

A type is more than the sum of its members; it also has all the members it inherits from its superclass as well. This chapter explains how .NET type inheritance works, when members are and aren't inherited, and how we can control and exploit it using C#. We also look at the role and use of interfaces and abstract classes.

❑ **Chapter 8 – Code Organization and Metadata**

When we code a class in C#, we have to make some decisions about where exactly to put it, both logically within a namespace structure, and physically, within a source file, and ultimately, within a .NET assembly. This chapter discusses these issues. We also see how to add data to our classes that may be of use to other code that makes use of them, using .NET metadata, and how to document our classes to provide information for other programmers about how they are used.

What Do You Need?

To make use of this book, you need to be able to compile and execute code written in C#. This means you will require either:

❑ The .NET Framework SDK obtainable from Microsoft's MSDN site (http://msdn.microsoft.com), in the Software Development Kits category. The download page at time of publication could be reached via the following URL:

http://msdn.microsoft.com/downloads/sample.asp?
url=/msdn-files/027/000/976/msdncompositedoc.xml

❑ A version of Visual Studio .NET that incorporates Visual C# .NET. The 2002 edition of the Visual C# .NET IDE is included with the following Microsoft products:

  • Microsoft Visual C# .NET Standard

  • Microsoft Visual Studio .NET Enterprise Architect

- Microsoft Visual Studio .NET Enterprise Developer

- Microsoft Visual Studio .NET Professional

The product homepage is at http://msdn.microsoft.com/vstudio/.

There are several .NET implementations for other platforms underway, and support for C# compilation on Linux, UNIX, and Windows is provided by the Mono project (http://www.go-mono.com/). Mono code does not have access to the full Microsoft .NET class library, but follows the same syntactic rules as Microsoft's C#, meaning the lessons in this book should apply in equal measure.

C#

Class Design

Handbook

1

1

Defining Types

C# is an object-oriented programming language, and one of the principles which guide its design is type safety. During object-oriented analysis and design, we identify the most important objects in our system, and consider how they will relate to each other. When we program in C#, classes are the main mechanism we use to define the behavior of the objects that will exist in our program at run time. However, C# offers us a great many ways to package up the code that defines our application – and not just in classes.

Whenever we code in C#, though, what we write are always **types**, and these types represent a combination of behavior and data storage requirements. When the program runs, it creates instances of types (which allocate the data storage required), and makes available the features of the types. Within the .NET environment, type-safe code only accesses the memory locations it is authorized to access and types interact only in well-defined, permitted ways. This is important for producing secure, stable applications that ensure even badly written code can't do too much damage, and plays by the rules.

This book aims to help C# developers gain a deeper and more confident understanding of how to build well designed classes that will behave correctly and consistently within the .NET Framework. Through exploration and examples, we will give you an awareness of the consequences of decisions made during the design and development phases, and will point out any not-so-obvious similarities with or differences from other object-oriented languages like C++ and Java.

We'll begin this book by looking at what exactly a type is. In this chapter, we'll examine .NET's type system, and the kinds of type available to us as developers.

Types

In programming, we use the term 'type' to describe a particular kind of value. For example, C++ and Java programmers will be familiar with types such as int, float, and double. For each type, the compiler knows the following information:

❑   How much memory to allocate when we create a value of this type

❑   What operations are allowed to be performed using this value

The concept of types is fundamental to strongly typed programming languages, including all .NET languages. In a strongly typed language, the type of value stored in each variable is known at compile time, so the compiler can predict how we intend to use each variable, and can therefore tell us when we are going wrong.

A type is a contract. A variable of a particular type guarantees contractually that it will contain all the data you would expect a value of the given type to have, and it can be processed in all the ways we would expect a value of that type to be processed. We sometimes call the contract of a type its *interface*.

> **C++ Note:** *Having been used to defining the interfaces of your C++ classes in header files, you will already be aware that C# has no header files. The definition of C# types is included in the compiled assembly as metadata. You should also remember that the C# compiler does not worry about the order of type declarations in your source code.*

To a computer all data is just chains of ones and zeroes. When we have a variable in our program, ultimately that variable is simply holding a binary number of some kind. So, when we ask the computer to display that variable on the screen, perform a calculation on it, or retrieve one of the variable's properties, the computer needs to know what type the variable contains in order to know how to interpret its value, and thus respond to our request. For example, an integer and a single-precision floating-point number can both be stored in four bytes of binary data. Take the following four bytes, for example:

```
00110110 11011011 10001010 01110100
```

If the value were interpreted as an integer, it would represent the number 920,357,492. Interpreted as a single-precision floating-point value, it has the approximate value of 6.5428267E-6. So, if a variable contains this binary number, and we ask .NET to add one to it, the result is going to depend not only on what value is in the variable, but also on the variable type.

A type describes the purpose of any string of ones and zeroes in memory. It enables us to compare values of two integers and see if one is greater than another, retrieve a string representing a value, or modify the value in a particular way.

The .NET Type System

The .NET Framework includes a large selection of types that assists software development in the .NET languages. All types we define and use in our own code must conform to the .NET Framework standards to ensure that they operate correctly in the runtime environment. There are two important specifications that define these standards, the **Common Type System** (**CTS**) and the **Common Language Specification** (**CLS**).

The Common Type System (CTS)

The Common Type System shows compiler writers how to declare and use types used in the .NET runtime. It defines rules that all .NET languages must follow in order to produce compiled code that can run within the Common Language Runtime (CLR). The CTS provides an object-oriented framework within which individual .NET languages operate. The existence of this common framework is crucial for ensuring type-safety and security at run-time, and also facilitating cross-language integration. In essence, the Common Type System is the backbone of the .NET Framework.

Figure 1 shows how the Common Type System is organized:

Figure 1

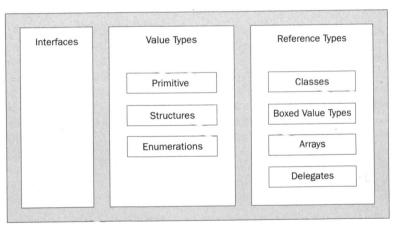

The diagram shows how the Common Type System makes a clear distinction between **value types** and **reference types**, which are discussed below. It also allows us to define pure interfaces; an interface is a simple definition of a contract, which is then implemented by another type (or types) – it separates out the definition of a contract from the implementation of that contract. All of the other types combine the above two things.

> **C++ Note:** Interfaces are akin to pure abstract classes. Unlike in C++, a C# class may only inherit from a single base class. However, a C# class may additionally inherit from multiple interfaces.

> *Java Note:* Like Java, C# supports single inheritance of classes but
> multiple inheritance of interfaces. Unlike Java-however, C# allows explicit
> implementation of interfaces, which avoids problems with naming
> conflicts. We'll see this in action later.

The Common Language Specification (CLS)

While the CTS defines how types are created and managed within the runtime, the
Common Language Specification is more concerned with language interoperability. The
CLS describes a minimum set of features that must be supported by any compiler
targeting the .NET runtime. While we're primarily C# developers, it is important to
understand the significance of .NET's language independence.

The CLS makes it extremely easy to use several different programming languages in the
same application. Whenever we compile source code written in a CLS-compliant
language, it is compiled into a standard .NET Framework byte code format called
Microsoft Intermediate Language (MSIL). The CLS ensures that certain types and
language constructs are all compiled to the same MSIL equivalents whatever the
language used. This means we can easily mix-and-match C#, Visual Basic .NET,
Managed Extensions for C++, Visual J#, or JScript .NET within the same application,
provided we only use CLS compliant types in any public interfaces declared in our
code. To ensure this, the C# compiler can be instructed to check the code and issue
warnings if we break any rules.

The use of an intermediate byte code format will be familiar to Java developers. Just as
Java is typically compiled to byte code before being run in a managed environment
(the Java Virtual Machine), so are C# and other .NET languages compiled to MSIL
before being run by the .NET Common Language Runtime (CLR). One difference is that
Java optionally allows the byte code to be interpreted at run time rather than compiled
to native code, while MSIL is always compiled, either by the Just In Time compiler
(JIT), or as a pre-JITted assembly loaded from the Global Assembly Cache (GAC). The
other important difference is that the language-neutral nature of MSIL was designed
into the .NET Framework from day one. As mentioned earlier, the CLS effectively
specifies a set of rules that define how different languages should compile to MSIL and
this facilitates language interoperability.

We need to make an important distinction here. We have a tendency to assume that
the C# language is so closely tied to the .NET runtime that CLS compliance is an
inherent property of the language. Actually C# is a type-safe, feature-rich,
object-oriented language in its own right, and it's perfectly capable of writing code
which is not CLS-compliant. It has primitive types that are not part of the CTS, for
example. In this book, while we will predominantly be talking about the .NET type
system, we will also talk about the way the C# compiler targets the .NET runtime when
it compiles your source code. We'll see, for example, how some of C#'s non-CLS
features are exposed to other CLS-compliant languages.

It is also worth pointing out here that language interoperability is not just a gimmick. The CTS and .NET runtime together support many more features than the subset defined by the CLS. Different languages expose different, larger subsets of these features, though at times they overlap. So it is possible that a particular language may be more suitable for certain parts of an application. As all languages share the common ground defined by the CLS, we have a guaranteed interface between these languages.

Apart from .NET languages, there are also a number of CLS-compliant languages from third-party vendors, such as COBOL (Fujitsu), Perl and Python (ActiveState), and Smalltalk (Quasar Knowledge Systems).

Before we look at the details of value types and reference types, it's useful to know that all the **types** in .NET are completely self-describing. This includes things such as enumerations and interfaces. A compiled .NET assembly (an `.exe` or a `.dll`) includes metadata, in which all the details of the types defined and used by the assembly are given. For those types defined in the assembly, we can use **reflection** to interrogate their definition. This is useful during development, where we don't need header files or type libraries to identify what properties and methods an object exposes. It is also crucial at run time, where the CLR uses this information to dynamically resolve method calls during JIT compilation. This information is stored in a compiled .NET assembly and is used extensively by the CLR. We'll cover metadata in more detail in Chapter 8.

Value Types and Reference Types

Value types often represent entities that are essentially numerical in nature, such as the date and time, colors, screen coordinates, and so on. Such entities can be represented by a simple binary number of a fixed length – the only complication is in interpreting the meaning of the number. Value types are typically small and exhibit quite simple behaviors, perhaps just providing an interface for reading and writing the underlying value.

Value Types and the Stack

An example of a simple value type is an eight-byte long integer that can be used to represent a very large range of dates and times. This number can be interpreted as an offset of a number of time intervals from a fixed point in time. .NET has a 64 bit `DateTime` type that does just that – it represents the number of ticks (units of 100 nanoseconds, or 10^7 seconds) since 00:00:00 on the first of January, 1 A.D (C.E.), at a particular point in time. Such values represent different instances in time quite effectively. The type, then, provides functionality allowing us to extract the year, the month, the day, the hour, minute, second, and so on, from the simple binary value, in a form that we can make use of.

Since this value type actually consists of very little data, it is easy to pass `DateTime` information around in a program. If we create a variable `aDate` to hold a `DateTime`, it will need eight bytes of storage exactly. If we create another variable `bDate` to hold a `DateTime`, it too will take eight bytes of storage. If we now write `bDate = aDate;`, the eight bytes of data in `aDate` can be quickly copied and placed into `bDate`.

When used as local variables or member fields, value types are allocated on the stack. This is an efficient (but limited size) area of memory used strictly for storing local variables (variables declared inside method bodies). The effect of the above actions may be shown schematically as follows. First, we declare two DateTime value types representing different dates:

```
DateTime aDate = new DateTime(1994, 08, 28);    // 28th August 1994
DateTime bDate = new DateTime(1996, 07, 23);    // 23rd July 1996
```

Then, we copy one date to the other:

```
aDate = bDate;    // copy date
```

The effect on the running thread's stack is shown in the following diagram. On the left is the situation immediately before the copy, and on the right is the situation after the copy.

Figure 2

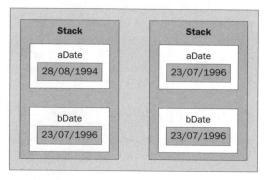

Value types exhibit **copy-by-value** semantics; when we copy one value type object to another, the compiler performs a byte-by-byte copy of our object. Value types are useful when we don't care how many copies of an object we create; all we care about is the value. When we pass a value type object into a method, the compiler creates a local copy of the object. When the method returns, the memory that the local copy of the value type object was using is automatically reclaimed. This means there are some important limitations to the kinds of uses to which we can put value types.

Reference Types and the Managed Heap

Since value types have fixed data size, they can be copied quickly and be processed faster then more complex types, such as arrays. We'll cover arrays in more detail towards the end of the chapter, but for now, we just need to appreciate that an array is not of a limited, fixed size. When we create a variable myArray to hold an array of integers, it is not clear how many bytes of storage it will need – it's going to depend on the size of the array we put into it. But, when .NET creates a variable, it needs to know how much space to allocate for it. .NET resolves this issue using a fixed size piece of data called a **reference**. The reference value is always the same number of bytes, and refers to a location in the part of the system memory called the managed heap.

The managed heap is a much larger area of memory than the stack but is slower to access. This is similar to a C runtime heap except that we only use it to allocate memory; we never specifically free memory from the managed heap. The CLR handles all of this housekeeping automatically (hence the term *managed*).

If we create an array of eight integers (which will require 32 bytes of space to store the array's members), it is created by allocating 32 bytes of the managed heap. When we place that array into the myArray variable, the location of the array on the managed heap (a reference to the array) is placed into the variable itself. The myArray variable that contains this reference is (like all local variables) held on the stack. The memory pointed to by the reference is on the managed heap.

If we then create another variable myArray2 to hold an array of integers, and then write myArray2 = myArray;, the value of that reference is copied into myArray2 so that it points to exactly the same array of integers that myArray did. Arrays, like all classes, are reference types.

We can see this happening schematically. First, we define two array variables, initializing one of them to refer to a new instance on the managed heap:

```
int[] myArray = new int[8];
int[] myArray2;
```

Then, we'll assign one array to the other. Remember, this only copies the reference:

```
MyArray2 = myArray;
```

The result of these operations is shown in the following diagram. On the left, we have the running thread's stack and the managed heap immediately before the above assignment; on the right the situation is shown after the assignment. Note that the reference variables myArray and myArray2 now both refer to the same array instance:

Figure 3

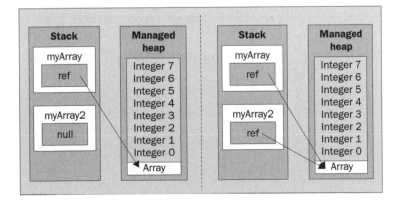

So, reference types represent entities that have a unique identity – they exist in one place on the managed heap, and are referenced from variables using this identity. When we defined an integer array and created an instance of this, the CLR allocated memory for the object and returned us a reference to this new object. When we copied the array into another variable, we just copied the reference. We still only have a single Array instance, but there are now two variables referring to it. Reference types exhibit **copy-by-reference** semantics. Likewise, when we pass a reference type into a method, the method receives a copy of the reference to our object, not a copy of its value.

Value Types and the Managed Heap

In a lot of .NET literature, you'll find the generalization 'value types are stored on the stack'. This is misleading. For example, an array is a reference type, so it is stored on the managed heap. But if we declare an array containing value-type entities, these values will be stored inline within the array, so they will actually be stored – as value types – on the managed heap. When we retrieve one of these values from the array, we don't get a reference to the location of the value on the heap, we get a copy of the value from the heap available for local use. The relevant distinction between value and reference types is that reference types are stored in a unique location on the managed heap; value types are stored wherever they are used.

Understanding .NET Memory Usage

Right now, Java developers will be thinking that value types are similar to primitive data types, while reference types are like classes and are heap allocated; C++ developers may be thinking of value types in terms of structs and reference types in terms of reference variables or pointers to dynamically-allocated memory. This is partly true in each case, but there are some important points to consider.

Where reference types are concerned, C++ developers will need to get used to not thinking in terms of pointers. Although this is more-or-less what happens behind the scenes, the CLR moves objects around on the managed heap and adjusts references on the fly while the application is running. Since we don't notice this at run time and it's not obvious from the source code, it confuses matters if you mentally try to translate between C# and C++ as you write. For example, in C# the syntax for accessing a value type is no different from that for accessing a reference type. In C++ you might have the following

```
SomeClass *pClassOnHeap = new SomeClass();
pClassOnHeap->DoSomething();
delete pClassOnHeap;
```

However, in C#, the '->' syntax is only used in unsafe code blocks for backward compatibility. In normal situations, the '.' should be used to access the type's methods as follows

```
SomeClass pClassOnHeap = new SomeClass();
pClassOnHeap.DoSomething();
pClassOnHeap = null;
```

Note also that we do not explicitly delete the heap-allocated variable when we have finished with it. We just nullify the reference and leave the rest to the garbage collector. Once the garbage collector determines that the object is no longer accessible through a reference stored anywhere else, it will become eligible for disposal. This will be familiar to Java and Visual Basic developers but may look like sloppy code to a C++ developer. This is discussed in more detail in Chapter 5 where we'll be looking at the object lifecycle.

Initializing Variables

When a variable of any type is created, it must be initialized with a value before being accessed. If we forget to put a value into a local variable and then try to use that variable in a calculation, the C# compiler will give an error. This is very different from C++ where it is the programmer's responsibility to check for this problem, and from Visual Basic where local variables are automatically initialized to suitable default values.

The only case in which the C# compiler will initialize variables on your behalf is for variables declared as fields in a `class` or `struct`. This simple compile-time check can save hours of debugging as it prevents you inadvertently retrieving junk values from memory left over from other programs.

Everything is an Object

It is important to remember here that any type within the .NET environment, whether a value or reference type, is an **object**. This means that every type will inherit explicitly, implicitly, or indirectly from `System.Object`. This is similar to the situation in Java, where there is a single rooted class hierarchy, with every class inheriting in some manner from `java.lang.Object` – except that in .NET it also applies to non-reference types. We'll explore some of the consequences of this throughout the book.

Value Types

There are three main kinds of .NET value types. In this section, we'll discuss each of these in some depth:

❑ **Primitive types**

All programming languages define primitive types such as integers, floating-point numbers, and so on. In .NET, such types are value types. We'll discuss the primitive types in C#, and see how these types map to Microsoft Intermediate Language (MSIL) data types.

❑ **User-defined value types**

We can define our own value types to represent simple objects or small pieces of data in our application. In C#, structures are user-defined value types, and are defined using the `struct` keyword. The .NET Framework defines custom value types, such as `System.DateTime` and `System.Drawing.Point`, in a similar manner.

❑ **Enumerations**

An enumeration is a special kind of value type, which represents a type that has a small list of allowable values. An enumeration might specify the values Yes, No, and Maybe for example. Underneath, each of these values is normally represented by an integer, but defining an enumeration type allows us to assign meanings to a specific set of integral values.

Unlike Java, both C++ and Visual Basic already support enumerations. The big difference with C# is that enumerations in the .NET world are strongly typed. For example, we might have a HairColor enumeration that allows Blonde, Red, Brown, and Black, and an EyeColor enumeration that can be Blue, Green, or Brown. This allows us to write readable code, while still ensuring that we can't accidentally give someone blue hair and red eyes.

Primitive Types

C# defines fifteen primitive types to represent integral numbers, floating-point numbers, Boolean values, and characters. Eleven of these primitive types are defined by the CLS to be interoperable with any other CLS-compliant programming language. The remaining four types are not CLS-compliant, so can only be used in private sections of a C# application or in any public interfaces where language interoperability is not required.

Each of these primitive types is actually just a synonym for a standard type in the .NET Framework's System namespace. There is no effective difference between a value type we define ourselves, and one of these special primitive types. However, these types do benefit from some special support in the C# language:

❑ **Literal syntax**: primitive values can all be created using a literal syntax. For example, when we write float pi = 3.142f; we are using a literal to specify a floating-point value. We could use 3.142d to indicate a double, or any of a range of suffixes to identify other numeric types. Similar notations exist for other primitive types, like true and false for Boolean literals.

❑ **Operator support**: primitive types can be combined using special operators. So we can use an addition operator (+) to add two numerical values, or the '&' or '|' operators to combine Booleans. In C#, it is also possible to define operators for our own types. We'll cover this in depth in Chapter 4.

The following table shows the mapping between C# primitive types and the equivalent structures in the System namespace. The table also shows how the C# .NET compiler translates these types into Microsoft Intermediate Language (MSIL) data types during compilation. Non-CLS-compliant types are marked with an asterisk:

Primitive Type	Equivalent .NET Structure	Equivalent MSIL Data Type	Description
bool	System.Boolean	bool	True/False value
byte	System.Byte	unsigned int8	8-bit unsigned integer
char	System.Char	char	Unicode 16-bit character
decimal	System.Decimal	System.Decimal	128-bit decimal value
double	System.Double	float64	IEEE 64-bit float
float	System.Single	float32	IEEE 32-bit float
int	System.Int32	int32	32-bit signed integer
long	System.Int64	int64	64-bit signed integer
object	System.Object	object	Base type of all types
sbyte*	System.SByte	int8	8-bit signed integer
short	System.Int16	int16	16-bit signed integer
string	System.String	string	Unicode string
uint*	System.Uint32	unsigned int32	32-bit unsigned integer
ulong*	System.Uint64	unsigned int64	64-bit unsigned integer
ushort*	System.Uint16	unsigned int16	16-bit unsigned integer

Notice that C# actually lists string and object as primitive types, although both of these are reference types, not value types. As object is the root of the whole .NET class hierarchy we'll discuss **System.Object** further in Chapter 2. However, while most programming languages include some form of string as a primitive type, the .NET Framework takes a slightly different approach. For now, we'll use this section to look at those primitives implemented as value types, and we'll discuss strings when we look at reference types a little later.

C and C++ developers should be aware that the descriptions given in the table for the C# primitive types will always be consistent within the .NET Framework. In particular, in C#, an int is always 32 bits. In C/C++ the size of an int is platform dependent— although this is commonly overlooked. Similarly, in C#, a long is 64 bits, where in C++ long represents "an integral type that is larger than or equal to the size of type int". These definitions obviously apply right across all of the .NET languages and this leaves a little less scope for error when operating in a mixed-language environment.

Visual Basic Note: Numeric types in C# include both signed and unsigned versions, which are not available in VB. Be careful when mixing these types, especially in comparisons. Also, C# does not automatically convert between numeric types in expressions, so you need to take care when rounding is important. For example, `float f = 1 / 3` *will return zero, while* `float f = 1.0f / 3.0f` *will return* `0.33333` *as expected.*

As all types in .NET are objects, we can even invoke methods on literals. This may seem strange and you'd probably never want to do it, but if we consider a line of code like `string s = 32.ToString();`, compile and run it, it should help fix in your mind the "everything is an object" message.

The following simple console application illustrates the use of primitive types in C#:

```
using System;

class MyClass
{
  static void Main()
  {
    int i = 100;      // use a primitive C# type
    Int32 j = i;      // use the equivalent .NET Framework type
```

We can use primitive C# data types (such as int) interchangeably with the equivalent .NET Framework types (such as `System.Int32`). For the sake of simplicity and familiarity, you should stick to one set of declarations in your code.

Microsoft is keenly advocating mixed-language programming using any combination of .NET Framework languages. If you are developing a multi-language solution, you might prefer to use the .NET Framework structure types explicitly, to emphasize the commonality across these languages. For example, `short` *in C# is the same as* `Short` *in Visual Basic .NET and* `short` *in Managed Extensions for C++; the equivalent .NET Framework type is* `System.Int16` *in all languages.*

```
Console.WriteLine("int:    {0}", typeof(int).FullName);
Console.WriteLine("Int32:  {0}", typeof(Int32).FullName);
```

We use the `typeof` operator to obtain information about data types at run time and write this information to the console. The following code asks the user for a numerator and a denominator and then calculates the quotient.

```
Console.Write("\nEnter a double: ");

string input = Console.ReadLine();
double num = Double.Parse(input);
```

```
        Console.Write("Enter another double: ");
        input = Console.ReadLine();
        double denom = Double.Parse(input);

        double res = num / denom;
        if (Double.IsNaN(res))
          Console.WriteLine("Not a Number.");
        else if (Double.IsPositiveInfinity(res))
          Console.WriteLine("Positive infinity.");
        else if (Double.IsNegativeInfinity(res))
          Console.WriteLine("Negative infinity.");
        else
          Console.WriteLine("Result is {0}.", res);
    }
}
```

We use various methods defined in the Double type to read and process double values in our application. The Parse method extracts a double value from a string; IsNaN() tests for "is not a number"; IsPositiveInfinity() tests for positive infinity (for example, dividing 100 by 0); and IsNegativeInfinity() tests for negative infinity (for example, dividing -100 by 0).

When the application runs, it displays the types for int and Int32 as System.Int32; this confirms that the int type in C# .NET is just another name for System.Int32. The application also asks us to enter two floating-point numbers; if we enter some arbitrary numbers, we can see the output on the console.

Save the code into a file called primitive_types.cs, and compile it. Now enter the following at the command prompt:

```
C:\Class Design\Ch01> primitive_types
int:      System.Int32
Int32:    System.Int32

Enter a double: 432.33
Enter another double: 4576.33
Result is 0.0944708969851387.
```

Viewing the Output from the Compiler

The .NET Framework SDK includes several useful tools for examining files generated when we build a project. One of the most important tools is the MSIL Disassembler; ildasm.exe. This tool enables us to see how the compiler has translated our C# source code into MSIL byte code. It also enables us to view detailed metadata for our types, which can help us understand how the Common Language Runtime works. This in turn can help us use C# more effectively. We'll look in detail at metadata in Chapter 8.

Some developers dismiss the MSIL Disassembler as being irrelevant and over-hyped, but that's not the case. We'll be using the MSIL Disassembler extensively in this book, to investigate how the C# .NET compiler has compiled our code.

To run the MSIL Disassembler tool, open a command prompt (if you are using Visual Studio .NET, make sure you start a Visual Studio .NET command prompt), then move to the folder that contains the executable file, and run `ildasm` as follows:

> `ildasm` *`assembly-filename`*

The name and location of the executable file depends on how we built the application:

❑ If we built the application using Visual Studio .NET, the executable file will have the same name as the project – although with an `.exe` or `.dll` extension – and will be located in the `bin\Debug` or `bin\Release` sub-folder. Also, Visual Studio .NET adds a namespace, which is the same as the project name.

❑ If we built the application using the command-line C# compiler, the executable file will have the same name as the source file, again with an `.exe` or `.dll` extension, and will be located in the same folder as the source file.

For example, if we built the `primitive_types` application using the command-line compiler, we could load up `primitive_types.exe` into the MSIL Disassembler. When you expand the MyClass icon, the MSIL Disassembler window displays the following information:

Double-click the Main icon, to open a view of the MSIL code for the `Main` method:

```
MyClass::Main : void(string[])                                    _ □ ×
.method private hidebysig static void  Main(string[] args) cil managed
{
  .entrypoint
  .custom instance void [mscorlib]System.STAThreadAttribute::.ctor() = ( 01
  // Code size       189 (0xbd)
  .maxstack  3
  .locals init (int32 V_0,
           int32 V_1,
           string V_2,
           float64 V_3,
           float64 V_4,
           float64 V_5)
  IL_0000:  ldc.i4.s   100
  IL_0002:  stloc.0
  IL_0003:  ldloc.0
  IL_0004:  stloc.1
  IL_0005:  ldstr      "int:     {0}"
  IL_000a:  ldtoken    [mscorlib]System.Int32
  IL_000f:  call       class [mscorlib]System.Type [mscorlib]System.Type::Get
  IL_0014:  callvirt   instance string [mscorlib]System.Type::get_FullName()
  IL_0019:  call       void [mscorlib]System.Console::WriteLine(string,
                                                            object)

  IL_001e:  ldstr      "Int32:   {0}"
```

In the MSIL code, the Main() method is marked with the MSIL managed keyword.
This indicates code that runs in the managed environment provided by the .NET
Framework Common Language Runtime. All code we write in C# will be managed
code. A variety of local variables can be found described with MSIL data types such as
float64, int32, and string.

Let's look at the end of the IL code for the Main() method:

```
MyClass::Main : void(string[])                                    _ □ ×
  IL_007a:  call       void [mscorlib]System.Console::WriteLine(string)
  IL_007f:  br.s       IL_00bc
  IL_0081:  ldloc.s    V_5
  IL_0083:  call       bool [mscorlib]System.Double::IsPositiveInfinity(float
  IL_0088:  brfalse.s  IL_0096
  IL_008a:  ldstr      "Positive infinity."
  IL_008f:  call       void [mscorlib]System.Console::WriteLine(string)
  IL_0094:  br.s       IL_00bc
  IL_0096:  ldloc.s    V_5
  IL_0098:  call       bool [mscorlib]System.Double::IsNegativeInfinity(float
  IL_009d:  brfalse.s  IL_00ab
  IL_009f:  ldstr      "Negative infinity."
  IL_00a4:  call       void [mscorlib]System.Console::WriteLine(string)
  IL_00a9:  br.s       IL_00bc
  IL_00ab:  ldstr      "Result is {0}."
  IL_00b0:  ldloc.s    V_5
  IL_00b2:  box        [mscorlib]System.Double
  IL_00b7:  call       void [mscorlib]System.Console::WriteLine(string,
                                                            object)

  IL_00bc:  ret
} // end of method MyClass::Main
```

Each line of IL code consists of a command, followed by any data the command needs to
operate on. Data that the program is working with is stored on the stack. Items are loaded
onto the stack using IL commands that begin ld for load. Each variable on the stack takes
up a fixed amount of memory defined by its type. For reference type objects, the stack
contains a reference to the location on the managed heap where the actual object is stored.

The first line in the screenshot loads a reference to a string onto the stack. The next loads the contents of the variable V_5 (which contains the result of the division operation) onto the stack. When an item is placed on the stack, it goes on top of any previous stack items. When items are taken off the stack, the top item is removed first.

We'll ignore the box command for a moment, and instead look at the call command. This call tells .NET to call a method, called WriteLine(), belonging to a class called System.Console, found in the mscorlib.dll assembly, which takes as arguments a string and an object. .NET looks up this method, takes the two items from the top of the stack and passes them to the method being called. The top item on the stack is our floating-point value, which is a result of the division we performed. This is not an object, it's a value type.

We'll look at boxing in depth later as there are some important performance considerations. For now, we just need to know that the box instruction in the IL code takes the item on the top of the stack, copies it to the managed heap, and places on the top of the stack a reference to the boxed value. This allows us to treat the value as an object and pass it in to this method call. So, when the call to the method comes, the items on the top of the stack are a boxed value and then a string, and these two values are passed to the Console.WriteLine method.

> *Close the MSIL Disassembler windows when you have finished. If you forget to close the MSIL Disassembler windows, the EXE file will remain locked by the MSIL Disassembler. If you try to recompile the application with these windows open, you'll get a compiler error because the EXE file cannot be overwritten.*

User-Defined Value Types (Structures)

Applications often require types to encapsulate essentially numeric quantities such as currencies, screen coordinates, and temperatures, which are not represented by the available primitive types. Using classes in these scenarios would be like using a hammer to crack a nut; the run-time overhead for garbage-collecting these simple objects would be unnecessarily high.

The .NET Framework provides user-definable **value types** as a solution to this problem. In C#, a value type is written as a struct. Remember that like value types, instances of structs are stored wherever they are used.

Value types are messy because they leave copies of themselves everywhere. However, they are very easy to clean up. .NET doesn't need to keep track of each copy of the value – if we need the value elsewhere, we'll just send a copy there. Thus if a value type is no longer reachable, the memory it was taking up is immediately available for use. With reference types though, we need the garbage collector to sweep up behind us. All the copies of a reference might have gone out of scope or been overwritten, but the memory on the managed heap is still being taken up with the referenced object. We'll see how the garbage collector handles that problem later on.

Because of the way value instances are passed around, value types should ideally be small. If we define large value types, inefficiencies start to creep in when we pass the value instances between methods in our application because of the amount of data that has to be copied into and out of the method. Large value types will slow down the allocation, management, and cleanup of objects and stack frames that use them.

In this section, we'll see how to define and use value types effectively in C# and how to use inheritance with value types.

Defining and Using Value Types

The rules for defining value types are essentially the same as for defining a class. For example, a value type can have fields, properties, constants, events, methods, and constructors. As we'll see in Chapters 3 and 4, we can also override methods and operators and provide indexers just as we can in classes.

Value types, or structures, are cut-down classes, although there are some important differences:

❑ Structures must have at least one field or event declaration.

❑ Structures automatically have a default parameterless constructor. The compiler will give an error if you try to define your own. This constructor performs default initialization for any fields you've declared. It initializes numeric fields to zero, Boolean flags to `false`, and sets object references to `null`.

❑ Although we cannot define our own parameterless constructor, we can (and should) provide parameterized constructors. Feel free to provide several parameterized constructors where appropriate, so that users of your value type can initialize their objects in a variety of useful ways.

❑ We cannot provide initializers for fields in a structure; we must perform initialization in a constructor (this is different from a `class`, where we can initialize fields at the point of declaration). However, we are allowed to provide initializers for `const` fields; that is, we can initialize `const` fields at the point of definition. When we look at `const`s in the next chapter, the reason for this will become clear.

❑ Structure objects have a much simpler deallocation mechanism than class objects. The garbage collector disposes of the class object, and then it calls the object's destructor just before the object disappears. Structure objects are deallocated when they go out of scope, or are overwritten with another value, rather than being garbage-collected. Therefore, it is not permitted to define a destructor, although we can define a `Dispose` method in the same way as we might for a class. However, since we can't guarantee it will be called, as we can in classes, it's best to avoid building value types that require their resources to be disposed. We'll see an example of this later, although object disposal is discussed in a little more depth in Chapter 5.

❑ Many examples show structures with `public` fields. This seems to contradict a basic rule of object-oriented development: "don't declare data public". The tradeoff is one of speed versus encapsulation; `public` data is (marginally) faster to access because it avoids the overhead of method calls to get at the data, but it clearly breaks the encapsulation of the structure. If in doubt, err on the side of caution and declare all your fields as `private`. If private fields are exposed as properties, the accessor code is usually in-lined by the compiler, resulting in an efficient implementation anyway. Don't optimize your code at the expense of maintainability; let the compiler optimize it for you.

❑ The .NET Framework does not allow us to inherit from a structure. Therefore, the methods defined in a structure cannot be overridden by methods in a subclass. One logical consequence of this is that it is not permitted to declare any member of a structure as `virtual`, `abstract`, or `sealed`. However, the compiler can predict with certainty which methods will be invoked when we use structure objects in our code. This insight enables the compiler to optimize the method invocation for efficiency; for example, the compiler can choose to expand the method body inline rather than executing a traditional method call. The net result is that method calls on structure objects can be less expensive than method calls on class objects.

❑ As value types, structures are always allocated where they are used. It doesn't make any difference whether you use the `new` operator when defining a variable containing a `struct`, or not. With reference types, if you declare a variable but do not use the `new` operator, the runtime will not allocate any storage on the managed heap, but will allocate a reference on the stack containing the value `null`. With value types, the runtime will allocate the space on the stack and call the default constructor to initialize the state of the object.

The following example, `value_types.cs`, illustrates some of these rules:

```
using System;

struct Money
{
  // private instance field
  private int centsAmount;

  // private class field
  private const string currencySymbol = "$";

  // public constructor
  public Money(int dollars, int cents)
  {
    centsAmount = (dollars * 100) + cents;
  }
```

```
    // another public constructor
    public Money(double amount)
    {
      centsAmount = (int)((amount * 100.0) + 0.5);
    }
  }

class MyClass
{
  static void Main()
  {
    Money freebie;
    Money salary = new Money(20000, 0);
    Money carPrice = new Money(34999.95);
  }
}
```

Note the following in this example:

❑ The fields in the structure are declared as private, to maximize encapsulation.

❑ The currencySymbol field is initialized at the point of declaration. This is allowable because currencySymbol is a const field.

❑ There are two constructors in the structure, to initialize structures in two different ways. Note the rounding adjustment needed in the second constructor when we cast from double to int.

❑ The Main() method in the separate class MyClass creates three structure objects, to show how to call the available constructors (including the compiler-generated parameterless constructor).

At the moment, this program doesn't provide any evidence that it's working. We'll add some more functionality to it in the next section.

Using Inheritance with Value Types

When we define a structure in C#, we cannot explicitly specify a base class. All value types implicitly inherit from System.ValueType, which is a standard type in the .NET Framework library. System.ValueType inherits from System.Object, and overrides some of the methods from System.Object (System.ValueType does not introduce any additional methods).

When we define our own value types, we can override some of the methods inherited from System.ValueType or System.Object. One of the most commonly overridden methods is ToString(), which returns a string representation of the object. For more information about System.Object, see Chapter 2.

Structures cannot be used as base classes for other classes to inherit; they are not extensible through inheritance. Structures can be very sophisticated types but they are not classes. This language restriction enables the compiler to minimize the amount of administrative code it has to generate to support structures.

Although structures cannot explicitly inherit from an arbitrary class, they can implement interfaces. For example, it is quite common to implement standard .NET Framework interfaces such as IComparable, which allows us to specify how objects should be compared, and so enables sorting. Value types will often implement this to interoperate well with other classes in the .NET Framework.

We'll be covering interfaces in more detail later in this chapter, but the following preview demonstrates how easily we can change our Money value type to implement an interface, and override the ToString() method inherited from System.Object:

```csharp
// value_type_inheritance.cs
using System;

struct Money : IComparable
{
  // private fields
  private int centsAmount;
  private const string currencySymbol = "$";

  // public constructors
  public Money(int dollars, int cents)
  {
    centsAmount = (dollars * 100) + cents;
  }

  public Money(double amount)
  {
    centsAmount = (int)((amount * 100.0) + 0.5);
  }

  // compare with another Money
  public int CompareTo(object other)
  {
    Money m2 = (Money)other;
    if (centsAmount < m2.centsAmount)
      return -1;
    else if (centsAmount == m2.centsAmount)
      return 0;
    else
      return 1;
  }

  // return value as a string
  public override string ToString()
  {
```

```
    return currencySymbol + (centsAmount / 100.0).ToString();
  }
}
```

The Money structure now implements the IComparable interface. The CompareTo() method, as specified by the IComparable interface, compares the value of this Money instance against another Money instance, and returns an integer to indicate the result of the comparison.

Money also overrides the ToString() method, which is defined in the System.Object base class. This returns a string representation of this Money instance. Let's see what effect these changes have:

```
class MyClass
{
  static void Main()
  {
    // create an array of 5 items
    Money[] salaries = new Money[5];
    salaries[0] = new Money(9.50);
    salaries[1] = new Money(4.80);
    salaries[2] = new Money(8.70);
    salaries[3] = salaries[2];
    salaries[4] = new Money(6.30);

    // display unsorted array
    Console.WriteLine("Unsorted array:");
    foreach (Money salary in salaries)
    {
      Console.WriteLine("{0}", salary);
    }

    // sort the array
    Array.Sort(salaries);

    // display sorted array
    Console.WriteLine("Sorted array:");
    foreach (Money salary in salaries)
    {
      Console.WriteLine("{0}", salary);
    }
  }
}
```

In the above example, the Main() method creates an array of Money instances, and when array element 3 is assigned the value of element 2, it obtains a copy of the value of element 2. Each Money instance in the array is displayed using Console.WriteLine, which implicitly invokes our overridden ToString() method. The Array.Sort() method sorts the array. For this to work, the array elements must implement the IComparable interface. Array.Sort() calls the CompareTo() method repeatedly on the array elements, to sort them in the specified order. Finally, the sorted array is displayed on the console.

The application displays the following output:

```
C:\Class Design\Ch01> valuetype_inheritance
Unsorted array:
$9.5
$4.8
$8.7
$8.7
$6.3

Sorted array:
$4.8
$6.3
$8.7
$8.7
$9.5
```

Enumerations

Enumerations are .NET value types that represent integral types with a limited set of permitted values. They may also be used to map bit flags onto an integer type to allow a convenient way to represent a combination of options using a single variable. Enumerations are present in many programming languages, but in .NET they are also object-oriented. This means that developers now have access to additional features, which are not present in other languages.

Enumerated Types

To declare an enumerated type, we use the enum keyword and specify symbolic names to represent the allowable values. We can also specify an underlying integral data type to be used for the enumeration (byte, short, int, or long), and optionally assign a specific number to each of the names.

The following example, enumerations.cs, declares a simple enumeration to represent medals in a competition:

```
// enumerations.cs
using System;

enum Medal : short
{
    Gold,
    Silver,
    Bronze
}
```

Enumerations inherit implicitly from System.Enum, and so inherit all of its members. Having defined an enumerated type, we can use it in our code as follows:

```
class MyClass
{
  static void Main()
  {
    Medal myMedal = Medal.Bronze;
    Console.WriteLine("My medal: " + myMedal.ToString());
  }
}
```

We have created an enumeration instance named myMedal and assigned it the value
Medal.Bronze. The scope of enumeration members is limited to the enumeration
declaration body.

If you compile and run this code, you will see that the output written to the console
contains the symbolic name Bronze instead of the equivalent numeric value. This is
one advantage of .NET enumerations over traditional C++ or VB style equivalents. This
facility is also used by the Visual Studio .NET IDE during development and debugging,
and it presents a much more meaningful picture to a developer.

As well as the ubiquitous ToString method, we can use the static Format() method
defined in System.Enum to convert a numeric value to a symbolic name without
needing an instance of the enumerated type. For example, the following statement
would produce the same output as the previous example:

```
Console.WriteLine("My medal: " + Enum.Format(typeof(Medal), 2, "G"));
```

As System.Enum implements the IFormattable interface, we can use format options
in combination with other .NET classes to access details of our enumerated type. For
example, we can create an array containing one element for each symbolic name and
display the numeric values together with the symbolic names:

```
Medal[] medals = (Medal[])Enum.GetValues(typeof(Medal));
foreach (Medal m in medals)
{
  Console.WriteLine("{0:D}\t{1:G}", m, m);
}
```

Replacing the body of the Main() method in the earlier example with the above code
produces the following output:

```
C:\Class Design\Ch01> enumerations2
0        Gold
1        Silver
2        Bronze
```

If we need to convert the other way, perhaps using a symbolic name entered by a user at run time to initialize an enumerated type, we can use the `Parse()` method. Replace the `Main()` method with the following code:

```
Console.Write("\nEnter a medal: ");
string input = Console.ReadLine();
Medal myMedal = (Medal)Enum.Parse(typeof(Medal), input, true);
Console.WriteLine("You entered: " + myMedal.ToString());
```

The Boolean parameter in the `Parse()` method controls case-sensitivity. In this example, case is not checked. We accept input of a matching symbolic name and echo this to the user:

```
C:\Class Design\Ch01> enumerations3
Enter a medal: gold
You entered: Gold
```

Note that entering a string that does not match any of the symbolic names defined will produce an `ArgumentException`, which may be trapped at run time using a `try...catch` block. Alternatively you might choose to use the `IsDefined()` method from `System.Enum` to validate user input before proceeding.

Bit Flags

Many developers are already familiar with bit flags. In essence, you start with a numeric type, say a byte consisting of 8 bits, and use a bit-mask (another binary number) together with some combination of logical operators to set, unset, or query individual bits in the variable. In this way you can carry around a combination of up to eight on/off settings in a single byte, which is a compact use of storage.

In C# we can define an enumerated type to do the same thing, which makes it much easier to read. We do this by defining an enumeration using the `[Flags]` attribute, and associating each symbolic name with a particular combination of bits. For example, the following code defines a single-byte enumerated type with four individual options:

```
using System;

[Flags]
enum Permit : byte
{
    Create = 0x01,
    Read   = 0x02,
    Update = 0x04,
    Delete = 0x08
}
```

The C# compiler allows us to use [Flags] or [FlagsAttribute]; they are synonymous. We can show how to use this enumerated type in the following code:

```
class TestBitFlag
{
  static void Main()
  {
    Permit perm1 = Permit.Create;
    Console.WriteLine(perm1.ToString());
    Permit perm = Permit.Create | Permit.Read;
    Console.WriteLine(perm.ToString());
    perm |= Permit.Delete;
    Console.WriteLine(perm.ToString());
  }
}
```

Notice how we can set individual bits in the variable by using the bitwise OR operator (|). We're also using the ToString() method to produce a readable representation of the variable. When we compile and run this code, it produces the following output:

```
C:\Class Design\Ch01> bitflags
Create
Create, Read
Create, Read, Delete
```

We can see how the System.Enum type produces different output once we identify our enumerated type with the [Flags] attribute. As before, we could use the Parse() method, this time with a comma-delimited set of options, in order to initialize a variable from user input.

The symbolic names we define don't have to map to individual bits. We can introduce values that represent a combination of bits and the functionality provided by System.Enum remains consistent. For example, redefine the enumerated type as follows:

```
[Flags]
enum Permit : byte
{
  Create = 0x01,
  Read   = 0x02,
  Update = 0x04,
  Delete = 0x08,
  AllExceptUpdate = 0x0B
}
```

Now, when you compile and run the example, should get the following:

```
C:\Class Design\Ch01> bitflags2
Create
Create, Read
AllExceptUpdate
```

You can see that the [Flags] attribute affects how the ToString(), Parse(), and Format() methods work within System.Enum and that the results still make sense. If the combination of bits set in the enumerated type matches one of the symbolic names exactly, then that name is output; if not then a combination of symbolic names is output in a comma-delimited list. We need to be a little wary though because it is perfectly legal to specify more than one symbolic name with the same value. In this situation, System.Enum will use one of these names in any converted output although which one it chooses will be indeterminate.

Inside an Enumerated Type

To sum up, there are two good reasons for using enumerations in your code:

❏   Enumerations use meaningful names to represent allowable values. These names make it easier for other developers to understand the purpose of these values.

❏   Enumerations are strongly typed. You cannot assign integer values to an enumeration instance unless you use an explicit cast; otherwise you must use one of the enumeration member names. This helps to avoid programming errors that might arise if you used raw integer values.

Now, C++ and Visual Basic developers will already be familiar with enums, even though the equivalent constructs in those languages are not strongly typed. Certainly, if you are new to C#, you will have noticed how enumerations are much more developer-friendly during debugging. The reason for this is because a .NET enumeration is a value type, which inherits directly from System.Enum. You don't see this relationship in the source code but it's obvious if you look at the MSIL with the IL disassembler. For example, here's the first sample application we coded at the beginning of this section:

Java doesn't have an enumeration construct. Java developers commonly use a class as the type, and various static instances of the class as the variable. If we observe the ILDasm output above we can see that an enumeration in C# isn't really a new idea, it's just a shorthand method for creating a specialized value type that provides certain limited but well defined behaviors. Unlike other value types though, it is not permissible to define methods, properties, or events within an enumeration.

There's nothing at all wrong with this except that there are cases where enumerations are not as appropriate as a custom-made value type. You can imagine that, with such a type, we could significantly enhance the facilities provided by an enum. We could add methods to an enum, and even have different enum members exhibiting different behaviors.

The point here is to think carefully about your design, especially if you are coding long switch statements that are based on values in an enumeration.

One final caveat with .NET enumerations: it's possible to cast any value of the underlying integral type to the type of the enumeration – whether it represents a legitimate value of the enumeration or not

For this reason, you should never assume that an enumeration value passed into a method could only possibly be one of the allowed values. Always perform validity checking on enumeration values.

Reference Types

These are some of the main reference types that exist in the Common Type System. In this section, we'll elaborate on each of these in turn.

❑ **Class types**
Most of the types we define in a typical application are class types. Classes specify the data and methods for the important objects in our application.

❑ **Delegates**
Delegates represent type-safe pointers to methods. We can use delegates to specify callbacks, and to register handlers for Graphical User Interface (GUI) events such as button clicks.

❑ **Arrays**
Arrays are allocated on the managed heap and accessed by reference. Arrays can be one-dimensional or multi-dimensional. You can also have arrays of arrays, which permit jagged array structures.

❑ **Strings**
The .NET Framework includes inbuilt comprehensive support for handling strings. This support extends deep into the CLR and includes features that help us to write applications that will work correctly on different runtime platforms and with different character sets.

Class Types

In object-oriented terminology, a class defines the methods and data for a specific type of object in the system. Many developers in the object-oriented community use the phrase **abstract data type** when they talk about classes. We need to be careful in .NET, because a class is only one kind of abstract data type – the term can equally be applied to structures. In addition, .NET uses the word abstract to refer to something quite different.

In the .NET Framework a class is a **reference type**; objects are allocated on the Common Language Runtime's managed heap, and the lifetime of these objects is controlled by the runtime. In this section we'll focus on defining classes, and during these discussions it is important to remember that classes are always reference types in the .NET Framework.

Defining Classes in C#

We use the `class` keyword to define a class. This is same as for C++ and Java. In fact the basic syntax for declaring a C# class is indistinguishable from Java. For example, the following code snippet will compile in either language:

```
public class MyClass
{
    private static int refCount = 0;
    public int someNumber;

    public void DoSomething()
    {
    }
}
```

This is also not so different from C++, where the above might have been written as follows:

```
class MyClass
{
public:
    int someNumber;
    void DoSomething()
    {
    }

private:
    static int refCount;
}

int MyClass::refCount = 0;
```

> **C++ Note:** Remember, in C#, there are no global variables or global functions. Everything must be defined within a class or structure. Also, if you don't supply a default constructor for a class, the C# compiler will generate one for you, which initializes all member fields to zero.

A class contains data and functionality. The following table describes the kinds of data members we can define in a class:

Kind of data member	Description
Field	A field is a piece of data that is stored in objects of this class. We can also use the `static` keyword, to define data that is shared by all objects of the class.
Method	A method is a function that provides some aspect of behavior for objects of this class. We can also use the `static` keyword to define methods that apply to the class itself, rather than to a particular object.
Property	A property looks like a field to anyone using your class, except that its value is always retrieved and modified through 'get' and 'set' methods defined in the class. A property presents functionality as if it were data.
Indexer	A type indexer is a kind of property that allows a class to be accessed using the `[]` notation. This is typically used to permit access to items in a collection.
Constant	A constant is a read-only value that is shared by all objects of the class.
Event	An event is a message that an object can send to interested listener objects. In the .NET Framework, we use the terminology **event source** to denote an object that can raise events, and **event receiver** to denote an object that can receive events. An event defined as a member of a type identifies all objects of that type as sources for that event.
Type	Types can contain nested types. This is only recommended for specific purposes, as illustrated in *Nested Classes*, later.
Constructor	A constructor is an initialization method. Every time we create an object of a particular class, a constructor is called to initialize the state of the object.
Destructor	A class can have a single finalization method. The CLR calls this method just before the garbage-collection process destroys an object. This is a good place to perform tidying-up operations before the object disappears from the scene.

C++ Note: As in C++, destructors are specified using the ~ symbol. Destructors can only be declared for reference types and cannot be overridden. Unlike in C++, a destructor cannot be called explicitly, as the garbage collector manages the objects' lifetimes. Each destructor in an object's hierarchy is called automatically before the memory for the object is reclaimed.

Just a quick note on constructors: in C#, we can define two kinds of constructors; instance constructors, which we are all familiar with, and **static constructors**, also referred to as type initializers or type constructors. A static constructor is similar to a static initialization block in Java. Static constructors are declared just like instance constructors, but by adding the static keyword. A class may have at most one static constructor, which takes no parameters. If defined, a static constructor is invoked before the first invocation of a static method in the class and before the first time an instance of the class is created. Static constructors are discussed further in Chapter 5.

The following class definition illustrates some of these kinds of members. It's unlikely we'd define all these in the same class, but we've listed them here for illustrative purposes. We'll consider the design heuristics for each kind of member in later chapters.

```
// class_members.cs - compile with /t:library option
class MyClass
{
    // Field (usually private, for encapsulation)
    private int aField;

    // Property (usually public, for ease of use)
    public int AProperty
    {
        get { return aField; }
        set { aField = value; }
    }

    // Constant (class-wide, read-only field)
    private const int aConstant = 43;

    // Delegate (defines a method signature)
    public delegate void ADelegate(int aParameter);

    // Event (to alert event receiver objects)
    public event ADelegate AnEvent;

    // Method
    public void AMethod()
    {
        // Method implementation code
    }

    // Instance constructor (to initialize new objects)
    public MyClass(int aValue)
    {
        aField = aValue;
    }

    // Destructor method (to tidy up unmanaged resources)
    ~MyClass()
    {
```

```
    // Finalization code
  }

  // Nested class definition
  private class aNestedClass
  {
    // class definition
  }
}
```

Defining Accessibility for Classes

When we define a type, we can specify its accessibility. We can make the type private to its declaration context, accessible from other code in the same assembly, or accessible from code in any assembly.

> *Assemblies are a key concept in the .NET Framework. In the simplest case, an assembly is a single file (.exe or .dll). When we write an application, we can decide whether we want to define all our classes (and other types) in the same assembly, or spread the classes across different assemblies for deployment purposes. Assemblies, as the name implies, can themselves consist of multiple files. For more information about assemblies, including a discussion on how to organize class definitions in assemblies, see Chapter 8.*

Defining the accessibility for types is an important consideration in large systems, where the number of types can easily run into the hundreds. The aim is to limit visibility as much as possible. By hiding types from other parts of the system, we make the system more decoupled and easier to maintain. We can change a type more easily if there are fewer dependencies on it elsewhere in the system.

The following examples show how to specify class accessibility using C#:

```
class MyClass1
{
    // members
}
```

In the absence of an access modifier, `MyClass1` is *implicitly* private, which means no other class from the same, or any other assembly can access it. On the other hand, `MyClass2` is *explicitly* public to all assemblies:

```
public class MyClass2
{
    // members
}
```

It is important to be aware that the default accessibility depends on the context in which it is being defined. It is good practice to make accessibility explicit by always declaring an accessibility modifier to avoid other code changes having unwanted side effects. For example, simply enclosing `MyClass1` in a namespace declaration would change the default accessibility from `private` to `internal`.

Public and private accessibility of classes in an assembly is similar to Java's convention, except that the default accessibility is `private` rather than `package`. However, there are a few more access modifiers that can be used on members defined within a class, including with nested classes.

There are three additional access modifiers that may be used to control the accessibility of your classes (nested or otherwise) or their members. These are:

Access modifier	Description
internal	The member or class may only be accessed from within the same assembly.
protected	The member or class may only be accessed from its parent class or from any types derived from the parent class.
protected internal	The member or class may be accessed from anywhere within the same assembly, or from its parent class, or from any types derived from the parent class.

Accessibility is covered in more detail in the next chapter.

Nested Classes

All the things declared in a class are effectively nested within it. There is nothing to stop you nesting any type within a class, including other classes. For instance, you may want to declare a data structure that is only useful inside a particular class, and the simplest way to do this is use a nested class. A nested class is not only a self-contained class just like any other, but also has access to all of the members defined in its parent class.

Let's see a brief example using the access modifiers shown in the previous section.

```
// class_visibility.cs
public class MyClass
{
  class MyPrivateClass
  {
    // members
  }

  internal class MyInternalClass
  {
```

```
    // members
    }

    protected class MyProtectedClass
    {
      // members
    }

    protected internal class MyProtIntClass
    {
      // members
    }
}
```

Compile this example to a DLL, and view the MSIL code in the MSIL Disassembler:

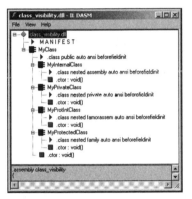

Notice the following in this screenshot:

- ❏ MyClass is qualified with the MSIL keyword public

- ❏ MyInternalClass is qualified with the MSIL keyword assembly

- ❏ MyPrivateClass is qualified with the MSIL keyword private

- ❏ MyProtectedClass is qualified with the MSIL keyword family

- ❏ MyProtIntClass is qualified with the MSIL keyword famorassem

The full implications of using the protected access modifier are covered in Chapter 7 *Inheritance and Polymorphism*. public, private, and protected access modifiers will be familiar to both C++ and Java developers although the meaning of these terms may initially be confusing; internal is a new access modifier for everyone.

> ***Java Note:*** *public and private have the same meaning as in Java. internal access is scoped to assemblies rather than namespaces (which would be more analogous to Java). internal protected is equivalent to Java's protected access, and C#'s protected access is equivalent to Java's private protected access, which was made obsolete in Java some time ago.*

39

Java developers will be familiar with two types of nested class: inner classes and static nested classes. In C#, a nested class is akin to Java's static nested class. There is no direct C# equivalent to a Java inner class, although the effect can be replicated by creating a nested class that holds a reference to its parent class and requires an instance to be passed to its constructor. This does have the advantage that the relationship between the nested class and its parent instance is made explicit in the code. Java developers should also note that there is no C# equivalent to anonymous inner classes; and C# classes may not be defined within method bodies.

Some useful guidelines are available on MSDN to help decide when the use of nested classes is a good design choice. Among these are the following:

❑ If your class is logically contained by another class and has no independent significance, then implement it as a nested class.

❑ If members of your class need to access private member fields of the object containing it, implement it as a nested class.

❑ If your class needs to implement an interface that returns another type of object that implements another interface (like `IEnumerable.GetEnumerator()`), you can create an implementation of that interface as a nested class and return the object through the required method. We'll look more at interfaces towards the end of the chapter.

❑ If other classes will reasonably need access, or will want to collect or contain your class, do not implement it as a nested class. A class that is accessed by several other classes should stand alone.

❑ In general, do not implement public nested classes. Nested classes should primarily be for the internal use of the containing class. If you do implement a public nested class, it should be a class that logically belongs to the containing type, and is used infrequently. One exception would be if an instance of the nested class were exposed as a property on the containing class.

Creating and Disposing of Class Objects

As with all object-oriented languages, we can write constructors in our class, to initialize objects when they are created. If we don't define any constructors in our class, the C# compiler will generate a parameterless constructor on our behalf. Static constructors are covered in Chapter 5.

We know that the Common Language Runtime tracks objects on the managed heap, and flags them for removal when they are no longer required in our application. The garbage-collection mechanism prevents memory leaks, and makes it easier for us to manage complex object relationships in our applications.

In C#, we can write a destructor method, to tidy up the object just before it is deallocated. A destructor is similar to a destructor in C++, or a class terminate method in Visual Basic 6, except that like a finalizer in Java, you have no control over the timing of this event. Destructors can also cause a significant run-time overhead because of the way the garbage-collection process executes finalization code. The garbage-collection process has to maintain a list of all defunct objects that require finalization, and ensure these objects are finalized at the appropriate time. Given the non-deterministic nature of object deallocation, we can never be sure when the finalization code will run.

Delegates

Delegates are an important part of the Common Type System in the .NET Framework. A delegate is like a type-safe pointer to a method in a class. We define a delegate to specify the signature of methods we would like to call through the delegate, since the delegate itself has no implementation. We can then create a delegate object and bind it to any method whose signature matches that of the delegate.

C++ developers can imagine delegates as type-safe function pointers. Java developers would probably use interfaces to achieve a similar effect. The availability of delegates in C# improves on the function pointer approach by being type-safe (and by being able to hold multiple methods), and it improves on the interface approach by allowing the invocation of a method without the need for inner classes.

Delegates are useful in the following scenarios:

❏ When registering a method as a callback method with another object. When something important happens to that object, it can invoke our callback method. An example of this usage is defining callback methods for events on Graphical User Interface (GUI) controls such as buttons and text fields.

❏ When choosing one of a series of methods (with the same signature) for use in an algorithm. For example, we might have methods to calculate the sine, cosine, and tangent of an angle. We can use a delegate to dictate which of these methods is used by the algorithm.

There are three required steps when defining and using delegates:

❏ Declare the delegate

❏ Create a delegate object, and bind it to a particular method

❏ Invoke the method by using the delegate object

Chapter 6 examines delegates in detail.

Arrays

As we mentioned earlier, unlike in many other programming languages, arrays in .NET are actually reference types. They are not just blocks of memory containing multiple copies of another type, but are in fact true objects that are allocated on the managed heap by the CLR. All arrays have an implicit base class of `System.Array`, which provides some useful functionality. We'll now find out how to declare arrays in C#.

Declaring Arrays

C# allows us to declare one-dimensional arrays (sometimes referred to as vectors), multi-dimensional arrays, or jagged arrays. Jagged arrays are effectively arrays of arrays, each of which may be of a different size. As in C++ and Java, arrays in C# are declared using the `[]` syntax:

```
// one-dimensional array
int[] oneDee = new int[10];

// two-dimensional rectangular array
int[,] twoDee = new int[10, 5];

// jagged array
int[][] jaggy = new int[3][];
jaggy[0] = new int[5];
jaggy[1] = new int[10];
jaggy[2] = new int[20];
```

Note that unlike with C++ the `[]` must always follow the type name, not the variable name. This is the same as the syntax used most commonly in Java. Also note that an array must be initialized using the new operator, because it is a reference type.

> **C++ Note:** *Arrays in C# are a much more predictable and usable datatype than the C-based arrays of C++. Their size and type is discoverable at run time, and if they are multidimensional, their dimensions can also be discovered. .NET array types are defined by the element type, and the number of dimensions they have – but not by the size of the array. It's not possible therefore to specify that a method's parameter must be an array of two integers, only that it must be an array of integers.*

Initializing Array Elements

When an array is created, all elements are automatically initialized to their default values. Alternatively, for all arrays (except jagged), we can use an array initializer to load some preset data. In this case, we don't need to specify the array dimensions as this can be determined at compile time:

```
int[] oneDee = new int[] {4, 4, 8, 2, 5, 9};
int[,] twoDee = new int[,] {{1, 3}, {9, 4}, {4, 4}, {8, 2}, {5, 9}};
```

C# also allows us to use a slightly simplified syntax, which has exactly the same effect:

```
int[] oneDee = {4, 4, 8, 2, 5, 9};
int[,] twoDee = {{1, 3}, {9, 4}, {4, 4}, {8, 2}, {5, 9}};
```

Here, each curly brace enclosed term relates to the items at indices [x,0] and [x,1], respectively, where x ranges from 0 to 4.

As each element in a jagged array is itself an array reference, it will be implicitly initialized to null. This is why we cannot specify an array initializer for a jagged array, but have to first create each of the sub-arrays:

```
int[][] jaggy = new int[3][];
jaggy[0] = new int[] {2, 8, 8, 9, 4};
jaggy[1] = new int[] {2, 3, 0, 7, 9, 6};
jaggy[2] = new int[] {1, 8, 1, 1, 1, 9, 5, 9};
```

Note that in this situation we cannot use the simplified initialization syntax, which is only permitted at the point of declaration.

Using Arrays

Individual array elements are accessed using the [] notation in a way similar to that used for array declaration. For example, we can access elements in our initialized arrays like this:

```
int numa = oneDee[2];     // numa now contains 2
int numb = twoDee[0, 1];   // numb now contains 3
int numc = jaggy[1][3];    // numc now contains 7
```

All developers should note that arrays in C# are by default zero based. Visual Basic developers should note the use of square brackets instead of parentheses to access array elements in C#.

As arrays inherit all of the functionality defined in System.Array, we have access to some useful properties and methods to query and manipulate the array and its elements. For some of these methods, the element types must support particular interfaces. We'll cover interfaces at the end of the chapter. Here are a few of the public members we can use from System.Array:

Member	Description
Rank	This read-only property returns the number of dimensions in the array.
GetLength()	Returns the number of elements in a specified dimension.
Sort()	Sorts the elements in one array, two arrays, or part of one array. Note that the array element type must implement IComparer or IComparable.

Table continued on following page

Member	Description
BinarySearch()	Uses a binary search algorithm to search a sorted array for a particular element. As with Sort(), the array element type must implement IComparer or IComparable.
IndexOf()	Returns the index of the first matching occurrence of an element in a one-dimensional array.

In addition to this, when we access array elements in our code, the CLR ensures that the array index is valid at run time. This means that we cannot accidentally or deliberately overstep the boundaries of an array and so gain access to memory outside the allowable range. This is not only useful for tracking bugs but also plugs a potential security hole.

Casting Arrays

With a few restrictions, C# and the .NET runtime allow us to cast arrays between reference types. For this to work both array types must have the same number of dimensions and an implicit or explicit conversion between the element types must exist. The CLR doesn't allow implicit casting of arrays containing value types but System.Array defines a Copy() method that allows us to achieve the same effect.

Casting an array to another type is similar to the conversion between any two types. If there is a valid conversion between two reference types, then the same conversion should be valid for arrays of those reference types. This is known as **array covariance** and because of this the CLR checks at run time whether any assignment to an element of a reference array is made from a valid type or not. For example, while it is legal to cast a string array to an object array, the third line of code in the following example would throw an exception:

```
string[] someStrings = new string[4];    // ok
object[] someObjects = someStrings;       // ok
someObjects[2] = 42;                      // throws exception!
```

It is more useful if we consider how to cast between arrays of value types. Perhaps you have an int array containing screen coordinates, on which you now wish to perform some algorithm requiring floating-point precision. You can use the Copy() method to quickly and efficiently perform this conversion on the whole array:

```
int[] points = {13, 145, 87, 209};
double[] work = new double[points.Length];
Array.Copy(points, work, points.Length);
```

You'll see a few more array handling examples in the next section.

Strings

The last section of our tour through standard .NET reference types deals with strings. Support for string handling in .NET is integrated tightly with the CLR and is very comprehensive. Hence, C# regards strings as primitive types, although they are actually reference types, and they are defined by the System.String class. In this section we'll see how to declare and use strings and just touch on some of the additional features. For more details, consult the *C# Text Manipulation Handbook*, Apress, ISBN 1-86100-823-6.

Declaring Strings

The fact that strings are considered as primitive types shows itself in a number of ways. For example, we initialize a string using a literal value:

```
string s = "Hello World";          // Ok
string s = new String("Hello world");   // Error!
```

You can initialize a string using a constructor, but only by passing in chars or char arrays (or memory pointers to byte arrays if writing unsafe, non-CLS-compliant code). C# defines the string keyword to indicate its primitive status and this is often a cause for confusion among new C# developers. In fact, string and System.String are synonymous and may be used interchangeably in your code, although it is always better to stick with one standard.

One great relief to C++ developers will be the C# syntax for specifying an @-quoted string, sometimes called a verbatim string. Simply prefixing the literal string value with the @ symbol will ensure that any escape sequences in the string are not processed, thus avoiding the need for doubling up escape characters. The following two statements declare identical strings; see which you think is clearer:

```
string s1 = "C:\\Winnt\\System32\\Write.exe";
string s2 = @"C:\Winnt\System32\Write.exe";
```

C# allows the use of the same escape sequences familiar to C and C++ developers. For example, we can use \t to encode a tab character, \n for a newline, and \r for a carriage return. However, there is a slightly more robust way of defining a newline character; as the System.Environment class defines a static NewLine property that is platform independent. Under Windows, this property contains "\r\n" and is used by other .NET Framework classes, such as by the Console.WriteLine() method.

Strings are Immutable

One of the most important things to be aware of in .NET is that strings are immutable. This is the same as for the java.lang.String class in Java, and it means that a string never changes once it has been initialized. It cannot shrink, grow, or have any characters altered.

Whenever you perform any manipulation on a string, a new instance is returned and the original string left intact. If we write the following statements, the test is performed on a temporary copy of our string, which is subsequently removed by the garbage collector:

```
string s = @"C:\Winnt\System32\Write.exe";
if (s.ToLower().EndsWith("dll"))
{
    // Do something
}
```

Mutability is covered in more detail in Chapter 2.

Using Strings

We'll finish off our brief look at strings with an example that includes arrays. First we define an array of strings using an array initializer:

```
using System;

public class StringClass
{
  public static void Main()
  {
    // Initialize at declaration
    string[] chapters = {"Managed heap", "Array handling",
                         "Reference types", "Year 2000"};
```

Strings and arrays are reference types, so what we have here is a stack variable, chapters, containing a reference to an array on the managed heap. That array contains references to strings elsewhere on the managed heap. If we attempt to change any of these array elements, this will result in the original element being replaced with a reference to a new string instance. Next we'll define a second string array, but this time we'll initialize individual elements in code:

```
    // Initialize by element
    string[] sections = new string[8];
    sections[0] = "Value types";
    sections[1] = "Language features";
    sections[2] = "Implementing interfaces";
```

We can concatenate strings using the '+' operator:

```
    // Concatenate strings
    sections[3] = "User-defined " + sections[0];
```

Again, this doesn't change the string objects on which it operates; it creates a completely new string object, and it is a reference to this object that we place in the third element of sections. Now, we'll use the CopyTo() method defined in System.Array to copy strings between our two arrays. This works fast since strings are reference types, and so only the references need to be copied. The CLR doesn't need to duplicate the actual strings themselves. Because strings are immutable, it doesn't matter if we perform any operations on the strings in the original array – the actual strings won't change. The effect of this is to make strings appear to behave in exactly the same way as value types, even though they are reference types. This behavior can be very useful, and is the reason for coding reference types immutably, which we'll examine in the next chapter.

```
// Copy elements between arrays
chapters.CopyTo(sections, 4);
```

Using the System.Array.Sort() method, we can sort either the whole array or, as in this example, just a subset of its elements. The String class implements the IComparable interface, which is necessary for it to be sorted by System.Array. In fact there are a range of comparison methods in the String class, which can cater for case-sensitivity and take into account the calling thread's CurrentCulture to ensure correct comparison of characters in different languages. For example, in German, the strings 'Strasse' and 'Straße' might need to be considered equivalent.

```
// Partial string sort
Array.Sort(sections, 0, 4);
```

Finally, as System.Array implements IEnumerable, we can use the C# foreach keyword to iterate through the elements in the array and display them to the console:

```
// Enumerate array
foreach (string s in sections)
{
    Console.WriteLine(s);
}
}
}
```

Save this file as string_array.cs, and compile it. The application produces the following output:

```
C:\> string_array
Implementing interfaces
Language features
User-defined Value types
Value types
Managed heap
Array handling
Reference types
Year 2000
```

Using Value Types as Reference Types

There are occasions when we would want to use a value type where a reference type is expected. Perhaps we need to pass an instance of a value type to a method that expects an object parameter; for example, say we need to insert a value instance into a .NET Framework collection.

Boxing and Unboxing

Converting an instance of a value type to an instance of a reference type is called boxing, and the reverse process is called unboxing. These are new concepts to most developers moving to .NET, and in C# this happens often without us even being aware of it. However, it is important to understand what's happening, so we'll spend a little time looking at these processes in detail.

Value Types as Objects

Consider the following code sample:

```
// Create an ArrayList object
System.Collections.ArrayList payroll =
    new System.Collections.ArrayList();

// Add some Money objects
payroll.Add(new Money(30500.0));
payroll.Add(new Money(54000.0));
payroll.Add(new Money(27900.0));
```

ArrayList is a standard .NET Framework collection class, and like all the other collection classes, ArrayList holds a collection of references to objects. These objects must be reference types, and so must be located on the managed heap. The Add() method of the ArrayList class expects an object as a parameter.

If we try to add an instance of a value type (a Money structure, defined earlier in the chapter in *Defining and Using Value Types*) to the ArrayList, the CLR automatically creates a boxed copy of the Money instance on the managed heap. In this sense, boxed means that the CLR has added a wrapper around the value instance to make it appear and behave like a reference type. This happens automatically in C#.

The boxed object holds a copy of the data from the value object; if the boxed object is modified, it won't affect the original value object. Likewise, if the original value object is modified, it won't affect the boxed object. This is what we'd expect from a value type.

The following code retrieves an element from the `ArrayList`:

```
Money myCash = (Money)payroll[0];
```

In C#, the `ArrayList` class contains an `Item` property, which serves as the indexer for the class. This allows us to use the `[]` syntax to return a reference to an object on the managed heap. When we try to assign this to a `Money` instance using an explicit cast, the CLR extracts the value from the boxed object and copies it into our local `Money` instance. Again, we have a copy of the value, and changes to it won't affect the original or the boxed value still on the heap. This is unboxing, and it also happens automatically in C#. However, because of the type-safe nature of C#, we have to use an explicit cast when unboxing. An exception will be thrown at run time if the object in the `ArrayList` is not of the correct type.

> **While we have shown boxing using an `ArrayList`, you should be aware that boxing does *not* occur when value types are declared in a normal C# array defined using the `[]` syntax. In this situation, memory is allocated on the managed heap to contain the value type array elements but these are not boxed.**

C# performs boxing automatically; and apart from supplying an explicit cast when unboxing, we don't need to write any special code to make that happen. This is a mixed blessing, because boxing and unboxing imposes an overhead at run time.

Performance Implications

In order to understand what effect this overhead may have on your application, and the situations in which this can occur, we'll go a little deeper into boxing and unboxing, because understanding these issues will help you decide whether it is better to implement a particular type as a `struct` or a `class`. Let's start by seeing what happens in the code snippet above when a `Money` value type is added to an `ArrayList`.

1. First a stack-based `Money` type is created as a result of the `new` operator. The relevant constructor is called to initialize the object's fields.

2. The C# compiler has recognized that the `Add()` method of the `ArrayList` class requires a reference type instead of a value type and so will have emitted MSIL code to perform the boxing operation.

3. Memory is allocated on the managed heap. This includes the memory required for the fields in the `Money` structure, plus some extra memory required to establish the boxed type as a reference type. For example, memory will be allocated for a method table pointer, which is not relevant for a value type.

4. The fields in the stack-based Money instance, created as a result of the new operator, will be copied byte-by-byte into the newly allocated heap memory.

5. Finally, the address of the heap-allocated object will be returned and passed to the Add() method of the ArrayList class.

This process is repeated three times, once for each Money instance that we add to the ArrayList. When it comes to unboxing, the following actions reverse the process:

1. First, memory is allocated on the stack for the myCash variable and the default Money constructor is called to initialize the member fields.

2. Next, the boxed reference is checked to see if it is null. If yes, then a NullReferenceException is thrown.

3. The type of the boxed object is then checked against the type declared in the explicit cast in the source code. In this example, if the object is not of the Money type, an InvalidCastException is thrown.

4. Finally, a pointer to the boxed value type on the managed heap is obtained and the contents of the Money fields are copied byte-by-byte into the stack-based variable myCash.

You can see that if your application is performing a lot of boxing and unboxing then the overhead in terms of performance and memory usage can be significant.

Other Boxing Scenarios

The previous example gives one scenario in which a value type is passed as a parameter to a method requiring a reference type. Boxing will also occur whenever you implicitly or explicitly cast an instance of a value type to a reference type. For example, the following code will create a boxed version of an int:

```
int number = 43;                    // define a value type
object o = number;                  // boxes a copy of number
int anotherNumber = (int)o;         // unboxes the copied value
```

Boxing also happens when you cast a value type to an interface. By definition interfaces are reference types. So if we wish to obtain the IComparable interface from our Money structure, the following code will cause a boxing operation:

```
Money someMoney = new Money(4.0); // define a value type
IComparable iface = someMoney;      // get reference to an interface
```

Another situation that you may be unaware of is when checking an object's type:

```
Money someMoney = new Money(4.5); // define a value type
Type t = someMoney.GetType();       // access type information
```

In this situation, someMoney is again boxed. This is because Money doesn't directly implement GetType(), as it is inherited from System.ValueType. In order to resolve this method call, the CLR needs to have a pointer to a Money() method table, which can only be obtained by boxing someMoney.

The best thing to do would be to limit the amount of boxing and unboxing. If you find your application is doing a great deal of boxing and unboxing, it will be more efficient to define your data type as a class rather than a struct.

> *Managed Extensions for C++ makes you work harder to achieve boxing and unboxing. In this environment, you must explicitly box and unbox value instances using the __box and dynamic_downcast operators respectively. The code is a little harder to read and write but at least you know when boxing and unboxing is taking place, and that can have its advantages.*

Interfaces

Now that we've seen how value types and reference types work in C#, let's turn our attention to interfaces. An interface is similar to a class, except that none of the methods in an interface have any implementation. An interface just specifies a set of related methods that must be implemented by other classes and structures. Because they contain no implementation, you cannot instantiate interfaces. In object-oriented design terms, interfaces are similar to pure abstract classes.

> *An interface can also contain properties, indexers, and events. For more information about these kinds of members, see Chapter 2.*

Interfaces play an extremely important role in object-oriented design. We can define interfaces to represent contractual obligations, without worrying about how these obligations will be satisfied by classes and structures in the application. Interfaces allow us to separate *what* an object can do, from *how* the object will do it.

By writing a generic method that takes an interface type as a parameter, and then implementing that interface in otherwise unrelated classes, we can provide a type-safe way of generalizing functionality across classes. If we access an object via an interface, the type of the object doesn't matter. For example, we only need to implement the IComparable interface in our own classes to allow them to be ordered correctly in a collection using, for example, the Array.Sort() method. The System.Array class only accesses instances of our class using this interface and doesn't care whether it's sorting strings, integers, apples, pears, oranges, or whatever.

Using interfaces in the design of our systems has several benefits:

❏　It enables us to defer decisions about how to implement a particular behavior. We can write the implementing classes and structures later in the development process.

❏　It allows us to provide several alternative implementations for the same interface.

❏　It provides a hook for future extensions to our code. We can come back to our application in six months time and define new implementing classes if necessary, without having to change code that relies on them as the interface stays the same.

C++ and Java developers should be familiar with this concept, but this will be new ground for Visual Basic developers.

By convention, all interfaces in the .NET Framework start with the letter I. This makes it easy to distinguish interfaces from classes and structures. The .NET Framework class library has interfaces such as IDisposable, ICloneable, IComparable, and so on.

Summary

In this chapter, we've seen how the .NET Framework defines a Common Type System that spans all .NET programming languages. We've investigated the use of primitive types, classes, structures, enumerations, interfaces, and delegates in C# applications.

❏　All primitive types (except String and Object) map to predefined value types in the .NET Framework class library. For example, if we declare an int variable in our C# code, the compiler maps this to System.Int32. This in turn translates into the int32 type in Microsoft Intermediate Language (MSIL) code.

❏　Classes represent reference types. When we create a class object, it is placed on the Common Language Runtime's managed heap. Class objects exhibit copy-by-reference semantics. When a class object is no longer referenced, the object becomes available for garbage collection.

❏　Structures represent value types. Value instances can be stored on the heap, or within managed objects. Value instances exhibit copy-by-value semantics. When a value instance goes out of scope, it is popped off the stack and deleted. Value instances are not subjected to garbage collection.

❏　Enumerations are integral data types that have a restricted set of allowable values. In the .NET Framework, enumerations are value types.

❏　Delegates represent pointers to methods. We can create a delegate to specify which method we want to invoke, and then invoke the method when we are ready. Delegates form the basis of the event mechanism in the .NET Framework.

❑ Interfaces specify a contractual agreement that we can implement in other classes and structures. Interfaces enable us to decouple the *what* from the *how* in our design.

Now that we've seen how to define types in C#, we'll investigate how to design and implement these types correctly and effectively in the following chapters.

C#

Class Design

Handbook

2

Type Members

One of the most basic building blocks in object-oriented programming is the class. Apart from interfaces and structs, the majority of application code that you will write for the .NET platform will be encapsulated in classes. Becoming an effective class designer is essential to becoming a successful object-oriented programmer.

Effective class designs also simplify maintenance and versioning. Once a class is designed and clients are consuming the class, it becomes difficult to change or version. If you remove functionality from a production class, you have violated the contract that consumers have coded against, and the consumer's code will fail. If you alter an existing class, you could possibly break all consumers using the class. Much like building a house, the original design and thought process is critical to avoid making future changes. It is much more difficult and expensive to redesign a finished house than one being sketched. Similarly, it becomes more difficult to change the design of your class structure once the class is in the production environment.

Members defined inside a type, or type members, are the fundamental programming constructs used to build classes within the .NET Framework. Type members within the .NET Framework include:

- ❏ Constants
- ❏ Variables (also known as fields)
- ❏ Properties
- ❏ Methods
- ❏ Constructors
- ❏ Events

All object-oriented programming languages (for example, C++, Java, C#, and VB.NET) offer differing levels of support for type members. For example, C++ and Java do not have support for a property; they make use of get and set methods. However, within the .NET Framework, all languages must support the CTS. The CTS enforces a set of common rules and requirements for describing type members.

This chapter introduces the .NET type members as described by C#. It is important to understand that other programming languages targeting the .NET platform (for example VB.NET), offer similar type members. Also, once compiled to the .NET native intermediate language, it becomes very difficult to tell what language the code was actually written in.

We also examine the class member accessibility levels that .NET provides to restrict the visibility of type members. At times, classes need the ability to restrict what type members are visible to different pieces of code. For example, a class may need to have a function that is only callable from within the same namespace. Applying the proper access modifier gives us the flexibility to provide such restrictions.

Lastly, we will also discuss inherent type members available to class designers. We will uncover functionality found in the .NET Framework's root class, System.Object. These inherent type members, or default methods are always present; this is due to the fact that every class is derived from System.Object. While the default methods are useful, it is also possible to override these type members to provide specific functionality. System.Object defines useful methods that client code can invoke on any kind of object; for example, the Equals() method indicates whether two objects contain the same value. We'll survey these methods during the chapter, and describe how to use the most important ones

Constants

A constant serves a very basic, yet extremely useful purpose. The constant is a symbolic representation of an unchanging value. Rather than hard-coding numeric and string values, they should be assigned to constants instead. A numeric value scattered throughout code without explanation is often referred to as a **magic number**. These magic numbers can make maintenance a tedious task and are prone to introduce bugs into code.

> **Java Note:** *Java does not have a constant type. Rather, Java achieves a similar function through the use of public variables declared as static final.*

To illustrate, we're going to create a simple guessing game (magicnumbers.cs). We have chosen to place the code for presentation in the main class, MagicNumbers. However, to encapsulate the rules of the game, we have placed the game logic in a separate class, GuessTheNumber:

```
using System;

public class GuessTheNumber
{
  public string tryGuess(int guess)
  {
    Random generator = new Random();
    int randomNumber=generator.Next(1,10);
    if (guess == randomNumber)
      return "You guessed it!";
    else
      return "Sorry, the number was " + randomNumber.ToString();
  }
}

class MagicNumbers
{
  [STAThread]
  static void Main(string[] args)
  {
    Console.WriteLine("We're going to play a guessing game!");
    Console.WriteLine("Please enter a number between 1 and 10:");

    try
    {
      int myGuess=int.Parse(Console.ReadLine());
      if ((myGuess > 10) || (myGuess <1))
        Console.WriteLine("Value must be between 1 and 10");
      else
      {
        GuessTheNumber gtn=new GuessTheNumber();
        Console.WriteLine(gtn.tryGuess(myGuess));
      }
    }
    catch
    {
      Console.WriteLine("You need to enter a number!");
    }
  }
}
```

While the example is a bit contrived, it does illustrate how magic numbers can cause problems. In our example, we need to store the minimum and maximum guess ranges in two classes. The problem is further compounded when we look at just the MagicNumbers class. Here, we reference the values multiple times for display to the user.

If, for any reason, we need to change the rules of our game, perhaps to make it a bit harder and let someone guess a number between one and twenty, then we would need to find all instances of our magic numbers and replace them. Of course, this is a rather easy task with our example, but just imagine a multi-thousand-line program with the same challenges as our example. The chance of bugs appearing in previously working code because a number was missed would be very high.

Now, let's fix that example up and show the power of constants. Again, the goal is to provide symbolic constants for values that will not change at runtime. It is good practice to group related constants together. The minimum and maximum number on our guessing game look to be a good place to use constants. The following code can be found in `magicnumbers_revised.cs`:

```csharp
using System;

public class GuessTheNumber
{
   public const int LOW=1;
   public const int HIGH=10;

   public string tryGuess(int guess)
   {
      Random generator = new Random();
      int randomNumber=generator.Next(LOW,HIGH);
      if (guess == randomNumber)
          return "You guessed it!";
      else
          return "Sorry, the number was " + randomNumber.ToString();
   }
}

class MagicNumbers
{
   [STAThread]
   static void Main(string[] args)
   {
      GuessTheNumber numberGame=new GuessTheNumber();

      Console.WriteLine("We're going to play a guessing game!");
      Console.WriteLine("Please enter a number between "
                        + GuessTheNumber.LOW + " and "
                        + GuessTheNumber.HIGH + ":");

      try
      {
         int myGuess=int.Parse(Console.ReadLine());
         if ((myGuess > GuessTheNumber.HIGH) ||
             (myGuess < GuessTheNumber.LOW))
               Console.WriteLine("Value must be between "
                                 + GuessTheNumber.LOW + " and "
                                 + GuessTheNumber.HIGH);
         else
         {
            Console.WriteLine(numberGame.tryGuess(myGuess));
         }
      }
      catch
      {
         Console.WriteLine("You need to enter a number!");
      }
   }
}
```

One important thing to note is that we are actually referencing the class GuessTheNumber to access the constant. Constants are not defined for each instance of the class. Rather, they are only defined once. We've also defined our constants as public. If a constant is only needed within the current class, then it is perfectly fine to declare the constant as private instead. We will cover other access modifiers later in the chapter.

The actual value of a constant is determined at compile time. When the code is compiled from C# into MSIL, the compiler will insert the constant's value in the resulting executable's metadata. One of the strong points of using constants, aside from tidying up code, is that inserting the constant value directly into the metadata does not require memory allocation. However, since the values are inserted straight into MSIL, constants may only be a primitive type.

Let's take a look at the resulting MSIL for the Main() method of the MagicNumbers class. After compiling the code, we will use the ildasm.exe utility included in the .NET Framework. This utility allows us to view the MSIL and metadata associated with .NET assemblies. The following code from the Main() method:

```
class magicnumbers
{
  [STAThread]
  static void Main(string[] args)
  {
    GuessTheNumber numberGame=new GuessTheNumber();

    Console.WriteLine("We're going to play a guessing game!");
    Console.WriteLine("Please enter a number between "
      + GuessTheNumber.LOW" + " and " + GuessTheNumber.HIGH + ":");
```

will be compiled into MSIL as shown in the screenshot below. Notice that the associated values for the HIGH and LOW constants of the GuessTheNumber class are embedded into the MSIL of the magicnumber class:

The fact that .NET embeds constants into the executable code presents a potentially serious downfall. Suppose the constant is defined within another assembly, a DLL for example, and our code was compiled against that DLL. At compilation time, the value of the constants are read from the DLL and placed directly into our code.

If the constants in the DLL change, then our code would need to be recompiled as well. Otherwise, our code is unaware of any changes in the other DLL. Both our code, and the DLL it is relying on, will continue to function, with one serious problem; the constants are no longer consistent.

Assume we are coding a class that uses a connection string to a database. Instead of typing the same string throughout the code, you code the connection string as a constant and use the constant instead. Without thinking, you have locked the code into that particular connection string. If any portion of that connection string changes (database name, IP address, protocol, data provider, and so on), you will be in perhaps a difficult position to recompile and redeploy the code just to fix the connection string.

Not-so Constants

Remember, a constant's value is substituted in at compile time. As such, it is restricted to primitive types. Additionally, because of this compile-time substitution, if a constant changes, then every other class that relies on that constant must also be recompiled.

However, there is another approach to achieve similar functionality to a constant. This method is to declare a variable as a static read-only variable. Where constants are resolved at compile-time, static read-only variables are resolved at run time. There are two main advantages of a static read-only variable:

- ❏ Unlike constants, they do not require dependent classes to be recompiled when they change.

- ❏ A static read-only variable can be assigned any type. It is not restricted to primitive types.

There is also a disadvantage to using static read-only variables, at least when compared to constants. A constant is directly substituted into the MSIL. As we demonstrated above, this is true even when a constant is referenced between classes. In contrast, a static read-only variable must maintain a link to the corresponding class.

In terms of syntax, creating and using static, read-only variables is not much different from defining and accessing a constant:

```
public class GuessTheNumber
{
    public static readonly int LOW=1;
    public static readonly int HIGH=10;

       . . . . .
       //code omitted for brevity
       . . . . .
}
```

However, the corresponding MSIL is much different. Now, rather than simply substituting in a constant value, we have to establish a reference to the class containing the read-only variable:

```
MagicNumbers::Main : void(string[])                              _ □ x
    IL_000b:  call        void [mscorlib]System.Console::WriteLine(string)
    IL_0010:  ldc.i4.5
    IL_0011:  newarr      [mscorlib]System.Object
    IL_0016:  stloc.2
    IL_0017:  ldloc.2
    IL_0018:  ldc.i4.0
    IL_0019:  ldstr       "Please enter a number between "
    IL_001e:  stelem.ref
    IL_001f:  ldloc.2
    IL_0020:  ldc.i4.1
    IL_0021:  ldsfld      int32 GuessTheNumber::LOW
    IL_0026:  box         [mscorlib]System.Int32
    IL_002b:  stelem.ref
    IL_002c:  ldloc.2
    IL_002d:  ldc.i4.2
    IL_002e:  ldstr       " and "
    IL_0033:  stelem.ref
```

A third option, which we will not review in detail here, is to use application configuration files. Application configuration is extremely flexible within the .NET Framework and proves to be an excellent mechanism for application-specific information. For more on application configuration files, check out the MSDN.

Configuration files are ideal for storing deployment-oriented information. For example, database connection information should be stored in a configuration file. Of course, with its ability to be resolved at run time, a static read-only variable could be used to access and store values from a configuration file.

Let's summarize what we've learned in this section to help you understand when to use constants, static read-only fields, or application configuration files:

❑ As a rule, only constants that do not change should be exposed to external classes. Of course, a constant is still a very useful mechanism when only used inside a class to minimize magic numbers. In this scenario, even frequently changing values will not be an issue, as the changes will be applied with each recompile.

❑ If a variable must be determined at run time, or must contain a reference to a complex type, as opposed to the primitive types that a constant is limited to, then a static read-only variable is the way to go.

❑ Lastly, a configuration file should be used to store information related to the setup, configuration, and deployment of an application. Constants serve a very useful purpose in .NET, but it is crucial to understand where constants are best applied and where another approach is better suited to solve a given problem in any programming language.

Fields

Fields, more commonly referred to as instance variables or class variables, are the most basic building blocks in most classes and structs. Quite simply, fields store data and references for classes and structures. A field is simply a variable defined in a class.

If not exposed and used correctly, fields can lend themselves to elusive bugs. You will see where some of the bugs can be introduced when we talk about accessibility. Fields can have five different levels of accessibility:

❑ `public`
The access is not limited. A consumer of your class can freely read and modify any public fields, without your class even being aware of the changes. Public fields should be used with caution.

❑ `internal`
Access to internal fields is restricted to the same namespace as your class. In essence, this is stating, "Only other types in my namespace can read or modify this field directly." As with public fields, your class will still not be aware of the changes. Internal fields should also be used with caution.

❑ `protected`
Access is limited to classes that are inherited or extended from your class, and your own class of course. Remember, an important part of OO design is the ability to inherit from other classes. This states, "Only myself and types that are derived from me can access this field."

❑ `protected internal`
This is the only valid two-keyword access modifier. This combines the meaning of both protected and internal to mean "Myself, other types in my namespace, or types derived from me, can access this field."

❑ `private`
This is the most restrictive of the access declarations. A private field means, "Only I can access this field. No other types in my namespace, nor any types derived from me can even see this field."

At this point, it is important to understand that proper exposure is essential in class design. For example, if a field is public, then it is possible for consumers of your class to modify the contents of a field without your class ever knowing about the changes.

A field is simply a variable defined in a class. When the .NET runtime creates an instance of the class, memory is allocated to hold the contents of the instance fields. Because the field is created at run time and has its own memory space, the field is not subject to the versioning problems associated with constants. This contrasts with a constant where the value is substituted in at compile-time. If a constant changes, the dependent classes must also be recompiled. If a field changes, the dependent classes are not affected as they simply hold a reference to the field.

Let's take a minute to demonstrate what a field looks like. As an added bonus, this will demonstrate why it is essential to pay attention to access modifiers on class fields. The following program (`fields_publicbankaccount.cs`) creates an object of type `Account`. The class `Account` is a very basic representation of a bank account with just one field (right now) to store the account's balance. Since the `balance` field is a `double`, the compiler will initialize it to a value of 0. Default values and class initialization are covered in greater detail in Chapter 5.

```
using System;

public class Account
{
  public double balance;
}

class AtTheBank
{
  [STAThread]
  static void Main(string[] args)
  {
    Account myAccount = new Account();

    Console.WriteLine("You have " + myAccount.balance + "
                      remaining.");
    myAccount.balance=10000;
    Console.WriteLine("You have " + myAccount.balance + "
                      remaining.");
  }
}
```

Compiling and running the above produces the following output:

```
C:\Class Design\Ch 02>fields_publicbankaccount.exe
You have 0 remaining.
You have 10000 remaining.
```

Looking at the MSIL created for the `Account` class, we notice the `balance` field is given its own location. The MSIL simply confirms that the `balance` variable is of type `float64` (double) with `public` access and that it is called `balance`:

By making this field public, we have made it part of the class's interface. This means that if we need to change the field name later, we will break binary compatibility. Additionally, and as you saw above, by making the field `public`, we have given unrestricted access to any other class that instantiates our class. In certain cases, this is acceptable and even desired. However, in most cases, and certainly in our bank account example, we do not want to allow others to change our field state. After all, it might not be desirable to let bank customers determine their own balances!

Public fields are simple to use, but are very dangerous and not recommended for two reasons:

- ❑ **Public fields are unrestricted**
  In this example, the AtTheBank class can change the value of the balance to any float64 value. If the requirement is that the balance can never be less than 0, then every piece of code that uses the Account class must enforce this rule before setting the public balance field. In other words, we allow clients to modify the field even if they don't understand all of the attendant business rules.

- ❑ **Public fields make the class difficult to version**
  Once deployed, we cannot change the name of the balance field, as the binary compatibility will be compromised. We also cannot turn the public fields into a property without compromising binary compatibility.

In practice, public fields should be avoided unless special justification can permit their use. For instance, sometimes it may be desirable to have a class or struct that simply stores state to be passed between other classes. However, as a rule, any data that is to be exposed on a public interface is more flexible in the form of a property.

Properties

Properties represent state in a class. However, properties are quite different from fields. Whereas a field stores data, a property provides a specific access point to that data. Properties extend the concept of the field by being able to restrict the incoming values and provide read-only and write-only data members.

> *Java and C++ Note: Java and C++ do not have a concept of a property. However, Java has a well-defined pattern for exposing fields in an equivalent manner. A standard practice in Java is to create getFieldName() and setFieldName() methods to perform a similar task to properties. Think of properties in .NET as a formalized implementation of this pattern.*

To build on the last example, if the business requirement stated the value of the balance could not be below zero, then the rules would be applied when the property is set. In our next example, if the argument violates the rule, then we will throw an ArgumentOutOfRangeException. The following program (properties_bankaccount.cs) illustrates this:

```
using System;

public class Account
{
    private double balance;
```

```
public double Balance
{
    get
    {
        return balance;
    }
    set
    {
        if (value < 0)
            throw
            new ArgumentOutOfRangeException("value","Balance must
                                            be greater than 0");
        balance=value;
    }
}
}
```

If you'll notice, we refer to value but have not declared it anywhere. The value keyword is implicitly set when the property is set. For example, myAccount.Balance=500 would load 500 into the value parameter that we reference in the set method:

```
class AtTheBank
{
    [STAThread]
    static void Main(string[] args)
    {
        Account myAccount = new Account();

        try
        {
            Console.WriteLine("You have " + myAccount.Balance + "
                              remaining.");
            myAccount.Balance=10000;
            Console.WriteLine("You have " + myAccount.Balance + "
                              remaining.");
            myAccount.Balance=-500;
            Console.WriteLine("You have " + myAccount.Balance + "
                              remaining.");
        }
        catch(ArgumentOutOfRangeException e)
        {
            Console.WriteLine("Bad value!");
        }
    }
}
```

Properties have greater flexibility in how to expose data to external classes. Properties provide data encapsulation. In our example, the user does not have direct access to the account balance any more. Rather, the account balance can only be accessed through the Balance property. The Balance property, in turn, enforces a basic business rule on setting the actual account balance. To the rest of the world, the balance is as easy to access as a public field, but now only the Account class is responsible for enforcing business rules.

The advantage of using data encapsulation comes when the implementation of the class needs to change. Data encapsulation allows us to control what values the user can assign to a property, giving us the power to prevent an invalid state since we can filter and possibly reject incoming values if they would incorrectly disrupt the object's state. In our example, if the rule later changes to allow negative balances, but only to $500, then we could change the Account class and not disrupt any other class that relies on Account. Properties also provide additional value over simply public fields in that a property can be defined as read-only or write-only.

In C#, defining a property as read-only or write-only is as simple as removing the appropriate setter or getter respectively. The compiler will throw an error at build time if we attempt to get the value of a write-only property or try to set a read-only value. This includes attempting to access a write-only property on the right-hand side of an expression or within a statement.

Within the .NET environment, properties are somewhat different from other type members. Within MSIL, properties are broken down into get_ and set_ methods. For example, our read-write property Balance would have both a get_Balance and set_Balance accessor method defined within the Account class's MSIL. The compiler will also emit a property definition into the MSIL to provide the association between the property and the get_ and set_ access methods. Let's go back to our Account Balance property:

```
using System;
public class Account
{
  private double balance;

  public double Balance
  {
    get
    {
      return balance;
    }
    set
    {
      balance=value;
    }
  }
}
```

However, the question may be, why even have properties at all. If the entire purpose of a property is to redirect to other accessors, then why not just add two methods to act as accessors to the private field and bypass the use of properties altogether.

Well, the easiest answer is that properties help immensely with readability. Consider the following two equivalent methods of setting the account balance:

```
Account myAccount = new Account();
double myBalance;

myAccount.Balance=1000;
myBalance=myAccount.Balance;
```

versus:

```
myAccount.setBalance(1000);
myBalance=myAccount.getBalance();
```

While both function well, the first is much easier to follow and seems a bit more natural to most people. Additionally, development tools like Visual Studio .NET use the property MSIL block to provide more detailed information about the class to the developer. For example, when Visual Studio .NET provides automatic code completion, it can distinguish between a method and a property and gives the property a different icon for display purposes.

However, the first approach of using properties does come with one downside. As you will recall, we discussed how fields could be assigned different accessibility levels. This holds true for properties as well. The downside is that an accessibility level can only be applied to the property; it cannot be applied to the get and set accessors separately. If, for any reason, the accessors must have different visibilities, such as a public get and a protected set, then a property will no longer be the right solution. In instances where you need separate accessibility levels, you will need to define your own getter and setter methods. Properties are covered in more detail in Chapter 4.

Methods

Methods are fundamental to designing classes in C#. They represent actions associated with a class. Methods typically perform actions that manipulate the object's state. However, this isn't always the case. For instance, you can declare a method as a static method. A static method might provide specific functionality, but it cannot work on an object's state. As with our other discussions around static things, a static method belongs to the class and not each specific instance.

All methods have a name, a parameter list, and a return type. As we will see, it is also possible to define multiple methods with the same name as long as they contain different signatures. Methods are discussed in more detail in the next chapter.

Method Overloading

The method signature includes the method's name, and the number and type of parameters. For example, if two methods with identical names differ only by their number and types of parameters, the .NET Framework considers the methods different. The practice of creating methods with same names and different signatures is called **method overloading**. If two methods exist in the same class or struct, with the same signature, the compiler will generate an error on compilation.

Note that our description of a method's signature does not include a return type. This is because methods in C# cannot be overloaded based solely on the return type. This rule is not enforced by the .NET platform, but rather by the C# language. The CLR supports the ability for two or more methods to only differ by return type, however the C# language (and many other .NET languages including VB.NET) do not. A compiler error will be generated if two methods in the same class differ only by return type. Each language enforces the restriction, not the .NET runtime. In practice, the issue is seldom a limiting factor in class design.

Properties versus Methods

Properties and methods are very similar. In fact, properties are syntactical shortcuts to defining methods. While both methods and properties can be used to perform activities, properties should be used to represent a piece of data and methods should be used to perform actions. Most often, a property is simply used to change (get or set) the state of one variable within a class. Methods are often used when we need to perform actions that change an overall object's state. In other words, methods perform the business functions of the object.

From the .NET point of view, there is no difference between properties and methods. Within .NET, properties are actually treated as methods. A property's get and set accessor are each compiled into their own method.

When designing classes, you will undoubtedly find yourself choosing between using properties and methods. The recommended approach to answering the question is to ask yourself if the purpose of the procedure to set or retrieve a piece of data or perform a more general action. Use properties to set and retrieve a piece of data; use methods to perform actions.

When naming your properties and methods, stick to nouns for properties to signify data and verbs for method names to signify an action. For example, if we expanded our `Account` class to carry customer information as well, then `Name`, `Address`, and `Telephone` would make ideal property names because they describe a piece of data. `Withdraw()`, `MakeDeposit()`, and `Transfer()` make ideal method names because they describe an action.

For more naming convention guidelines, refer to the specifications set forth in the .NET SDK's Design Guidelines for Class Library Developers. The .NET SDK can be downloaded freely from MSDN at http://msdn.microsoft.com.

Static Type Members

The fields, properties, and methods we have seen so far in this chapter are accessible only with a reference to an instance of a class. However, not all functionality is best implemented tied to an instance of a class. .NET allows us to define type members that are callable directly from the class without requiring an instance of the class to be created. Fields, methods, and properties can all be declared in this fashion.

Static type members are useful if a particular action is not tied to an instance of the class, but is functionality that can be used as a standalone. For example, a Time class may define a GetCurrentTime() method that returns the current system clock time. Creating an instance of Time just to call GetCurrentTime() is not ideal since all classes would return the same value. Since this method is general to the Time class and is not specific to each instance, it is best implemented as a static member.

Static type members are commonplace with the .NET base class library. A trivial example of a static type member can be found with the System.DateTime class. System.DateTime.Now is a static function returning the system date, as seen in static_time_example.cs. Note that the DateTime class is used directly; we do not need to create an instance of DateTime to call the Now type member. The Now property within the DateTime class is declared as static:

```
using System;

public class static_time_example
{
  [STAThread]
  static void Main(string[] args)
  {
    Console.WriteLine(DateTime.Now);
  }
}
```

Generally speaking, it is useful to think of static members as belonging to classes. Non-static, or instance members belong to objects, or instances of classes. If you'll recall, this is exactly how constants and static read-only fields perform. In fact, a constant is a special type of static field.

Remember, a field is a storage location for an object's data. A new storage location is created for each instance of an object. It is slightly different if a field is static. A static field denotes exactly one storage location. No matter how many instances of a class are created, there is only ever one copy of a static field.

Let's make one small change to our Account class to further explore how static fields affect our program. The following code is located in static_bankaccount.cs:

```
using System;

public class Account
{
  private static double balance;

  public double Balance
  {
    get
    {
      return balance;
    }
    set
    {
      balance=value;
    }
  }
}

class AtTheBank
{
  [STAThread]
  static void Main(string[] args)
  {
    Account mySavings= new Account();
    Account myChecking=new Account();

    mySavings.Balance=500;

    Console.WriteLine("Savings balance: " + mySavings.Balance);
    Console.WriteLine("Checking balance: " + myChecking.Balance);
  }
}
```

The only change we've made to the Account class is in how we define the balance field:

```
private static double balance;
```

However, while this change is small, the corresponding effect on the program is quite noticeable. Look again at the two instances of Account, mySavings and myChecking:

```
Account mySavings= new Account();
Account myChecking=new Account();

mySavings.Balance=500;

Console.WriteLine("Savings balance: " + mySavings.Balance);
Console.WriteLine("Checking balance: " + myChecking.Balance);
```

If `balance` were an instance variable, then `mySavings` and `myChecking` would each have their own balance field. We would expect that the output of the above program would show that the `mySavings` instance had a balance of 500 while `myChecking` only had the default value of 0. However, balance is not an instance field. Rather, it is a static field. Because of this, the value of balance is shared across all instances of `Account`.

If a method is declared as static, then that method will perform an action on the class, not an instance of the class. A static member can only access and modify static fields. Let's modify the account one more time to show off the use of a static method. The following code is in `static_bankaccount2.cs`:

```
using System;

public class Account
{
    private static double balance;

    public double Balance
    {
        //...omitted for brevity
    }

    public static void addTen()
    {
        balance=balance+10;
    }
}

class AtTheBank
{
    [STAThread]
    static void Main(string[] args)
    {
        Account mySavings= new Account();
        Account myChecking=new Account();

        mySavings.Balance=500;
        Account.addTen();

        Console.WriteLine("Savings balance: " + mySavings.Balance);
        Console.WriteLine("Checking balance: " + myChecking.Balance);
    }
}
```

Static methods act on the class, not the instances of the class. Static methods can access static fields, static properties, and other static methods. As such, you cannot call `AddTen()` through the `mySavings` or `myChecking` instances of the `Account` class. Rather, you must make the call directly against the `Account` class. However, as you can see from the output, the call does still affect the balance of every instance. This is because `AddTen()` adds to the static `balance` field. Here is the output of the above program:

```
C:\Class Design\Ch 02>static_bankaccount2.exe
Savings balance: 500
Checking balance: 500
Savings balance: 510
Checking balance: 510
```

Care must be taken when using static methods and fields. Only fields that truly must be shared across all instances should be marked as static. Similarly, only methods and properties that must act on static fields should be marked as static. An ideal situation to use static methods and fields is in conjunction with the read-only attribute.

Events and Delegates

Events are fairly simple to think about. Up until this point, we've told our classes what to do. Any feedback has been as part of the method call. That is, if we want to make a deposit, we tell our Account class to make a deposit. If we want to know our balance, we can ask our Account class. With an event, we can let our class tell us when something happens.

Suppose we have a BankManager class now, and that the Bank Manager wants to know whenever someone tries to deposit more than $10,000 into an account. One way to write this, and a rather inefficient approach, is to have the BankManager ask every Account instance if it has had a large deposit. Another way is to have every Account instance hold a reference to the BankManager. When the Account receives a large deposit, it can let the Bank Manager know. This approach works fine, at least for a while. As soon as the bank hires an Auditor who wants to know of all deposits, then we need to revisit Account and add another reference, this time to the Auditor.

A much simpler approach would be for any interested classes to simply watch the Account. This way, the Auditor would be free to watch and notice every deposit. Meanwhile, the Bank Manager would only pay attention to the large deposits. In a sense, the Bank Manager and Auditors are observers of a subject, the Account.

The heart of the event is another type member – the delegate. Basically, a delegate is a reference to a method of another class. If you have a C or C++ background, you might remember a similar ability through the use of function pointers. One of the big disadvantages of function pointers, though, was that they were not type-safe. In other words, 'they could attempt to access an invalid memory address'. With a delegate, .NET changes all of that. We now have a first-class member that both allows for callback functions and better ensures things won't blow up at run time.

Events are very powerful and useful mechanisms for designing classes. Rather than constantly monitoring an object for a certain change, that object can simply raise an event. Additionally, it is quite simple to add more subscribers in the future. In this manner, the publishing object is not tied to the subscribers.

However, events, and delegates, should only be used where they make the most sense. They are another tool in your design toolbox, but not the only tool. One large drawback to events is that they do not have to be acted upon. There is no requirement that any class must catch an event thrown by your class. There is a chance that no subscribers have requested to listen for a particular event thrown by your class. As such, you should not throw events that are critical to a class's proper operation. For instance, we couldn't design our Account class to rely on the Auditor class responding to an event. This is because there is no way, using just events, for us to ensure that an Auditor has subscribed to the event. We will cover events and delegates in much more detail in Chapter 6.

Operators

Like most programming languages. C# also gives us the ability to define our own implementation of an operator. Although it can be confusing to see in action, operator overloading as it is called, is a useful feature that you can easily use to provide custom arithmetic or comparison operations in a class.

> **Note:** *The ability to create your own operator is very much in tune with C++. Java does not natively support this functionality, as there is some need for a preprocessor. However, there packages available to allow this type of development with Java as well.*

Almost any unary or binary operator can be overridden with a default behavior. Some operators require that other operators be implemented as well. For example, if the less than (<) operator is defined then the greater than (>) must be defined as well.

There are also a few rules for defining operators. First, the signature of the operator must always be public static. Second, only value types can be passed to the operator. Attempting to pass a reference type will throw a compile-time error. Operators are covered in more detail in Chapter 4.

Constructors

When an object is created, it is given a default initial state. Fields can be set to an initial value when they are declared, or they accept the default value of their declared type. More often than not, you need more control over the initial state; the creating code would like to perform initialization routines that cannot be done with simple assignment statements.

Constructors are type members that are called to initialize an object's state before the reference is returned to the caller. They are similar to methods in that they can have zero or more arguments. Constructors do not have a return type, and they are executed after the instance state fields are assigned their initial values. Also, like methods, constructors can be overloaded.

Constructors are different from normal methods because they can only be called, implicitly, at the time the object is created. After creation, the constructor cannot be called and is not in the object's declaration space. If a class does not specify a constructor, then it will still have a default, parameterless constructor.

If your object needs to have certain values from the start, perhaps as part of a business rule, then you should not provide empty constructors.

As with other type members, it is possible to set accessibility levels on the constructor as well. Sometimes it might be desirable to have one constructor `protected` or `internal` so that derived classes or classes in the same application have one method of creating objects and have another constructor available to enforce defaults that must be set at object creation.

Another important aspect about constructors comes into play when a base class is extended. As part of object construction, the derived object can defer part of initialization to its base class. We will be covering them in much greater detail in Chapter 5.

Destructors

A constructor is called at object creation. It follows that a destructor is called when an instance is destroyed. A destructor cannot have any parameters. As such, a destructor cannot be overloaded. A class can have, at most, one destructor. Also of note, is that a destructor cannot be inherited.

> *C++ Note: In C++, the programmer is virtually required to write a destructor to manage releasing memory and performing any other clean up. In Java, there is no destructor. Rather, the approach is to allow the garbage collector to handle cleanup. In C#, the best of both approaches is combined. We can rely on the Garbage Collector to manage everything related to disposing of our instance, or, we can write our own destructor, which will be called when the instance is garbage-collected.*

We will cover destructors in much greater detail in Chapter 5.

Working with System.Object

All classes within the .NET Framework ultimately derive from .NET's root class System.Object. If we do not inherit from another class, the class will implicitly inherit from System.Object. The compiler enforces this requirement, which means that we don't need to write:

```
public class Account: System.Object
```

because it is implicit. As all classes derived from System.Object either directly or indirectly, it is quite easy to forget the functionality that System.Object provides. Several of the members of System.Object are virtual methods. You can override these virtual methods to provide our own implementations. Overriding System.Object's members makes classes more consistent with those found in the .NET base class library set. The vast majority of the .NET classes override System.Object's methods to provide functionality tailored to the class. The following System.Object methods are commonly implemented in classes:

- ❑ ToString()
- ❑ Equals(object)
- ❑ GetHashCode()

In the following section, we will explore how each of these functions works and how we can override them in our Account class. But first, let's examine another very useful method provided as part of System.Object.

GetType()

A very straightforward, and rather useful, member of the System.Object class is the GetType() method. Consider the following program:

```
using System;

public class Account
{
// Code omitted for brevity
}

class AtTheBank
{
  [STAThread]
  static void Main(string[] args)
  {
    Account myAccount= new Account();

    Console.WriteLine("myAccount is an object of type : " +
                      myAccount.GetType());
  }
}
```

Compiling and running the above code produces the following output:

```
C:\Class Design\Ch 02>sysobject_gettype_bankaccount.exe
myAccount is an object of type : Account
```

As you can see, GetType() returns the type of the instance. In this case, the returned value is Account as myAccount is an instance of the Account object.

ToString()

ToString() is typically the default class member. For example, if we have a function call as below:

```
Console.WriteLine(Object);
```

it is equivalent to:

```
Console.Writeline(Object.ToString());
```

This is because, if you don't specify a class member then it defaults to a call to ToString(). This call returns a string representation of the current object. By default, the System.Object.ToString() method will only return the instance's type name. The following code is located in sysobject_tostring_bankaccount.cs:

```
using System;

public class Account
{
    private double balance;

    public Account(double startingBalance)
    {
        balance=startingBalance;
    }
}

class AtTheBank
{
    [STAThread]
    static void Main(string[] args)
    {
        Account myAccount= new Account(500);

        Console.WriteLine("ToString:" + myAccount.ToString());
        Console.WriteLine("Same as above:" + myAccount);
    }
}
```

Compiling and running the above code results in the following output:

```
C:\Class Design\Ch 02>sysobject_tostring_bankaccount.exe
ToString:Account
Same as above:Account
```

The majority of the time, the default implementation of ToString() is not very useful. After all, we can retrieve the same information by calling GetType(). With the default ToString() method, the same results are returned for every instance of the class, regardless of the instance state of the object. What we need is a descriptive string that is particular to the object instance. Overriding System.Object.ToString() allows us to customize the string representation for a particular instance, as can be seen in sysobject_tostring_bankaccount2.cs, below:

```csharp
using System;

public class Account
{
  private double balance;

  public Account(double startingBalance)
  {
    balance=startingBalance;
  }

  public override string ToString()
  {
    return "Object: " + GetType() + " balance: " + balance;
  }
}

class AtTheBank
{
  [STAThread]
  static void Main(string[] args)
  {
    Account myAccount= new Account(500);

    Console.WriteLine("ToString:" + myAccount.ToString());
  }
}
```

Compiling and running the above code provides the following output:

```
C:\Class Design\Ch 02>sysobject_tostring_bankaccount2.exe
ToString:Object: Account balance: 500
```

Equals()

Quite often we need the ability to compare objects for equality.
`System.Object.Equals()` gives us such ability. .NET defines two forms of equality:
reference equality and **value equality**. By default, `System.Object.Equals()` will
test for reference equality. Reference equality occurs when two references point to the
same underlying object. The following example,
`sysobject_equals_bankaccount.cs`, illustrates this:

```
using System;

public class Account
{
  private double balance;

  public Account(double startingBalance)
  {
    balance=startingBalance;
  }
}

class atthebank
{
  [STAThread]
  static void Main(string[] args)
  {
    Account myAccount = new Account(500);
    Account mySavings = new Account(500);

    Console.WriteLine(myAccount.Equals(mySavings));
    mySavings=myAccount;
    Console.WriteLine(myAccount.Equals(mySavings));
  }
}
```

The first test of equality returns a `false`. While `mySavings` and `myAccount` both have
the same value, they do not reference the same instance. After setting `mySavings` to
`myAccount`, the next test of equality returns `true`. The resulting output is:

```
C:\Class Design\Ch 02>sysobject_equals_bankaccount.exe
False
True
```

Many real-world objects need the ability to test for value equality. Value equality is
satisfied if two objects have the same state. Overriding the
`System.Object.Equals()` method allows us to perform a custom value equality test.
The following code, saved as `sysobject_equals_bankaccount2.cs`, provides an
example for overriding the default `Equals()` implementation:

```
using System;

public class Account
{
  private double balance;

  public Account(double startingBalance)
  {
    balance=startingBalance;
  }
```

In the first two statements below, we perform a check to ensure that we were not passed a null object and that the object we were passed is of the same type. If neither of those cases is true, then there is little sense in continuing on with the comparison. Otherwise, we cast the object to an Account type and proceed to test equality on the balance instance field. The cast is necessary, as the default object does not have a balance field.

```
  public override bool Equals(object obj)
  {
    if ((obj == null) || (GetType() != obj.GetType()))
      return false;
    Account acct=(Account)obj;
    return acct.balance == balance;
  }
}

class AtTheBank
{
  [STAThread]
  static void Main(string[] args)
  {
    Account myAccount = new Account(500);
    Account mySavings = new Account(500);

    Console.WriteLine(myAccount.Equals(mySavings));
  }
}
```

When this code is executed, it will return that the two objects are equal. This is because we have provided our own Equals() implementation. Our implementation actually tests for value equality. As a side note, we need to point out that our comparison is a bit weak. After all, we would probably never try to determine if two accounts were the same value. However, it should illustrate how to easy it is to set up your own equality tests.

When you compile the above example, it will work, but you will get a warning about not overriding the GetHashCode() method. Let's explore the use of GetHashCode() next.

GetHashCode()

GetHashCode() returns a hash code. This function is used in hashing algorithms and certain data structures, like the hash table. The .NET Framework includes the Hashtable as a fundamental collection object available to developers. Hashtables store objects according to an object's integer hash code. The Hashtable class uses the hash code to sort the objects internally in order to provide faster sorting and searching.

Storage by hash code allows the Hashtable to find a particular object or set of objects within a larger set with minimal effort. The obvious question is where the hash code comes from. In order to develop a hash code for you class, you must override System.Object.GetHashCode().

The default implementation of System.Object.GetHashCode() can only guarantee that the same hash code can be returned for the same instance every time. It cannot guarantee that different instances will have different hash codes. It also cannot guarantee that different instances with the same value will have the same hash code. Overriding System.Object.GetHashCode() gives the programmer the opportunity to return a consistent hash code dependent on the object's state.

There are a couple of rules that should be followed when overriding the GetHashCode() method:

❑ If two objects are of the same type and have the same value, they must return the same hash code.

❑ The hash code should be based on immutable members. An immutable member's value cannot change once it is created. Imagine getting a hash for an object, storing the object, and then changing a value that the hash relies on. It would likely become impossible to retrieve the object as the hash, used for lookup, has changed.

❑ Ensure that hash values are fairly randomly distributed. Well-distributed hash values lend to better search performance.

❑ Hash codes should be inexpensive to compute. Simply, it shouldn't take seconds to compute an instance's hash code.

If you are not overriding the GetHashCode() method, do not rely on the hash code for persisting objects. Different versions of .NET might generate different hash codes for the same instance. As such, you cannot guarantee that a hash used in conjunction with persisted objects, say as a primary key when saving state to a database, will always remain valid.

Let us implement a simple GetHashCode() for our Account class, this can be found in sysobject_gethashcode_bankaccount.cs:

```
using System;

public class Account
{
  private double balance;
  private int pin;

  public Account(double startingBalance, int PIN)
  {
    balance=startingBalance;
    pin=PIN;
  }

  public override int GetHashCode()
  {
    return (pin ^ Convert.ToInt32(balance));
  }
}

class AtTheBank
{
  [STAThread]
  static void Main(string[] args)
  {
    Account myAccount = new Account(500,1234);

    Console.WriteLine(myAccount.GetHashCode());
    Console.ReadLine();
  }
}
```

As a warning, our above implementation is nowhere near being a sound hash code implementation. While, in real life, an account's PIN is immutable (or at least immutable enough), there is an obvious problem in that, at least at a large bank; many accounts could have the same PIN value.

Equals() and GetHashCode()

It is important to implement both GetHashCode() and Equals() together. The Hashtable class uses the GetHashCode() to determine how to sort data, and uses Equals() to verify the objects are indeed equal. If the Equals() method is omitted, the Hashtable cannot verify if two objects are indeed equal. If GetHashCode() is omitted, the Hashtable cannot sort efficiently. The Hashtable class uses both Equals() and GetHashCode() in its design. Omitting one would return unpredictable results.

Regardless of if you use the Hashtable class in your application, overriding Equals() and GetHashCode() is good programming practice and makes the class interface more intuitive and predictable for developers using the class. Many algorithms implement sorting and comparison. Implementing GetHashCode() and Equals() allows your classes to participate in many of .NET's pre-built objects (like Hashtable) and enables developers writing the sorting and searching algorithms to generalize their procedures for objects taking advantage of these members.

Summary

Type members are the programming constructs used to build a class or struct. This chapter briefly touched on each type member and usage guidelines associated with their usage.

Constants are used to provide readability and act as a single point of change for known values. Constants are shared members by default and are used whenever values are guaranteed not to change.

Fields are variables used to hold state in a class or struct. To provide data encapsulation, fields are commonly created with the `private` access modifier. Public fields lock the class interface and data together, making it difficult to change the code without breaking compatibility.

Properties represent a piece of data exposed by the class. Properties extend the concept of a field by adding a layer of abstraction between a class's internal and external representation. Properties give the designer the ability to change how state is managed within the class while not affecting how state is managed outside the class. Properties can be designated as read-only or write-only, simply by excluding the getter or setter, to prevent unwanted usage of the property.

Methods perform the functionality of the class. Multiple methods can have the same name with different signatures to provide multiple implementations. Such a practice is called method overloading.

Fields, properties, and methods can all be declared as static. Static type members are accessible without an object reference and normally address things that you would associate with the class's general concept not a specific instance.

Events provide a way for classes to notify listeners when certain actions have occurred. Since events are not required to be handled, they should typically be used to send information not critical to the central operation of the class.

Constructors allow you to customize the object creation process. If no constructor is specified the C# compiler will inject a default constructor into the class's MSIL.

Type members have levels of accessibility. A public member has no access restrictions. Protected members are accessible externally from derived classes only. Internal members are accessible from any code contained in the same namespace. Private members are accessible only from within the containing class.

`System.Object` is the root of every type in the .NET Framework. Because all types inherit from this base, all types have certain methods available to them..

C#

Class Design

Handbook

3

Methods

Methods are fundamental both to C# class design and also to the MSIL code emitted by the C# compiler. This chapter explores both of these areas and explains how to design and code effective methods in your classes.

Methods represent actions associated with a class. A method is a sequence of statements that encapsulate a discrete task or process. At run time, the inner working of your method is hidden from the client code, and the client code will invoke methods in the class without any knowledge of the actual working of the method. In object oriented programming terms, this is known as encapsulation. In essence, methods represent the behavior of your class.

Methods should be named to describe the task that they perform. Choosing the name of the method is an important consideration of the class design process as the method name forms part of the semantic contract between the class designer and the class-consuming client code. As C# is a case-sensitive language, it is possible to create two methods that only differ by the case of the name of the method. This should be avoided as it causes ambiguity.

Invoking Methods

In this chapter we will illustrate the different kinds of methods, parameter types, and other considerations when designing classes in C#. First, let's consider what happens inside the .NET Common Language Runtime when a method is actually invoked. Method invocation consists of a number of pre-processing and post-processing activities. Initially, the CLR allocates memory to the method, by creating a **stack frame**. A stack frame is a block of stack-based memory that is large enough to accommodate the arguments that are passed to the method as well as local variables defined within the method itself. A stack frame is a temporary block of memory because when method execution ends, the frame is popped off the stack immediately freeing up memory.

All applications from simple console ones through to large multi-tier distributed systems are ultimately built up through sequences of method calls. When sequences of methods are invoked, a stack frame is created for each method and added to the call stack. This process builds up a **stack trace**. Since a stack trace is an ordered collection of stack frames, it actually provides a detailed log of the sequences of method calls made within an application. Each stack frame contains the arguments passed into the method and all variables within it.

Stack frame and stack trace information is most useful in debugging situations where you need to know the sequence of calls from one area of the application to the next. You also need to know what arguments were passed to each method and what happens to those arguments inside the method.

The .NET Framework permits access to the stack frame and stack trace data through the StackFrame and StackTrace classes in the System.Diagnostics namespace. The following example shows how to use these classes, and the source code can be found in stack_trace.cs:

```
using System;
using System.Diagnostics;

class Foo
{
  static void Main()
  {
    Bar.BarMethod(42);
  }
}

class Bar
{
  public static void BarMethod(int x)
  {
    StackTrace st = new StackTrace();

    for(int i=0; i < st.FrameCount; i++)
    {
      StackFrame sf = new StackFrame();
      sf = st.GetFrame(i);
      Console.WriteLine(sf.GetMethod());
    }
  }
}
```

This example invokes a static method called Bar.BarMethod(). This method dumps a simple stack trace to the console window by iterating through the internal collection of stack frame objects returned from the StackTrace.GetFrame() method. The following output should be displayed in the Console window:

```
C:\Class Design\Ch 03>stack_trace
Void BarMethod(Int32)
Void Main()
```

We can see both the methods making up the stack trace, with the most recent first. The information displayed here is quite similar to some of the debug messages produced in Visual Studio .NET when creating your own applications. The System.Diagnostics namespace classes provide a good way to help debug the methods in your application. Using guidelines from the above example, you can create your own custom stack traces and discover which methods called your methods.

Method Scope and Visibility

As with all type members, we can specify the scope and visibility with the familiar keywords public and private, and so on. These keywords are known as **access modifiers** and must be the first keyword in the method declaration. These work in the same way as with other class members as we saw in the previous chapter.

When designing your class, spend time figuring out the correct levels of visibility for all class members. In order to preserve the rules of encapsulation, data hiding, and abstraction, only those members that need to form part of the external contract should be public. Utility and helper routines used internally within a class should always have private visibility for class-level scope, or internal visibility for assembly-level scope.

The rules governing protected members are more complex and are determined by the inheritance design requirements. protected members are discussed in Chapter 7.

Method Types

Depending on your class design pattern, some methods will perform actions on specific instances of your class and other methods will be more neutral in purpose and will perform generalized actions that are not specific to any particular instance of your class. These two types of methods are known as **instance methods** and **static methods** respectively.

Instance methods perform actions that are specific to an instance of a class. When a method is invoked on an object, it has no direct effect on any other object. Instance methods can have an indirect effect on other objects if they share common resources such as databases, and can also use a keyword called this. As you may know, the this 'variable' is a reference to instance of the object on which this method was invoked. this can be used to access other object instance members such as private methods and private fields.

Of course, in a user-defined value type, we can still have instance methods, and the this keyword is still available. But it's not a reference to the instance on which the method was invoked; that would make no sense in a non-reference type. When we call a method on a value type, the value itself is copied into the new stack frame, where we can access it using the name this, and then when method execution completes, the value is copied back into the location from which it came. This actually means that in an instance method in a value type, we can assign a new value to this, and it will be this value that is copied back on method termination.

Static methods are used when the purpose of the method does not apply to a specific instance of a class. Unlike instance methods, static methods cannot access this, and can also only access other static members in the class.

Instance and Static Method Example

The following example called method_types.cs illustrates the above-mentioned points. The example is based on an Account class to represent a bank account. The class supports two methods – GetAllAccounts() and DepositMoney():

```csharp
using System;
using System.Data;

public class Account
{
  public static DataSet GetAllAccounts()
  {
    return (new DataSet());
  }

  public void DepositMoney(decimal amount, string accountNumber)
  {
    if (this.validateAccount(accountNumber))
    {
      // Deposit Money to the correct account
    }
  }

  private bool validateAccount(string accountNumber)
  {
    return true;   // Assume Account Number is ok
  }
}

public class Payments
{
  static void Main()
  {
    DataSet dsAccountList = Account.GetAllAccounts();
```

```
      Account account = new Account();
      account.DepositMoney((decimal)249.99, "56329SVZ");
  }
}
```

Here are the observations you should make in this example:

❑   GetAllAccounts() is a static method. Static methods must be invoked by specifying the name of the type first followed by the method name. In this example we use Account.GetAllAccounts().

❑   DepositMoney() is an instance method. Instance methods can only be accessed by creating an instance of the object account.DepositMoney(). DepositMoney invokes a private instance method called validateAccount() using the hidden this parameter this.validateAccount().

Instance and Static Method Best Practice

When designing your method types, here are guidelines to help you design better instance and static methods:

❑   When designing your classes, it's best not to have lots of static methods in a class that also has many instance methods. If this situation arises, consider splitting instance and static methods into two separate classes to make your design clearer. The class with the static methods is called a **group abstraction**.

❑   Static methods can only be invoked by specifying the type name first. This differs from C++, which allows static methods to be invoked from an object instance. This enforcement by the C# compiler should be considered a positive thing because of the nature and purpose of static methods – it makes sure that the programmer's intentions are always clear from the code.

❑   Be careful of concurrency issues if a class with a static method is used in multi-threaded code. Because each thread will access the same static method and therefore access the same static fields, static data and shared resources will be volatile if accessed concurrently. This is less of an issue with instance methods, provided instances are not shared between threads.

❑   If an instance method invokes other instance members, use the this keyword to make the code clearer.

Arguments and Parameterized Methods

Implementing useful methods that don't accept arguments can be quite limiting. Most methods will process data in some way; therefore the data (or a reference pointer to the data) should be passed to the method. Variables passed to methods are usually referred to as **arguments** and the values that refer to those arguments within the method are called **parameters**. Methods that accept arguments are therefore called parameterized methods.

Parameter Types

Passing arguments to parameterized methods is not a trivial consideration. Deliberation must be given to the type of data being passed, how the data will be processed within the method, and how the processing (if any) should be passed back or made visible to the client code. We also need to consider if the argument must be initialized before it is passed and also consider how many arguments the method will require and if the number of arguments is arbitrary.

When an argument is passed to a method, we are initially given two main choices over how the argument is passed. We can pass the actual value of the argument (passing by value) or we can pass a reference (passing by reference) to the argument. Passing an argument by value is the default in C# and is the same in all languages that target the .NET Framework.

Passing by Value

Passing an argument by value involves making a physical copy of the data from the client code (the argument) into the method (the parameter). Both the client code and the method then have variables holding their own separate copy of the data. At the time the method is invoked, this data is exactly the same. However, the method will then proceed with its sequence of statements and potentially change the value of this data locally within the method itself. Changes to the value of the parameter do not affect the value of the argument, which is separate.

Passing an argument by value requires no additional keywords within the method declaration. The following example called `passing_by_val.cs` demonstrates passing data by value:

```
using System;

namespace parameter_types
{
  public class Calculator
  {
```

```
    public static decimal CalculateInterest(decimal balance)
    {
      decimal interest = (decimal)45.11;
      balance = balance + interest;
      return (balance);
    }
}

class BatchRun
{
  static void Main()
  {
    decimal balance = (decimal)4566.54;

    Console.WriteLine("Balance = " + balance);
    Console.WriteLine("Balance + Interest = " +
        Calculator.CalculateInterest(balance));
    Console.WriteLine("Balance = " + balance);
  }
}
}
```

This example calculates the interest on the balance of a bank account. The simple
`CalculateInterest()` method takes a `balance` argument and adds the interest.
The following output is produced:

```
Balance = 4566.54
Balance + Interest = 4611.65
Balance = 4566.54
```

Notice how the account balance has remained unchanged after calling
`CalculateInterest()`. This is because the value of the argument has been copied
to the method parameter. Both the argument and parameter hold separate values.

Passing by Reference

Passing arguments by reference involves copying a reference to the data instead of the
data itself. We think of this as if we are passing a pointer to the location in memory
where the data is to the method. Both the client code and the method hold separate
references to the same data. Because of this, changes made to the parameter by the
method are visible to the client code. The changes a method makes to a parameter that
can affect the client code are called **side effects**. When an argument is passed by
reference, think of the parameter as an alias to the argument.

What actually happens is that the value is copied in to the method, just as it is when
passed by value; when the method terminates, the value is copied back out again into
the location from which it came, along with any changes that have been made to the
value in the course of the method executing.

Passing an argument by reference requires the use of the additional `ref` keyword in *both* the method declaration, *and* the calling client code. Failure to use the `ref` keyword in the calling program results in a compile-time error:

Argument 'n': cannot convert from '<type>' to 'ref <type>'.

The `ref` keyword overrides the default pass by value behavior. The following example demonstrates passing data by reference:

```csharp
using System;

namespace parameter_types
{
  public class Calculator
  {
    public static decimal CalculateInterest(ref decimal balance)
    {
      decimal interest = (decimal)45.11;
      balance = balance + interest;
      return (balance);
    }
  }

  class BatchRun
  {
    static void Main()
    {
      decimal balance = (decimal)4566.54;

      Console.WriteLine("Balance = " + balance);
      Console.WriteLine("Balance + Interest = " +
          Calculator.CalculateInterest(ref balance));
      Console.WriteLine("Balance = " + balance);
    }
  }
}
```

The `CalculateInterest()` method has been modified to accept the argument by reference by using the `ref` keyword. The calling client code has also been modified to pass the arguments by reference using the `ref` keyword. This means that the parameter and argument hold a reference to the same value.

Arguments passed by reference using the `ref` keyword must be initialized before being passed to the method. Failure to initialize an argument results in the following compile time error: Use of unassigned local variable <variable name>.

When running the program, the following should be displayed –

```
Balance = 4566.54
Balance + Interest = 4611.65
Balance = 4611.65
```

Notice how the account balance has been changed as a side effect of calling the CalculateInterest() method. In this example, the CalculateInterest() method also returns the new account balance. This is redundant because the account balance is changed automatically by virtue of the fact that it was passed by reference. Thus we have two options:

❏ Pass arguments by value and get a return value back from the method

❏ Pass arguments by reference, declare the method as void, and do not return a value

The most important factor influencing our choice here is this: if you need a method to return several values, passing by reference can simulate this. A method can only return one value; passing by reference can be used to produce side effects on all arguments passed.

If you are considering passing arguments by reference to alter several arguments, read on to the next section, which discusses output parameters. Output parameters can sometimes provide a more elegant and appropriate solution to this problem.

Output Parameters

Output parameters solve the problem of getting a method to simulate the manipulation and passing back of more than one value. Similar to ref parameters, output parameters are also passed by reference and the out parameter also behaves like an alias to the argument, but there is one subtle and important difference to ref arguments, and that is that:

> **Arguments passed by reference using the out keyword do not have to be initialized before being passed to the method.**

By implication, if an argument has no value (or if it is a null reference), then the method cannot inadvertently do any harm to the argument. Output parameters are also considered unassigned within a method; methods with out parameters must therefore initialize all out parameters before the method returns.

The following example parameter_types.cs demonstrates passing data by reference using out parameters:

```
using System;

public class Calculator
{
  public static decimal CalculateInterest(out decimal balance)
  {
    decimal interest = (decimal)45.11;
    balance = (decimal)4566.54;
    balance += interest;
    return (balance);
  }
}

class BatchRun
{
  static void Main()
  {
    decimal balance;

    Console.WriteLine("Balance + Interest = " +
        Calculator.CalculateInterest(out balance));
  }
}
```

When you run this program, the following should be displayed in the console window:

```
C:\Class Design\Ch 03>parameter_types
Balance + Interest = 4611.65
```

Looking at the program, here are the main points to note:

❑ The account balance (balance) is uninitialized before it is passed to CalculateInterest().

❑ Output parameters are always assumed to be uninitialized; CalculateInterest() must initialize the balance parameter before returning.

❑ If output parameters have already been initialized before being passed to the method, the method must ignore this and assign its own value anyway. In this example, assigning the balance first and then attempting the interest addition operation will cause a compile-time error because balance must be initialized in the method before it returns.

❑ Both the calling program and the method declaration explicitly use the out keyword, in the same manner as ref parameters.

Output parameters are currently unique to C# within the .NET Framework. Visual Basic .NET does not support the concept of output parameters. C# output parameters are treated the same as regular by-reference parameters when consumed by other .NET programming languages. Therefore, both C# out parameters and C# ref parameters behave like Visual Basic .NET ByRef parameters.

Output parameters are very useful for methods that need to simulate returning several values. Because out parameters are treated as uninitialized, the method must assign a value to all out parameters before returning. This is similar in principle to methods that return a single value where the method must assign and return a single value of the correct type.

The C# compiler forces the use of the out keyword in both the client code and the method signature; this provides very clear indications to a developer as to the purpose of the parameter within the method.

Passing Reference Types versus Value Types

Choosing whether to pass arguments by reference (ref or out) or by value not only depends on how you want the method to behave in terms the method side effects, performance, and return values; but also on the type of data that you want to pass to the method.

.NET types are either value types or reference types. As discussed in Chapter 1, value types include primitive data types, structures, and enumerations. A simple assignment of a value type to another value type variable results in two variables containing separate data. In fact, all value type assignments, including passing arguments to method parameters by value, result in the copying of data to the new variable. The lifetime of a value type can be directly controlled by the method or client code because when a method returns all value types fall out of scope and their memory allocation is immediately released. When a value type variable goes out of scope, the variable and all of its data are removed from the stack, immediately freeing up memory.

Reference types can be of any object type (including arrays and strings), and they are heap based. Reference type variables contain references. It is these references that are the values that are passed by value or by reference in calling methods.

A reference type can have many references pointing at it. This happens when more than one stack-based variable points to the same heap-based reference type. Reference types will not go out of scope on the heap (and consequently be made available for garbage-collection) until all references are removed from the stack. The garbage collector governs the heap and an object will consume memory until the garbage collector removes it from the heap. We'll look at these issues further in Chapter 5 where we discuss object lifecycle in more detail.

To compare and contrast the difference between passing reference types and value types, we also need to reconsider the parameter types discussed in the previous section. We actually have four primary combinations for passing arguments to methods:

❏   Passing a value type by value

❏   Passing a value type by reference (ref or out)

❏   Passing a reference type by value

❏   Passing a reference type by reference (ref or out)

The following sections cover each of these combinations in detail. Here's what happens with each of the four possible combinations:

The following sections do not explicitly cover output parameters (out), these are really a variation of a ref parameter.

Passing Value Types by Value

When we think about value types, numbers such as integers tend to be the first kind of value type that springs to mind. Structures are also value types and are ideal candidates for creating complex value type entities such as a type to represent a fraction, coordinates on a graph, or maybe some credit-card details. All of these examples are usually represented as a structured set of numbers. Structures are chosen over classes when dealing with relatively simple *real-world* objects that cannot be represented using a single primitive type.

When a structure is passed by value, a copy of the structure is made to the method parameter. Both the argument and parameter hold separate copies of the structure. Any changes made by the method to its copy of the structure will not be reflected in the client code.

Passing a value type by value is the deafult, and it is a logical default. You should not consider changing it unless one of the conditions listed in the next section applies.

In the following example, we can demonstrate passing a value type by value. This example is based on a `CreditCard` entity represented as a structure. We will implement a `GetBalance()` method that simulates retrieving the credit card balance details from a database. Because of the sensitive nature of credit card details, it is important that bugs cannot creep to the `GetBalance()` method that might accidentally change the credit card details. The following example is named `val_by_val.cs` in the source code file.

```csharp
using System;

public struct CreditCard
{
    double cardNumber;
    DateTime expiryDate;

    public double CardNumber
    {
        get
        {
            return cardNumber;
        }
        set
        {
            cardNumber = value;
```

```
      }
    }

    public DateTime ExpiryDate
    {
      get
      {
        return expiryDate;
      }
      set
      {
        expiryDate = value;
      }
    }
  }

public class Authorization
{
  public static decimal GetBalance(CreditCard creditCard)
  {
    creditCard.ExpiryDate = creditCard.ExpiryDate.AddMonths(12);
    return (decimal)845.21;
  }
}

class Payments
{
  static void Main()
  {
    CreditCard card = new CreditCard();
    Decimal balance;

    card.CardNumber = 1111222333444;
    card.ExpiryDate = Convert.ToDateTime("01/03/2003");

    balance = Authorization.GetBalance(card);

    Console.WriteLine("Card Number - " + card.CardNumber);
    Console.WriteLine("Expiry Date - " +
        card.ExpiryDate.ToShortDateString());
    Console.WriteLine("Balance      - " + balance);
  }
}
```

When running this program, you should see the following output in the console window:

```
C:\Class Design\Ch 03>val_by_val
Card Number - 1111222333444
Expiry Date - 01/03/2003
Balance     - 845.21
```

Note that the deliberate modification of the credit card expiry date in the GetBalance() method has not permanently affected the state of the credit card structure. This is a good example of when to pass a value type by value because we do not want the GetBalance() method to have any side effects.

Passing Value Types by Reference

When we pass a structure using the ref keyword, a reference to the structure is passed to the method, instead of a copy of the structure itself. When this happens both the argument and the parameter are said to have **referential equivalence**. This means that changes made by the method are visible to the client code.

Passing a value type by reference should be chosen:

❑ When the argument can be represented in a simple form such as a number or a simple structure.

❑ When the method needs to make changes to the structure that **should** be reflected in client code.

❑ When several structures need to be passed to the method and the method will alter all of them. This resolves the issue of a method only being able to return a single value back to the client code.

To demonstrate when to pass a value type by reference, add the following RenewCard() method to the Authorization class. The new file is called val_by_ref.cs:

```
public static void RenewCard(ref CreditCard creditCard)
{
  creditCard.ExpiryDate = creditCard.ExpiryDate.AddMonths(12);
}
```

Now change the Payments class as follows:

```
class Payments
{
  static void Main()
  {
    CreditCard card = new CreditCard();
    Decimal balance;

    card.CardNumber = 1111222333444;
    card.ExpiryDate = Convert.ToDateTime("01/03/2003");

    balance = Authorization.GetBalance(card);

    Console.WriteLine("Card Number - " + card.CardNumber);
    Console.WriteLine("Expiry Date - " +
```

```
            card.ExpiryDate.ToShortDateString());
        Console.WriteLine("Balance     - " + balance);

        Authorization.RenewCard(ref card);

        Console.WriteLine();
        Console.WriteLine("Card Number - " + card.CardNumber);
        Console.WriteLine("Expiry Date - " +
            card.ExpiryDate.ToShortDateString());
        Console.WriteLine("Balance     - " + balance);
    }
}
```

When running the program, the following output should be displaye in the console window:

```
C:\Class Design\Ch 03>val_by_ref
Card Number - 1111222333444
Expiry Date - 01/03/2003
Balance     - 845.21

Card Number - 1111222333444
Expiry Date - 01/03/2004
Balance     - 845.21
```

Notice how the credit card expiry date has incremented by 1 year. This is a good example of passing a value type by reference because we want the RenewCard() method to have side effects that are visible in the client code.

Passing Reference Types by Value

When reference types are passed by value, we are asking to pass the value of an object. The value of an object is not the value of one of its properties, or a value returned by one of its methods. The method parameter actually receives the value of the object's location on the heap.

The side effects of passing a class by value are exactly the same as passing a structure by reference. But the route taken by the CLR is a different one. When a structure is passed by reference, the structure is referenced from the called method. The argument and parameter hold a reference to the same structure. When a class instance is passed by value, the reference is copied to the called method. The argument and parameter both hold a reference to the same object on the heap.

The route taken by the CLR might be different but the effects are still the same. If the object is mutable, we can change the state of the object passed by value, and those changes will be visible to the calling code.

Passing a reference type by value is the default; again this is a natural default, and you shouldn't change it under normal circumstances.

When an instance of a reference type is passed in to a method, remember that the reference is still held by the calling code. If you put a copy of the reference into a class variable, say, it refers to the same object that the calling code's reference refers to – and will still refer to that same object after your method has returned. So with reference types, not only can a called method change the state of objects passed in to it by the calling code, the calling code can change objects after passing them in to a method, and have the effects persist. Sometimes this is desirable, sometimes it isn't. If you want to avoid these issues with reference types, consider making your types immutable.

The following example, ref_by_val.cs, is based on an employee entity. The employee will be represented as a class because an employee entity is typically complex. Note that only the Salary property will be used in this example to reduce space. We will then implement a Taxation class and a Calculate() method to calculate the employee's net salary:

```csharp
using System;

public class Employee
{
    int salary;

    public int Salary
    {
        get
        {
            return salary;
        }
        set
        {
            salary = value;
        }
    }
}

public class Taxation
{
    public static void Calculate(Employee employee)
    {
        employee.Salary = employee.Salary - (employee.Salary*22/100);
    }
}

class Calculate
{
    static void Main(string[] args)
    {
        Employee employee = new Employee();

        employee.Salary = 40000;
        Console.WriteLine("Gross salary before tax - {0}",
```

```
        employee.Salary);

    Taxation.Calculate(employee);

    Console.WriteLine("Net salary after tax     - {0}",
        employee.Salary);
    }
}
```

When running the program, the following should be displayed in the console window:

```
C:\Class Design\Ch 03>ref_by_val
Gross salary before tax - 40000
Net salary after tax     - 31200
```

Notice how the salary has changed even though the Employee was passed by value. This is because Employee is a class and therefore a reference type.

We can avoid this behavior by temporarily reassigning the Employee parameter inside the Calculate() method. The new code file is called ref_by_val2.cs. Change the Calculate() method as follows:

```
public class Taxation
{
    public static void Calculate(Employee employee)
    {
        Employee temp_employee = new Employee();

        temp_employee.Salary = employee.Salary;

        temp_employee.Salary = temp_employee.Salary -
((temp_employee.Salary/100)*22);

        employee = temp_employee;
    }
}
```

This time, when running the program, the following should be displayed in the console window:

```
C:\Class Design\Ch 03>ref_by_val2
Gross salary before tax - 40000
Net salary after tax     - 40000
```

Notice how the salary has remained unchanged after the method call. By using a temporary instance of an object of the same type as the parameter, then copying each property, we can perform the same calculation on the temporary object. Even after reassigning the parameter to the temporary object at the end of the method, the changes to the Salary property are not visible in the client code. Reassignments of reference types passed by value are not permanent and the client code sees no side effects.

101

Passing Reference Types by Reference

To pass an object to a method, we pass the variable holding the object reference. If the method parameter is declared as `ref` or `out`, the parameter is actually a reference to a reference to the object. We then have a double reference – the method parameter is a reference to the calling argument, which in turn is a reference to our object on the heap.

The difference between passing a reference type by reference and passing a reference type by value is subtle, yet important. Unlike passing reference types by value, passing a reference type by reference allows us to permanently reassign the parameter and the argument to a different object instance. This can improve the safety of passing objects to methods that change the state of an object. A parameterized method can be declared to receive an object as an argument, the method can then create a new second object of the same type and change its state, and then if conditions apply, the parameter object can be reassigned against the second object.

Passing a reference type by reference should be used when:

❏   The argument must be represented as a class

❏   The method needs to conditionally change the state of the argument

❏   The method needs to permanently reassign the parameter to a new instance of the same type

As well as allowing a called method to reassign a reference to a new instance of the same type, it also allows it to unassign it – to set its value to `null`.

To demonstrate this, change the `Calculate()` method as follows:

```
public class Taxation
{
  public static void Calculate(ref Employee employee)
  {
    Employee temp_employee = new Employee();

    temp_employee.Salary = employee.Salary;

    temp_employee.Salary = temp_employee.Salary -
        ((temp_employee.Salary*22/100);

    employee = temp_employee;
  }
}
```

Now change the `Calculate` class:

```
class Calculate
{
```

```
static void Main()
{
  Employee employee = new Employee();

  employee.Salary = 40000;
  Console.WriteLine("Gross salary before tax - {0}",
      employee.Salary);

  Taxation.Calculate(ref employee);

  Console.WriteLine("Net salary after tax    - {0}",
      employee.Salary);
  }
}
```

When running the program, the following should be displayed in the console window:

```
C:\Class Design\Ch 03>ref_by_ref
Gross salary before tax - 40000
Net salary after tax    - 31200
```

Notice how the salary has changed after calling the Calculate() method. We can see in this example that passing a reference type by reference always has side effects in the client code, even when the parameter is assigned to a new instance.

Variable Length Parameter Lists

Sometimes when designing a class, we do not know how many arguments a method should accept. Classes that exhibit this behavior are common in the .NET Framework. The Console.WriteLine() method is a good example. This method accepts a variable number of arguments of type System.Object, which are used as arguments to a string format.

A technique known as a parameter array can be used to code a method that accepts an arbitrary number of arguments. The params keyword can be used in the method declaration to achieve this behavior. The file shown next (var_para.cs) demonstrates this:

> **The parameter immediately following the params keyword must be declared as a single dimensional array – [ ].**

```
using System;
class Statistics
{
  public static double AverageScores(params int[] scores)
  {
```

```
        int total = 0;
        double average = 0;

        foreach(int score in scores)
        {
            total += score;
        }

        average = total*1.0 / scores.Length;

        return average;
    }
}
```

Create the client code to execute the `AverageScores()` method:

```
public class params_example
{
    public static void Main()
    {
        Console.WriteLine("Average - " +
            Statistics.AverageScores(7, 2, 5, 8, 9, 6, 8, 1));
        Console.WriteLine("Average - " +
            Statistics.AverageScores(3, 4, 2, 5));
        Console.ReadLine();
    }
}
```

which produces the following output:

```
C:\Class Design\Ch 03>var_para
Average - 5.75
Average - 3.5
```

The way in which the CLR resolves parameter array method calls differs from the normal means of resolution, where the number of arguments matches the parameters list one for one. When a mismatch occurs between the number of arguments and the number of parameters, the compiler checks for the presence of the params keyword in the method declaration. The compiler then creates a temporary internal stack of parameters of the declaring type until there are enough parameters to accept the total number of arguments. In addition, **each item in the array is passed by reference**. Ensure, therefore, that you know of the side effects if you manipulate the values.

Because of the dynamic processing that occurs to match the arguments against enough parameters, parameter arrays must be the last parameter within the method declaration. For instance, the following code will *not* compile:

104

```
public static double AverageScores(params int[] Scores, int PassMark)
{
  //
}
```

> **The params parameter must be the most rightmost parameter of a method.**

Using a parameter array does cause a small additional operation to take place before the method can be called – the parameters need to be packaged up into an array, which must be allocated on the heap – but this is hardly a large performance penalty given the flexibility they provide.

Passing Strings – Immutable Objects

Although string objects are reference types, they are instances of the System.String class. This class overrides some of the typical behavior of a reference type, making strings behave in a similar manner to (but not the same as) a value type.

String objects are immutable – that is, they cannot be changed from their initial value. Simple string operations that seem to change the value of a string actually return a different string object, rather than a modified version of the original. This is an important consideration in methods such as XML and HTML builders that extensively process string parameters, because these activities can drain system resources. As they are reference types, changing a string actually results in two strings on the heap, the original, and the modified version. The string variable will reference the new string object following new assignments. If the only reference to the original string was from the variable which we've changed, then we now have an orphaned string on the heap which the garbage collector will have to find and dispose of. Obviously if we're doing this a lot, we'll have some performance problems.

> **Extensive string manipulation should be performed using the System.Text.StringBuilder class, which limits the number of objects that have to be created to represent strings.**

The Apress publication, C# Text Manipulation Handbook, *ISBN 1-86100-823-6, covers the use of the* StringBuilder *class and other classes to perform efficient text manipulation.*

Passing Arrays and Upper Bound Checking

Arrays are reference types in the .NET Framework, and the rules detailed in *Passing Reference Types by Value* and *Passing Reference Types by Reference* are observed while dealing with arrays. This even applies to arrays containing value types only.

Changes to the members of an array passed in by value will be visible to client code, because they are accessed through a reference to the same array. However, an array passed by value can't be reassigned as a different array reference, so the size of the array will remain constant. So, if you want to obtain exactly eight bytes of data from a method, you could pass it an eight byte array by value, and have the method fill it; you would be guaranteed that the array, after the method had finished with it, was still an eight byte array, but the contents of each element could have been changed by the called method.

To prevent the client code from gaining access to any manipulation the method performs on the array, create a temporary array within the method. With an array of value types, it is adequate to `Clone()` the array, because that creates a new array containing a new set of copies of the same values. We can then manipulate these values to our heart's content, without affecting the client code's array. If our array contains reference types, this may not be completely adequate. The `Clone()` method performs a shallow copy of the array and so the references in the new array point to the same objects on the heap as do the references in the parameter array. If you want the elements in the array to be cloned as well, you'll need to do some more work to ensure the array contents are duplicated as well.

Passing Enumerated Values

Enumerations provide an excellent way to pass arguments to methods where the argument has a finite set of allowable values. Enumerations are used to clarify lists of data internally represented as numerical values such as validation tables and lookup lists. Enumerations can also be considered collections of constants.

Calling a method with an enum parameter makes full use of IntelliSense in the Visual Studio .NET IDE. The developer can select a valid entry from the `CloseDownOptions` list, or pass a variable declared as the same type as `CloseDownOptions`. Enums make code clearer and more concise because they eliminate the need for *magic numbers* (hard-coded values), and multiple constant values, and reduce the risk of an incorrect value being passed to the method.

Method Overloading

It is a basic object-oriented design principle that a method name should reflect what the method actually does. Often, several methods are required that do similar things, but accept different arguments. In some programming languages, convoluted method names such as `PrintString()`, `PrintImage()`, and `Print()` methods might be used to cope with this. In languages that target the .NET Framework, such as C#, we can call all of these methods by what they do: `Print()`.

Overloading is used extensively within the .NET Framework base-class libraries and can be identified in the IntelliSense information displayed when coding a method call in Visual Studio .NET. The first version of the method is displayed with '1 of n', followed by the method signature. The spinner controls, or the up-down arrow keys can be used to navigate to each version of the method.

Overloading is particularly useful in utility type classes, where a consistent approach of two (or more) variations on *every* method could be implemented. For example, we may have a class to abstract a data-access component. The class supports retrieving customers from the database using a `GetCustomer()` method. Two versions of this method could be coded to accept a customer ID as an `int` value, and the customer ID embedded in an XML node.

Overloading methods allows us to specify several variations of the same method all with the same name, and differing only by the method signature. The **signature** (sometimes referred to as prototype) of a method is the combination of both its name and its parameter list.

Below is a method, `DisplayCalculatedCost()`, which accepts two arguments: an `Order` object and a `Double`:

```
private void DisplayCalculatedCost(Order order, double orderCost)
{
  // Display the details
}
```

This has the following signature:

```
DisplayCalculatedCost(Order, Double)
```

While the `CalculateCost()` method:

```
private double CalculateCost(double orderCost, double deliveryFee)
{
  // Calculate order cost
}
```

has the following signature:

```
CalculateCost(Double, Double)
```

As you can see the return type is not considered part of the method's signature. This defines one of the rules of overloading:

> **Two or more methods cannot overload each other if they differ only by return types.**

Consider the signature resulting from a `params` argument type. As discussed earlier, the compiler creates a signature reference for each possible outcome of the function. In the case of a parameter array, this list is potentially infinite. This is demonstrated by:

```
public static int AverageScores(params int[] scores)
{
  int total = 0;
  int average = 0;

  foreach(int score in scores)
  {
    total += score;
  }

  average = total / scores.Length;

  return average;
}
```

resulting in the signatures:

```
AverageScores(ref int)
AverageScores(ref int, ref int)
AverageScores(ref int, ref int, ref int)
...and so on
```

When you want to overload a method, a number of rules apply:

❑ Each overload must differ by one (or more) of the following:

- Parameter count

- Parameter data types

- Parameter order

❑ Each method should use the same method name; otherwise, you are simply creating a totally new method.

❑ You cannot overload a method with a property of the same name or vice versa.

You might be surprised to see that just changing the order of parameters overloads a method, as shown below (`argument_order.cs`):

```
using System;

public class MethodOverload
{
  public int Add(int number_one, double number_two)
```

```
  {
    return (int)(number_one + number_two);
  }

  public int Add(double number_two, int number_one)
  {
    return (int)(number_two - number_one);
  }
}

public class Test
{
  public static void Main(string[] args)
  {
    MethodOverload overload_meth = new MethodOverload();

    Console.WriteLine("Add (int, double) "+ overload_meth.Add(4,3.2));
    Console.WriteLine("Add (double, int) "+ overload_meth.Add(4.2,3));
  }
}
```

Here we have defined two methods called Add(), which both take two arguments, an int and a double. The only difference is the order in which the arguments are passed:

❑   Add(int, double)

❑   Add(double, int)

The first method really does add the numbers but the second subtracts them:

```
C:\ClassDesign\Chapter03>argument_order
Add (int, double) 7
Add (double, int) 1
```

Simply by switching the order in which we pass parameters we can call different methods. While you would **never** implement a design quite this bad, it does demonstrate that overloading methods by parameter order alone is usually a bad idea. It will make your code hard to read and people calling your methods will get confused.

Here is an example of overloading a function in a more useful manner:

```
private double CalculateCost(double orderCost)
{
  // Calculate total cost
  return (this.CalculateCost(orderCost, 0, 0));
}

private double CalculateCost(double orderCost, double deliveryFee)
{
  // Calculate total cost
```

```
    return (this.CalculateCost(orderCost, deliveryFee, 0));
}

private double CalculateCost(double orderCost, double deliveryFee,
                            double handlingFee)
{
    // Calculate total cost
    return (orderCost + deliveryFee + handlingFee);
}
```

These methods have the following finite signatures:

- ❑   CalculateCost(Double)

- ❑   CalculateCost(Double, Double)

- ❑   CalculateCost(Double, Double, Double)

These methods calculate the cost of some goods with an optional delivery fee and handling charge. Notice the use of the this keyword to identify that we are calling the local version of the overloaded method. The first two methods call the third overload passing the appropriate number of zeros.

There are advantages of overloading methods. Method overloading should be used to provide different methods that do semantically the same thing. More than one method with the same name can be defined within a type as long as the signatures differ. You should always carefully consider whether giving two methods different names would create greater clarity in your class interface than creating two methods that only differ by their signatures. To use the Add() example we showed earlier, we could have several versions of this method that all took different types of number as arguments, so long as they all returned the sum of the two (or more) values passed in. Although if we were to create a method that concatenated strings, or combined non-numerical values, or worse did some mathematical operation on numbers other than adding them, it would be unwise to give it the same name.

Exception Handling

When designing methods, a defensive approach should always be taken. This means that you have to assume that your methods will at some point encounter a problem that forces the method to terminate prematurely. As a designer or developer of a class, you are bound to handle these exceptions in a graceful manner. This is because exception-handling (or the lack of it) forms as much of a part in the semantic contract between a class and its client as any other design consideration. Exception handling means either dealing with the exception internally, and taking an appropriate course of action, or catching the exception and throwing a more meaningful exception back to the client code. If our methods lack exception handling, then any exceptions that occur in the course of their execution will be passed on to the calling code anyway. The decision not to handle an exception delegates the obligation to handle the exception should it arise to the code that called our method.

Failure to anticipate the possibility of exceptions being thrown in your methods results in extra work when developing the client code. Without exception handling in our code, client code itself will have to anticipate and second-guess what has gone wrong when one of your methods is invoked. This breaks the first law of object-oriented programming – encapsulation. Only documented exceptions should ever be thrown by your methods, so that client code always knows what to expect.

As an example, consider a method that stores a customer's details. It may do this by performing an update on a database. A number of things could go wrong, for example the database might be unavailable, or a foreign key constraint violation may have occurred. If we later change the implementation of this method so that it calls a web service, we might encounter a different class of problems; network failures, or XML parsing errors. If we passed these on to client code written with the assumption that it needed to handle only database exceptions, it would likely fail to handle these new exceptions. The upshot is, allowing exceptions to permeate up from our methods exposes the inner workings of our classes, and breaches the purpose of encapsulation. If something goes wrong, the underlying cause of the exception should generally be hidden from the calling program. In this example, all the client code needs to know is that *the customer details have not been stored*. It can then take appropriate action to deal with this situation. An application without exception handling usually results in meaningless error messages appearing on the user's screen or worse still, the application will just crash for no apparent reason.

What Is an Exception?

An exception is thrown when a method encounters an unanticipated problem or processing error, which causes the method processing to terminate prematurely. An example of this would be a 'file not found', or 'divide by zero' exception. Unlike some programming languages that generate meaningless error numbers, the .NET Common Language Runtime throws an exception, which is a special type of object.

An exception is an object that ultimately derives from System.Exception, which is the base class for all exception classes and provides the core contract supported by all exception classes. Although System.Exception is the super type of exceptions, there are two main sub-classes of exceptions – System.SystemException, from which all .NET Framework Class Library exceptions are derived and System.ApplicationException, from which all user-defined application-specific exceptions are derived.

System.Exception exposes a number of useful read-only properties that are common to all exception classes. These properties can be examined and reported on to enhance the debugging process:

❑   HelpLink:
    The HelpLink property sets or gets a URN or URL that links to an appropriate help file. This is useful in applications with user interfaces that might need to display meaningful additional information to the user.

❑ InnerException:
This property can be used to create nested exceptions. This is used when the original exception is handled by throwing a different exception class. The original exception can be embedded in InnerException to create a nested exception.

❑ Message:
The Message property is used to embed a meaningful error message usually describing the cause of the exception.

❑ Source:
The Source property holds the name of the object or application that caused the exception. If this property is not set, the name of the offending assembly is used instead.

❑ StackTrace:
This property returns a string representation of the call stack. This can be used to track the sequence of method calls leading up to the exception.

❑ TargetSite: This property contains the System.Reflection.MethodBase of the offending exception when the StackTrace property is not a null reference.

These properties form the baseline contract for all exception classes, but most specialized exceptions extend this list of properties to include information specific to that exception class. For instance, the System.ArgumentException class also includes a ParamName property, which is used to indicate the name of the offending parameter when an invalid argument is passed to a method.

When an exception is thrown, execution of the method terminates prematurely. The method will not return a value back to the client code and any arguments passed by reference may or may not have been changed by the method. The source of the exception will immediately attempt to find an exception handler. An appropriate exception handler is found by matching the type of the exception against an exception handler for that type.

Try...Catch...Finally

try, catch, and finally statement blocks form the basis of structured exception handling. This is achieved by organizing a method into:

❑ The code that might throw an exception (the try block)

❑ Code to handle the exception (the catch block)

❑ Code to perform any cleanup and releasing of system resources (the finally block)

A `try` block is used to isolate a block of code to be tested for an exception. The code that is tested for an exception is wrapped within a `try {}` statement. `try` blocks must always be followed by either or both of a `catch` and `finally` block.

Catch blocks are used to catch specific exception types. Although `catch` blocks are not mandatory, at least one `catch` block usually follows a `try` block. To catch different types of exceptions, more than one `catch` block can be used for different types of exception.

If a `finally` block exists, it is always executed regardless of whether an exception has been thrown and handled. `finally` blocks are not mandatory unless there is no `catch` block. However, because `finally` blocks are always executed following `try` and `catch` blocks, they should be used to perform the housekeeping necessary for graceful exception handling. This includes the release of application resources such as database connections and so forth. `finally` blocks are extremely useful because they are always guaranteed to execute even after an exception has been thrown. It is for this reason that `finally` blocks should almost always be used. Here are some guidelines for using try, `catch`, and `finally` blocks:

- ❑ Only use `try` blocks around the code that you want to catch exceptions for.

- ❑ Catch only those exceptions that the specific class and method is responsible for. Leave other exceptions to propagate back to the client code.

- ❑ At the root of your application (usually a user interface), include a general exception handler that catches `System.Exception`; this can be used to handle all exceptions that propagate from the lower tiers of your application.

- ❑ Catch exceptions starting with the most specific exceptions first then move on to general exception handlers. Catch blocks have precedence based on their order and the correct exception handler will be ignored if it is below a general exception handler.

- ❑ In an application divided into several logical and physical tiers, try not to let all exceptions propagate from the lower tiers to the user interface. The performance overhead of retreating back up a stack trace for an appropriate exception handler can be excessive in an environment like this. The problem can also be compounded if `finally` blocks of code are used.

- ❑ Use `finally` blocks around code that must be executed regardless of exceptions. This should include code to release system resources.

Throwing Your Own Exceptions

Exceptions can be thrown in your own code by using the `throw` statement. This should be done when the processing in the method encounters a terminal issue that cannot be ignored, such as an invalid argument being passed to a method:

```
throw (new System.ArgumentException("Error Message",
                                    "Parameter Name"));
```

It is customary to specify the details of the exception in one of the exception class constructors when throwing a new exception. The `System.ArgumentException` permits the specification of the error message and the name of the offending parameter. These details are then made available through the properties of the `System.ArgumentException` class. These were discussed earlier in this section, but you can see from this example that a `ParamName` property has been added to the `System.ArgumentException` class to provide additional information to the caller.

If the calling code provides an invalid argument, it's a clear cut case for throwing an exception. The calling code is responsible for ensuring that it passes in valid data, and if it fails to do so, your method can't be expected to complete normally. Throw the exception, and you immediately pass responsibility back to the calling code.

When throwing exceptions from your classes, consider whether the exception makes sense to the calling code. If the calling code thinks it's calling a simple method that adds two numbers together, there's no point throwing a `FileNotFoundException` because your code logs all of its additions, and the log file is missing. The calling code won't anticipate that exception and won't be able to do anything about it. Consider catching the `FileNotFoundException` in your code, and then throwing a different exception that makes sense to the caller.

`System.ArgumentException` is built into the .NET Framework Class Library, but you can also create your own exception classes. Creating your own exception class is possible by creating a class that derives from an existing exception class. Since existing exception classes are either implicitly or explicitly derived from `System.Exception`, your own exception classes will be derived form it too. This means that the minimum set of properties provided by `System.Exception` must be supported in your exception class; however, some of these properties can be overridden and new properties can be added to specialize your exception class.

Depending on the kind of error your exception class represents, it is usually best to derive your own exceptions from `System.ApplicationException`. Exceptions can also be based on existing .NET Framework exceptions, but doing so means that your own exceptions may become indistinguishable if your `catch` blocks are not explicit enough or are in the wrong order.

To create your own exception classes follow these steps:

❑ Create a class that inherits from an existing exception type. `System.ApplicationException` is usually the best choice.

- ❑ Your exception should support three common constructors found in all exception classes. These constructors permit the setting of the Message and InnerException properties, the Message property on its own, and a default constructor that sets no properties. If you are deriving from an exception class other than System.ApplicationException you may also need to provide additional constructors.

- ❑ From each of the three constructors, call the equivalent base-class constructor passing the Message and/or InnerException arguments, or the default constructor.

- ❑ Include any additional properties that add value to your exception type. These properties should be read-only because their values can only be set through a constructor.

- ❑ Include any other additional constructors that permit the additional property values to be set.

- ❑ Make your exception class serializable by specifying the [Serializable] attribute. This will allow your class to cross AppDomains and CPU process boundaries when thrown.

The following is an example of an exception class for a bank account. The code file is called InsufficientFundsException.cs, and it has to be compiled as a .dll file. The exception can be thrown when trying to withdraw money when there are insufficient funds in the account:

```
[Serializable]
public class InsufficientFundsException : System.ApplicationException
{
  private decimal balance;

  public InsufficientFundsException() : base()
  {
  }

  public InsufficientFundsException(string message) : base(message)
  {
  }

  public InsufficientFundsException(string message,
      Exception   innerException) : base(message, innerException)
  {
  }

  public InsufficientFundsException(string message,
      Exception innerException, decimal balance)
      : base(message, innerException)
  {
    this.balance = balance;
  }
```

```
public InsufficientFundsException(string message, decimal balance)
    : base(message)
{
    this.balance = balance;
}

public decimal Balance
{
    get { return this.balance; }
}
}
```

Aside from following the necessary steps required to create your own exception classes, there are a number of best practices to follow. When creating your own exception classes, follow these guidelines:

- ❑ Always suffix your exception classes with the word Exception, as in this example, InsufficientFundsException. This will help distinguish the exception class from other classes.

- ❑ Create your exception classes within descriptive namespaces that include the name of your organization and the name of the application. This permits custom exception classes to be fully qualified where necessary, which can help to distinguish between built-in .NET Framework Class Library exception classes, and your own application exception classes. This is also a good way of grouping exception classes by functional areas within your application.

- ❑ Consider carefully which existing exception base class you will base your exception class on. All exception classes either implicitly or explicitly derive from System.Exception, which is the base class. The best option is to explicitly derive from System.ApplicationException, unless you need to specialize an existing exception type.

- ❑ Custom exception classes can override some of their base-class members such as the Message property, and they can also extend the base class by providing additional properties and corresponding constructors. In our example, we include the current account Balance as a property; this adds value to the InsufficientFundsException type by returning an additional reason for the exception being thrown.

- ❑ When catching an exception and throwing a different exception, the original exception should be nested within the InnerException property, which returns a reference to the original exception type. This technique is used to provide additional detail to the client code should it be required.

- ❑ Don't go overboard creating exception classes for every exception you can think of. Consider creating generalized exceptions for functional areas of the application and using meaningful error messages instead. A good idea is to start by having an exception type for each logical tier of your application.

❑ Try not to create elaborate hierarchies of exceptions. Try to stick to two or three levels of inheritance at the most. This will simplify your catch blocks and reduce the possibility of getting your catch blocks in the wrong order.

❑ For exception classes that propagate back to the user interface, assign the HelpLink property that can be used to hyperlink to an HTML help file providing further assistance.

Methods and MSIL Code

The final subject in this chapter on methods will be a discussion on MSIL code. MSIL is the low-level programming instruction set produced by all compilers that target the .NET Framework.

Looking at the MSIL code produced by the C# compiler in this chapter is important because we can see how the different types of methods are compiled into MSIL code, and also show the broader importance of MSIL methods that are covered in the remaining chapters. This insight will change the way you will think about the elegant and sometimes complex object-oriented C# code you produce.

To look at how simple methods are compiled into MSIL code, create the following program, which includes an example of the main types of methods. This program can also be created in Notepad and is saved in the source code as msil.cs:

```
using System;

class MSILMethods
{
    static void Main()
    {
        int result = 0;
        int total;
        int net = 0;

        MethodExamples examples = new MethodExamples();

        result = examples.ByValueMethod(7);
        examples.ByRefMethod(ref result);
        examples.OutputMethod(out total, result);
        result = result + examples.OverloadMethod(total);
        total = examples.OverloadMethod(result, total);
        net = examples.ParamsMethod(result, total);

        Console.WriteLine(net);
    }
}

class MethodExamples
```

```
{
  public int ByValueMethod(int a)
  {
    return a++;
  }

  public void ByRefMethod(ref int b)
  {
    b = b * 2;
  }

  public void OutputMethod(out int c, int d)
  {
    c = d / 4;
  }

  public int OverloadMethod(int e)
  {
    return e + 2;
  }

  public int OverloadMethod(int e, int f)
  {
    return e + f;
  }

  public int ParamsMethod(params int[] g)
  {
    int total = 0;

    foreach(int num in g)
    {
      total = total + num;
    }

    return total + 1;
  }
}
```

Compile msil.cs and examine the MSIL code produced by the C# compiler using the utility ildasm:

```
C:\Class Design\Ch03>ildasm msil.exe
```

Once ildasm loads, first expand the MSIL methods node, select msil.exe, and click on View, and then Show Token Values. Now expand the msil node. The following screen should be displayed, which displays all of the members of the MSILMethods class:

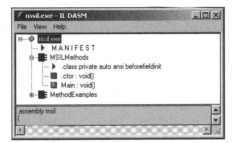

Double click on .ctor : void() and the following screen should be displayed:

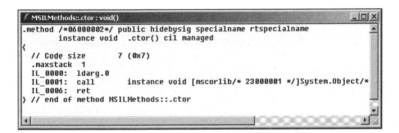

From the MSIL code emitted by the C# compiler we can make the following observations about the implicit constructor of the MSILMethods class:

❏ We can tell from this that for the MSILMethods class, that constructor is actually a method from the .method declaration. Constructors are actually compiled into MSIL code as methods. This is important because, when considering the design and usage of constructors, we know that constructors are really methods, although quite specialized methods in terms of their purpose in class design.

❏ The constructor method (.ctor) makes a call to the System.Object constructor. It is from this that we can tell the base class of our type. The MSILMethods class does not explicitly derive from any type within the original .cs file, but implicitly derives from System.Object. This is why a call is made to the System.Object constructor.

Close the .ctor window and double click the Main() method node. The following window should be displayed:

```
/ MSILMethods::Main : void()                                    _ |□| x|
.method /*06000001*/ private hidebysig static
        void  Main() cil managed
{
  .entrypoint
  // Code size        88 (0x58)
  .maxstack  4
  .locals /*11000001*/ init (int32 V_0,
            int32 V_1,
            int32 V_2,
            class MethodExamples/* 02000003 */ V_3,
            int32[] V_4)
  IL_0000:  ldc.i4.0
  IL_0001:  stloc.0
  IL_0002:  ldc.i4.0
  IL_0003:  stloc.2
  IL_0004:  newobj       instance void MethodExamples/* 02000003 */::.ctor() /* 06000009 */
  IL_0009:  stloc.3
  IL_000a:  ldloc.3
  IL_000b:  ldc.i4.7
  IL_000c:  callvirt     instance int32 MethodExamples/* 02000003 */::ByValueMethod(int32)
  IL_0011:  stloc.0
  IL_0012:  ldloc.3
  IL_0013:  ldloca.s  V_0
```

From the Main() method, note the following:

❏   We can tell from the MSIL code that Main() is implemented as .NET
    managed code through the cil managed flag in the method declaration.

❏   Because we have created a console application, Main() is also the entry
    point to the program. We can tell this from the .entrypoint directive.
    This is what distinguishes .exe files from .dll files. All .exe files always
    have one method with the .entrypoint directive.

❏   In the Invoking Methods section, we discussed how stack frames are
    created to allocate a fixed block of memory on the stack to be used for
    parameters and local variables. The .maxstack directive tells us the
    maximum number of stack-based variables our method needs to execute
    this method. In the example, we have four stack-based variables – total,
    result, and net, (which are all of type int), and example (a reference
    pointer to a stack-based object of type MethodExamples). The actual size
    of the Stack Frame is calculated by the C# compiler and emitted into the
    MSIL code. The value of the .maxstack directive is actually optimized to
    allow parts of the stack frame to be reused when variables are either no
    longer required, or go out of scope. The optimized calculation for
    .maxstack is based upon the maximum stack size the method requires to
    execute, which is not necessarily the number of variables within the
    method. The optimized calculation depends on a number of factors
    including variable type (int, bool, reference, and so on), maximum
    number of arguments passed to other methods, and variable scope.

Next, close the Main() window and expand the MethodExamples node. This node
contains all of the members of the MethodExamples class:

Double-click on the first OverloadMethod member and the following screen should be displayed:

```
/ MethodExamples::OverloadMethod : int32(int32,int32)                    _|□|×
.method /*06000007*/ public hidebysig instance int32
        OverloadMethod(int32 e,
                       int32 f) cil managed
{
  // Code size       8 (0x8)
  .maxstack  2
  .locals /*11000002*/ init (int32 V_0)
  IL_0000:  ldarg.1
  IL_0001:  ldarg.2
  IL_0002:  add
  IL_0003:  stloc.0
  IL_0004:  br.s       IL_0006
  IL_0006:  ldloc.0
  IL_0007:  ret
} // end of method MethodExamples::OverloadMethod
```

In between the `.method` directive and the `public` access modifier we can see a token tag of 06000007. The token tag uniquely identifies this member within the assembly. Now close this window and double-click on the second OverloadMethod member of MethodExamples. The following screen will be displayed:

121

```
MethodExamples::OverloadMethod : int32(int32)                          _ |□| x|
.method /*06000006*/ public hidebysig instance int32
        OverloadMethod(int32 e) cil managed
{
  // Code size       8 (0x8)
  .maxstack  2
  .locals /*11000002*/ init (int32 V_0)
  IL_0000:  ldarg.1
  IL_0001:  ldc.i4.2
  IL_0002:  add
  IL_0003:  stloc.0
  IL_0004:  br.s       IL_0006
  IL_0006:  ldloc.0
  IL_0007:  ret
} // end of method MethodExamples::OverloadMethod
```

Here we can see that the second overload of OverloadMethod() has a different token tag 06000006. Because token tags are unique within an assembly, this means that overloaded methods are in fact compiled as completely separate methods and the token tag is actually used to resolve which overloaded method to call. We can prove that this resolution process is made at compile time by reexamining the Main() method of the MSILMethods class:

```
MSILMethods::Main : void()                                            _ |□| x|
  IL_001e:  callvirt    instance void MethodExamples/* 02000003 */::OutputMeth

  IL_0023:  ldloc.0
  IL_0024:  ldloc.3
  IL_0025:  ldloc.1
  IL_0026:  callvirt    instance int32 MethodExamples/* 02000003 */::Overload
  IL_002b:  add
  IL_002c:  stloc.0
  IL_002d:  ldloc.3
  IL_002e:  ldloc.0
  IL_002f:  ldloc.1
  IL_0030:  callvirt    instance int32 MethodExamples/* 02000003 */::Overload

  IL_0035:  stloc.1
  IL_0036:  ldloc.3
  IL_0037:  ldc.i4.2
  IL_0038:  newarr      [mscorlib/* 23000001 */]System.Int32/* 01000003 */
  IL_003d:  stloc.s     V_4
  IL_003f:  ldloc.s     V_4
  IL_0041:  ldc.i4.0
  IL_0042:  ldloc.0
  IL_0043:  stelem.i4
  IL_0044:  ldloc.s     V_4
  IL_0046:  ldc.i4.1
```

You might need to scroll across the window to view the token tags called by Main().

By examining the MSIL code emitted by the C# compiler, we can deduce the following:

- Class members, including overloaded members with the same name are implemented as separate members in MSIL code. The resolution of an overloaded member by comparing the method signature against the argument list is made by the C# compiler.

- The C# compiler calculates the size of each stack frame required to invoke a method. This calculation is optimized to use the least amount of memory possible.

- Constructors are also implemented as methods. The same is also true of properties and operators, which are discussed in the next chapter.

Design Summary

To recap this chapter, we will finish with some issues to bear in mind when designing methods:

- Passing reference types by reference (ref) allows you to reassign the object. The method parameter effectively becomes a double pointer, first to the client code variable reference, then to the object itself.

- Using enumerated lists of values as method arguments rather than integer magic numbers aids code clarity and helps prevent bugs. Enumerated lists are displayed in IntelliSense allowing the programmer to accurately select an appropriate value. This will provide some degree of safety when evaluating method parameters within the method itself.

- Try to standardize the overloading of methods. Overloaded methods can be confusing when developing client code, as several implementations of the same method are available, each accepting a different set of arguments. This confusion is amplified when each of these methods also returns a different value type. Consider that overloaded methods coded in this manner should have been coded as separate methods as they serve different purposes. Only use overloading if the methods are semantically related. Each overload of a method should achieve the same goal based on a different set of arguments.

- When invoking a static method, refer to the class name rather than an object instance variable; static methods belong to the class itself and may be used by other objects of a different class type, without having to instantiate an actual object.

- Exceptions form part of the semantic contract for a class. Handle only those exceptions your method is responsible for, leaving other exceptions to propagate automatically.

C#

Class Design

Handbook

4

Properties and Operators

In this chapter, we will look at the role of properties and operators in C# class design. We'll see plenty of examples along the way to illustrate how properties can improve the encapsulation, usability, and robustness of our types. We will also look at Indexers, which are a special kind of property. We'll see how operator overloading can be used to simplify application development by allowing your own types to be used with arithmetic or Boolean operators, just like primitive types. Explicit and implicit conversion operators will be covered in Chapter 7.

By the end of this chapter, you should understand how to create meaningful properties and when and how to implement operators for your classes and structures. You should also understand the connection between properties and operators. Before continuing with this chapter, it is recommended that you first read the previous chapter on *Methods*. Many of the techniques you will learn in the *Methods* chapter directly apply to this chapter.

Properties in C#

Properties represent the attributes of a class unlike methods (which represent the actions of a class). For example, consider a Person class that has attributes such as Name and Salary. The Person class also has actions such as Update and CalculateBonus. We must decide how to represent the Name and Salary attributes in our code during implementation. One option would be to define Name and Salary as private fields in the Person class; however, this will prevent the information from being accessed elsewhere in the program. Declaring Name and Salary as public fields is not a good idea because it breaks the encapsulation of the class. It exposes the data directly so that it can be read and modified by any other part of the program; so much for data hiding! Properties solve this problem by providing indirect access to private variables through get and set accessors.

Property accessors are just methods that permit conditional abstract access to the underlying data. Property get and set accessors are sometimes called property procedures in other languages such as Visual Basic .NET.

> **Properties represent the attributes of a class. They provide indirect access to private fields through get and set accessors.**

From the perspective of a programmer using a class, a property can be accessed like a public field in a class. Users of the class can access the property name directly, as if the class really contains a public field with that name. The only difference is that we can make a property read-only or write-only; this is not possible with public fields.

Properties enable us to expose data to the client code, while at the same time preserving the encapsulation of how that data is represented within the class. For example, we can write validation code in the set accessor to ensure the user doesn't assign an illegal value to the property. Likewise, we can perform computations in the get accessor to recalculate the value of the property on request. We will discuss accessors later when we look at the MSIL code emitted by the C# compiler for properties; for now, understand that an accessor is an entry into the class like a method.

C# Property Syntax

Properties, like methods are implemented within classes. The public and private access modifiers discussed in Chapter 3 also apply to properties and the same rules apply. Properties can also be instance and static class members; these differences are discussed in a short while.

Let's start by defining how properties are implemented in C#. This example is actually a scalar property, but the principles of the get and set accessors are the same as an indexer:

```
public class Person
{
  private string name;

  public string Name
  {
    get { return name; }
    set { name = value; }
  }
}
```

In this example, we can see a private field called name. This field can be accessed through the get and set accessors of the Name property. We can omit either the get or set accessor for a property, but not both:

❑ If we omit the set accessor, the property becomes read-only. This can be useful for properties that might need to be recalculated each time they are used, such as the days a person has worked at a company.

❑ If we omit the get accessor, the property becomes write-only; this can be useful for a password property on a security object for example. However, since making the property readable is rarely a bad idea (you never know when someone might need to query it), this situation will not be common.

Java Note – Java properties are also defined as get and set methods but they must also be accessed as get and set methods too.

The CLS in the .NET Framework supports two different kinds of properties:

❑ **Scalar Properties**
A scalar property represents a single class attribute. A property can be a primitive value such as an int or reference type such as a string, or a more complex type such as a DateTime, a Color, or a BankAccount class. Unlike with Visual Basic .NET, C# scalar properties cannot be parameterized. However, both C# and Visual Basic .NET offer a more elegant solution in the form of Indexers.

❑ **Indexers (indexed properties)**
An indexer is a construct that allows array-like syntax to be used on a class. The client code uses array syntax to access a specific value in a private collection or array.

We'll examine both kinds of properties in detail during this chapter. During these discussions, remember that properties are a standard feature in the .NET Framework. This means client code written in any CLS-compliant language can use any property defined in our C# classes providing the property is of a CLS-compliant type.

Scalar Properties

Let's start with scalar properties. The following example was used on the previous page and shows a simple read/write property called Name, in a class called Person. We've compressed the syntax a little, so you can see how properties provide a neat way to write accessor code. We'll explain how properties can be used, after the code listing. The source code for this example is called simple_scalar_property.cs:

```
public class Person
{
  private string name;

  public string Name
  {
    get { return name; }
    set { name = value; }
  }
}
```

Note the following points in this example:

- ❏ The Person class has a field called name, which holds the person's name. This field is declared as private, to prevent direct access by client code. As we've said several times already, one of the most important aims of object-oriented development is to preserve the encapsulation of the class.

- ❏ The Person class has a property called Name, to get and set the person's name. The property acts as a wrapper for the name field. The Name property is declared as public, so that it can be used in client code. Most properties tend to be public, because the essence of properties is to provide a convenient public interface to a class. Nevertheless, situations do arise where a private, protected, or internal property might be required. For example, we can define a private property that can only be accessed by the other members in the same class. The Name property is also of type string; the get accessor must also return a value of type string. The underlying private field is usually of the same type too, as in this example.

- ❏ The set accessor includes a hidden parameter called value. The value parameter contains the value that was passed from the client code.

> **When you define a property, specify the type of the property by including the type between the access modifier and the name of the property. In this example, the Name property is of type string, but it can be any other publicly available type.**

It is important to devise a consistent naming scheme that differentiates between fields and properties in a class. This will make the code more self-documenting, which will make it easier to write and (hopefully) reduce the bug count. Also, our code will be easier to maintain because our intentions are clearer for the maintenance programmer.

Defining a naming scheme for properties and fields is simplified in C# because C# is case-sensitive. In other words, name is not the same as Name. It is often necessary, particularly when considering properties, to represent the data in a number of ways; primarily fields for internal use and public properties for external consumption. As a developer, you need to use both meaningful field and property names that imply the same purpose. Using the same word for both the public property and its underlying type is a good idea because the connection is obvious.

The approach we've taken in this chapter is to use camel Case (xxXxx) for fields (for example, name or dateOfBirth) and Pascal Case (XxXxx) for properties (for example, Name or DateOfBirth). Some developers prefer to use a leading underscore for fields (for example, _Name). Properties should also be named using nouns.

It really doesn't matter what naming convention you choose, as long as you use it consistently within and across classes.

The following code snippet shows how to use the Name property defined in the Person class:

```
public class SimpleScalarProperty
{
  static void Main()
  {
    Person person = new Person();
    person.Name = "James";

    Console.WriteLine(person.Name);
  }
}
```

Note the following in the Main() method:

❑   The client code has no direct access to the name field; all access to this data must be made indirectly through the Name property. This means the Person class developer retains control over how the data is implemented privately inside the class. This is called encapsulation.

❑   The client code uses field-like syntax to access the property. This is more convenient than method-call syntax. For example, if Person defined a pair of methods called GetName() and SetName() (similar to Java), the client code would have to use this rather more cumbersome syntax to get and set the person's name:

```
person.SetName("James")
Console.WriteLine(person.GetName())
```

Now that we've seen how to define and use a simple property, it's time to roll up our sleeves and discuss the design and implementation issues that enable us to use properties correctly in our classes, starting with the MSIL code emitted by the C# compiler.

Compiling Scalar Properties into MSIL

In Chapter 3, we discussed the role of MSIL code. We looked at how different kinds of methods compiled into MSIL code. When properties are compiled, the MSIL code emitted from the C# compiler also produces the MSIL .method routines for properties. This is because properties are specialized types of methods, and this is how they are compiled into MSIL code.

When we define a read/write property in a class, the C# compiler generates a pair of methods for the MSIL code. For example, if our property is called Name, the compiler generates methods called get_Name() and set_Name() in the MSIL code. Whenever these properties are used in client code, the compiler implicitly generates code to invoke the get_Name() and set_Name() MSIL methods.

We can use the MSIL Disassembler tool ildasm to illustrate this behavior.

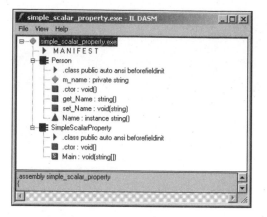

Notice the following members of the `Person` class:

Member name	Description
m_name	This is a `private string` field, to hold the person's name
get_Name	This method is generated by the compiler, to get the `Name` property as a `string`
set_Name	This method is generated by the compiler, to set the `Name` property as a `string`
Name	This is the `Name` property itself, which contains the `get` and `set` methods

The following screenshot illustrates how the `Name` property is implemented in MSIL; this is obtained by double-clicking on the `Name` property in the above window:

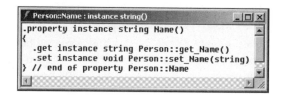

Notice that the `Name` property contains two MSIL statements that identify the `get` and `set` methods for this property. The following is the MSIL generated for the `Main()` method:

```
SimpleScalarProperty::Main : void(string[])                        _□×
.method private hidebysig static void  Main(string[] args) cil managed
{
  .entrypoint
  // Code size       29 (0x1d)
  .maxstack  2
  .locals init (class Person V_0)
  IL_0000:  newobj      instance void Person::.ctor()
  IL_0005:  stloc.0
  IL_0006:  ldloc.0
  IL_0007:  ldstr       "James"
  IL_000c:  callvirt    instance void Person::set_Name(string)
  IL_0011:  ldloc.0
  IL_0012:  callvirt    instance string Person::get_Name()
  IL_0017:  call        void [mscorlib]System.Console::WriteLine(string)
  IL_001c:  ret
} // end of method SimpleScalarProperty::Main
```

The statements marked in the above screenshot set and get the Name property by setting the compiler-generated code to invoke the set_Name(), and get_Name() methods respectively.

By understanding how our code is compiled into MSIL, we can use language features effectively and appropriately in our code. For example, we have just seen that properties are implemented as methods in MSIL code. Whenever client code uses a property, the compiler uses a method call.

Some .NET Framework languages are much more explicit about the way properties map onto methods. A good example is Managed Extensions for C++; to create a read/write property called Name, we would explicitly define separate property functions called get_Name() and set_Name(). However, these differences at the source-code level are leveled when we compile our code into MSIL. MSIL code always looks the same, regardless of which programming language we use to write the source code.

It's worth thinking here for a moment about what happens to the MSIL code at run time. The JIT compiler compiles this code, which performs some optimizations based on what it knows about the code that's been loaded in. This means that while the indirection introduced by properties generates more lines of MSIL instructions, the JIT compiler is able to optimize some of the operations and generate tight, fast code. In fact, in many cases, the JIT compiler can make property access faster than field access, which sounds impossible. However, method calls can be optimized efficiently, and access to member data in the same instance can be faster than remote access to member data in other instances. This makes a property an excellent technique to quickly access the state of an object.

Read/Write, Read-Only, and Write-Only Properties

The Name property in the previous example was a read/write property. We can also define read-only properties and write-only properties. Read-only properties are quite useful, because they enable us to expose data without allowing the client code to modify the data. For example, we might want to provide a read-only property to get a person's date of birth. Similarly, we could use a write-only property to set a security password.

The following example illustrates read/write properties, read-only properties, and write-only properties. The Person class has the following properties:

❑ A Name property that gets and sets a person's name. The person's name is allowed to change, for example if the person gets married or decides they don't like the name they were born with.

❑ A DOB property, to get the person's date of birth. The person's date of birth must be set in the constructor, and cannot change thereafter (a person's date of birth cannot change after the person has been born).

❑ An EmailAlias property, to set the person's e-mail alias. The e-mail alias represents the first part of an employee's e-mail address, before the domain name. The e-mail alias can be modified, but it can never be retrieved on its own (instead, the client program retrieves the full e-mail address).

❑ An EmailAddress property, to get the person's full e-mail address. The e-mail address is computed every time it is requested, by appending the company's domain name to a person's e-mail alias.

The source code for this example is located in the file readable_and_writable.cs:

```
using System;

public class Person
{
  private string name;
  private DateTime dob;
  private string emailAlias;

  public Person(string name, DateTime dOB)
  {
    name = name;
    dob = dOB;
  }

  public string Name
  {
    get { return name; }
    set { name = value;}
  }

  public DateTime DOB
  {
    get { return dob;}
  }

  public string EmailAlias
  {
    set { emailAlias = value; }
  }

  public string EmailAddress
  {
    get { return emailAlias + "@MyCompany.com"; }
```

```
    }
  }

  class ReadableAndWritable
  {
    static void Main()
    {
      Person person = new Person("Steve", new DateTime(1972, 8, 22));

      person.EmailAlias = "Steve.S";

      Console.WriteLine("Name - " + person.Name);
      Console.WriteLine("DOB - " + person.DOB.ToShortDateString());
      Console.WriteLine("Email Address - " + person.EmailAddress);

    }
  }
```

When we run the program, we get the following output in the console window:

```
C:\Class Design\Ch 04>readable_and_writable.exe
Name - Steve
DOB - 22 August 1972
Email Address - Steve.S@MyCompany.com
```

We can use the MSIL Disassembler tool to investigate how read-only and write-only properties are compiled into MSIL code.

Run the MSIL Disassembler on readable_and_writable.exe and you should see the following:

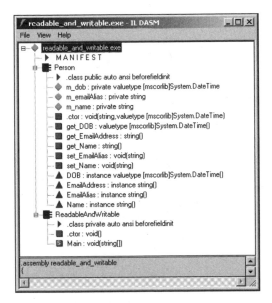

Notice the following items in the MSIL Disassembler window:

- ❑ The get_Name() and set_Name() methods get and set the Name property

- ❑ The get_DOB() method gets the DOB property

- ❑ The set_EmailAlias() method sets the EmailAlias property

- ❑ The get_EmailAddress() method gets the EmailAddress property

- ❑ The C# compiler did not emit a set_DOB() method; this is because the DOB property is read-only

- ❑ The C# compiler did not emit a set_EmailAddress() method; this is because the e-mail address is derived from EmailAlias, and is a read-only property

Static Properties

A static property represents a piece of type-wide information that we want to expose as part of the class, rather than as part of a particular instance. In the same way as static methods discussed in the previous chapter, client code accesses static properties through the class, rather than through an instance of the class.

The following example shows how to define a static property named Domain, to represent the domain name used as part of a person's e-mail address. The assumption here is that all people in our application have the same domain name. Therefore, the domain name is not specific to an instance of the Person class, but the Person class as a whole.

The source code for this example is located in the file static_properties.cs:

```
using System;

public class Person
{
  private string name;
  private DateTime dob;
  private string emailAlias;
  private static string domain;

  public Person(string Name, DateTime dOB)
  {
    name = Name;
    dob = dOB;
  }

  public string Name
  {
    get { return name; }
    set { name = value; }
  }

  public DateTime DOB
```

```
  {
    get { return dob; }
  }

  public string EmailAlias
  {
    set { emailAlias = value; }
  }

  public static string Domain
  {
    get { return domain; }
    set { domain = value; }
  }

  public string EmailAddress
  {
    get { return emailAlias + "@" + domain; }
  }
}

class ReadableAndWritable
{
  static void Main()
  {
    Person person = new Person("Steve", new DateTime(1972, 8, 22));

    person.EmailAlias = "Steve.S";
    Person.Domain = "AnotherCompany.com";

    Console.WriteLine("Name - " + person.Name);
    Console.WriteLine("DOB - " + person.DOB.ToShortDateString());
    Console.WriteLine("EMail Address - " + person.EmailAddress);
  }
}
```

Note the following points with this example:

❑ The Domain property is static

❑ The EmailAlias property uses the domain name to generate the full e-mail address for the person

❑ The Main subroutine sets the Domain property by using the class name (Person) rather than an instance (such as person)

Guidelines for Writing Get Procedures

When we define a read-write or read-only property, we need to consider how to write the get accessor.

The get accessor shouldn't make any changes that affect the state of the object in any way. This is because calling a get accessor is logically comparable to accessing a public field. If we find ourselves updating state in our get accessor, we should implement it as a method instead. Methods may, and often do, have side effects. We suggest two distinct scenarios where get accessors are useful:

❑ To get the value of an existing field in the class. In this scenario, the get function simply acts as a wrapper for a private field that is already present in the class. The get function returns the value directly.

❑ To calculate a derived value in the class. In this scenario, the get accessor uses data in the class to compute the new value. In UML, for object-oriented analysis and design, this is known as a **derived attribute**.

Guidelines for Writing Set Procedures

When we define a read/write or write-only property, we need to consider how to write the set accessor. Perhaps the most important decision is how to handle illegal values. One way to do this is to throw an exception to indicate to the client code that an illegal value is unacceptable. Since values are passed to property set accessors in the same way as arguments are passed to parameterized methods, we can throw a System.ArgumentException like an ArgumentOutOfRangeException or an AgrumentNullException, either because the value is out of range, or it is null.

> **Structured Exception Handling is discussed in Chapter 3. Exceptions can be handled and thrown inside properties just like methods.**

Complete Example of Scalar Properties

The following example illustrates all of the issues we've discussed in this section on scalar properties. In this example, we define a class named FootballTeam to represent a football team. Among other members, the class has properties for the soccer team's name, the color of their jerseys, and the number of points the team has earned so far (3 points for a win, 1 point for a draw, and 0 points for a defeat).

Read through the code to understand how the properties are defined in the class. The System.Drawing class is used for the Color class, whereas System.IO is used for file handling classes. The source code for this example is located in scalar_properties_complete.cs:

```
using System;
using System.Drawing;
using System.IO;

class FootballTeam
```

```
{
  private string name;
  private Color jerseyColor;
  private short wins, draws, defeats;
  private bool logging;

  public FootballTeam(string teamName, Color teamColor)
  {
    name = teamName;
    jerseyColor = teamColor;
  }

  public string Name
  {
    get { return name; }
  }

  public int Points
  {
    get { return ((wins * 3) + (draws * 1)); }
  }

  public Color JerseyColor
  {
    get { return jerseyColor; }
    set {
      if(value.Equals(Color.Black))
      {
        throw(new ArgumentException(
          "Teams cannot have Black jerseys"));
      }
      else
      {
        jerseyColor = value;
      }
    }
  }

  public bool Logging { set { logging = value; } }

  private FileStream LogStream
  {
    get {
      try
      {
        return (new FileStream(name + ".log", FileMode.Append,
                               FileAccess.Write));
      }
      catch (System.IO.IOException)
      {
        return (new FileStream("Default.log", FileMode.Append,
                               FileAccess.Write));
      }
```

```
      }
   }

   public void PlayGame(string opponent, short goalsFor,
           short goalsAgainst)
   {
     if (goalsFor > goalsAgainst)
       wins++;
     else if (goalsFor == goalsAgainst)
       draws++;
     else
       defeats++;

     if (logging)
     {
       StreamWriter sw = new StreamWriter(LogStream);
       sw.WriteLine("{0} {1}-{2} {3}", name, goalsFor,
           goalsAgainst, opponent);
       sw.Flush();
       sw.Close();
     }
   }
 }
```

Note the following design points in the `FootballTeam` class:

❑ The constructor explicitly initializes name and `jerseyColor`. The other
fields are initialized implicitly; wins, draws, and defeats are implicitly
initialized to 0, and logging is implicitly initialized to False. It's good
practice to rely on implicit initialization where it is suitable; in our example,
the implicit initialization for wins, draws, defeats, and logging is fine.

❑ The Name property gets the name of the soccer team. There is no set
accessor for Name, because a soccer team cannot change its name once it has
been created (unlike US football teams, where the name of a team can
change when the franchise is sold to another city).

❑ The Points property calculates and returns the number of points earned
by the team so far. This property is never stored in the object, but is always
recalculated on demand. If the Points property is accessed frequently, an
alternative strategy would be to have a points field that is updated every
time a game is played. However, if the Points property is seldom used,
the overhead of keeping the value up to date might not be worth the effort;
this design assumption led us to recalculate the Points value only
when requested.

❑ The JerseyColor property gets and sets the color of the team's jerseys.
The set accessor includes validation, to prevent teams from having black
jerseys (since only referees can wear black). An ArgumentException is
thrown in this case.

❑ The `Logging` property is a rare example of a write-only property. This property enables client code to enable or disable logging of results to a file. If this property is `True`, we write the result of every game the team plays to a log file. There is no `get` accessor for the `Logging` property as the client program should never need to query whether logging is enabled or disabled.

❑ The `LogStream` property is a `Private` property. This means it can only be used within the `FootballTeam` class. The purpose of the property is to create and return a `FileStream` object, which can be used to write results to a log file. The accessor encapsulates logic that decides which file to use for logging. This is a good example of a property being more appropriate than a field.

❑ The `PlayGame()` method increments `wins`, `draws`, or `defeats`. The subroutine also tests the `Logging` property to see if logging is enabled; if it is, the subroutine uses the `LogStream` property to get a `FileStream` object to use to log the result to file.

We can use the `FootballTeam` properties (and other members) as shown in the following client code:

```
class Season
{
  static void Main()
  {
    FootballTeam myTeam = new FootballTeam("Wolves", Color.Gold);

    myTeam.Logging = true;

    myTeam.PlayGame("Portsmouth", 2, 1);
    myTeam.PlayGame("Manchester United", 2, 3);
    myTeam.PlayGame("West Bromwich Albion", 4, 0);
    myTeam.PlayGame("Stoke City", 3, 2);
    myTeam.PlayGame("West Ham", 1, 1);

    Console.WriteLine(myTeam.Name + "
                      (" + myTeam.JerseyColor.Name + ") - " +
                      myTeam.Points.ToString());

  }
}
```

Note the following points about the `Main()` method:

❑ We use the `Name` read-only property to display the name of the soccer team

❑ We use the `JerseyColor` read/write property to change the color of the team's jerseys, and then display the new jersey color

❑ We use the `Logging` write-only property to enable file logging

❑ We use the `Points` read-only property to calculate the number of points earned by the team

When you run the application, it should display the following output in the console window:

```
C:\Class Design\Ch 04>scalar_properties_complete.exe
Wolves (Gold) - 10
```

The application also logs the football results to a file named `Wolves.log`. The file contains the following:

```
Wolves 2-1 Portsmouth
Wolves 2-3 Manchester United
Wolves 4-0 West Bromwich Albion
Wolves 3-2 Stoke City
Wolves 1-1 Newcastle United
```

Indexers

Now that we've seen how to use scalar properties, let's take a look at **indexers.**

C# does not permit parameterized scalar properties. In other languages that do support parameterized scalar properties, they tend to be used in conjunction with private arrays or collections of data. For instance, if we have a `Person` class with a property called `Child`, the `Person` class must support the possibility of several children. The `Child` parameter would be used to reference each element of an array.

This technique is not allowed in C#; however, C# does support indexers, which are a more elegant technique for solving this problem.

> *C++ Note: C# Indexers are called Indexed Properties in C++.*

We've already considered a `Person` class with a `Child` property, but what if we need to deal with people instead of a single `Person`? Here we have a requirement for an object hierarchy of `Person` objects each with `Child` objects. Indexers allow types such as a `Person` to be treated like an array:

❑ Indexers are declared like a scalar property

❑ Indexers provide indirect access to the underlying `private` fields using `get` and `set` accessors

❑ Indexer `set` accessors have a hidden and implicit parameter called `value`

❑ Indexers can be any value or reference type

Unlike scalar properties, however, indexers have the following characteristics:

❑ Indexers allow a class to be treated like an array using the `[ ]` operators

❑ Indexers are parameterized and accept arguments

140

- ❑ Indexers almost always provide indirect access to hidden collections or arrays of types

- ❑ Indexer properties must be declared as this

- ❑ Indexers add a hidden property called Item to a class

- ❑ Indexers behave like a default property because the client code does not need to refer to the name of the indexer

- ❑ Classes can only have one indexer because a class can only have one default type member

When a class exposes an indexer, it is sometimes referred to as a container class because it acts as a container for a collection of other types. Those types in turn can also be containers for other types creating a hierarchy of object types. A good example of this within the .NET Framework is a DataSet object, which is a container of Table objects. Table objects in turn are collections for Row and Column objects.

When indexers are used to create an object hierarchy like this, the object relationships then become similar in principal to database one-to-many or parent-child relationships.

Defining a Single Indexer in a Class

Recall that indexers provide indirect access to private variables, just like scalar properties. Unlike scalar properties though, this private data is almost always some kind of collection such as an array of classes or structures. This is because we normally want to index whole entities rather than a single attribute of an entity.

For example, if we create an indexer property in a Person class to represent the person's Name, we could write code like this:

```
Person[1] = "James";
Person[2] = "Steve";
```

This would provide an array-like syntax but limits us for other class attributes such as Email, Address, and so on. We cannot add additional indexers because indexers are default properties and only one default property is allowed in a class.

To use an indexer, we need to index the Person entity as a whole and not just the person's name. To do this, we need a containing class an indexer of the type Person. This supports the sensible requirement of being able to index a Person and not just one attribute of the Person.

The following example (indexers_simple.cs) demonstrates this idea:

```
using System;

public class Person
{
   private string name;
```

```
      public Person(string Name)
      {
        name = Name;
      }

      public string Name
      {
        get { return name; }
      }
   }

   public class Authors
   {
      private Person[] persons = new Person[5];

      public Person this [int index]
      {
        get { return persons[index]; }
        set { persons[index] = value; }
      }
   }

   public class SingleIndexer
   {
      static void Main()
      {
        Authors authors = new Authors();
        authors[0] = new Person("James");
        authors[1] = new Person("Roger");
        authors[2] = new Person("Ben");
        authors[3] = new Person("Richard");
        authors[4] = new Person("Teun");

        for(int i=0; i<5; i++)
          Console.WriteLine(authors[i].Name);
      }
   }
```

When you compile and run this program, the following list will be displayed in the console windows:

```
C:\Class Design\Ch 04>indexers_simple.exe
James
Roger
Ben
Richard
Teun
```

Let's now consider the main points of interest with our first indexer:

❑   The Person entity is represented as a class with properties and respective private fields to store and access the attributes of the Person.

142

❏   The `Authors` class is the container class for `Person`. It is called a container class because it contains a hidden private array of type `Person` and because it contains the indexer. The indexer is also of type `Person`.

❏   The indexer property is parameterized and accepts an argument of type `int`. Like scalar properties, the indexer also provides indirect access to a `private` field. However, the `private` field is an array of `Person` objects. The `int` parameter represents the ordinal value in the array.

❏   The indexer is created with the `this` keyword, which implicitly creates a default property called `Item`. The indexer is accessed in the C# client code without specifying the name of the property – `Item`, because it is the default property.

❏   The `SingleIndexer` client code class has a very intuitive coding style. We are using the container class (`Authors`) with the array syntax but each element is of type `Person`.

❏   The management of the array of `Person` classes is hidden from the client code. This is called encapsulation or data hiding because the array of persons can only be accessed through the `Authors` class indexer.

The fact concerning the default property called `Item` is important when the C# class containing the indexer is accessed through non-C# client code. Because `Item` is a default property, it can never be referred to in the C# client program. Though other languages such as Visual Basic .NET, using our C# `Person` class can explicitly refer to the `Item` property. Compare the following example in Visual Basic .NET with the C# client code above:

indexers_simple.vb:

```
Module Module1
  Sub Main()

    Dim i As Integer
    Dim authors As New Authors()

    authors.Item(0) = New Person("James")
    authors.Item(1) = New Person("Roger")
    authors.Item(2) = New Person("Ben")
    authors.Item(3) = New Person("Richard")
    authors.Item(4) = New Person("Teun")

    For i = 0 To 4
      Console.WriteLine(authors.Item(i).Name)
    Next i

  End Sub
End Module
```

Here the Visual Basic .NET client code can make explicit reference to the `Item` indexer property. If your C# classes are likely to be consumed by Visual Basic.NET client code, the default property name for an indexer can be overridden. Change the `Authors` class as shown below. (The complete code listing can be found in `indexers_indexer_name.cs`.)

```
public class Authors
{
  Person[] persons = new Person[5];

  [System.Runtime.CompilerServices.IndexerName("Person")]
  public Person this [int index]
  {
    get { return persons[index];  }
    set { persons[index] = value; }
  }
}
}
```

Applying the above attribute allows Visual Basic.NET client code to refer to a `Person` property instead of an `Item` property:

```
authors.Person(0) = New Person("James")
authors.Person(1) = New Person("Roger")
authors.Person(2) = New Person("Ben")
authors.Person(3) = New Person("Richard")
authors.Person(4) = New Person("Teun")
```

Let's recap the main observations so far:

❏ We have seen how to define a single indexer on a class to create a parent-child relationship similar to a one-to-many database relationship.

❏ The term container class has been introduced. A container class is the parent in the parent-child relationship.

❏ The container class has a private array of objects of the same type as the indexer; in our example the container or parent class was the `Authors` class, and the child was a `Person` class. The private array within `Authors` was also of type `Person`.

❏ Child classes can themselves contain indexers making them parent classes for other child classes. This is similar to an `ADO.NET DataSet` object, which contains `Table`, which in turn contains `Columns` and `Rows`.

❏ An indexer is actually a default property called `Item` that is hidden in C# client code. C# client code does not refer to the `Item` property when using the array `[]` operators.

❏ Visual Basic .NET clients can refer to the `Item` property.

- The default indexer property name of Item can be changed using an attribute – [System.Runtime.CompilerServices.IndexerName ("DefaultPropertyName")]. This can make Visual Basic.NET client code more legible.

- Indexers differ from scalar properties in that they are parameterized, the parameter though, is used as an identifier for the child class – in the examples so far, the ordinal position in the private array. Indexers can accept different and multiple arguments as we will shortly see.

Compiling Indexers into MSIL

To gain a deeper view of how indexers work, compile the C# example above and examine the executable output using ildasm. From the command prompt, type the following:

```
C:\Class Design\Ch 04>ildasm indexer_single_vb.dll
```

The following screen should be displayed after you have expanded the Authors and Person nodes:

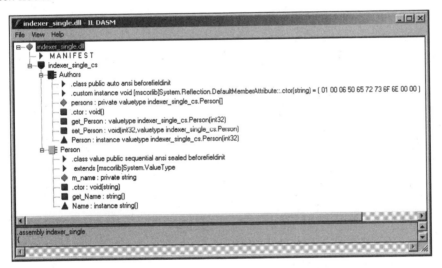

The MSIL code emitted by the C# compiler confirms our earlier observations:

- We can see the indexer defined in the Authors class. Its definition is the same as a scalar property, as it has both get and set accessors.

- Notice that the indexer is called Person and not Item. This is because the default name of the indexer has been overridden.

- Indexers are in fact default properties; the Authors class contains a DefaultMemberAttribute that allows the indexer (default property called Person) to be referenced implicitly through C# client code.

- In Visual Basic .NET, the default Person property can be explicitly referenced.

Using Indexers with ArrayLists

The previous example worked well enough as a demonstration of indexers, but lacked much functionality for a production-quality component. The array in our example had a fixed length of five. The boundaries of the array are stored internally within the Authors class and there is no functionality to add or remove Person classes from the Authors class.

We need to make our Authors class more useful by adding :

❑   A method to Add Person classes

❑   A method to Remove Person classes

❑   A method to Count the Person classes

> **When considering the use of indexers in your class, familiarization with the Systems.Collections namespace is a good idea. This namespace provides many useful variations on the array and collection theme. One of the most useful is the ArrayList, which will be used predominantly through the rest of this topic.**

We will now extend the previous example by including our wish list of functionality detailed above.

Modify the Authors class from the indexers_simple.cs file as follows. The complete listing can be found in indexers_simple_arraylist.cs:

```
public class Authors
{
  private ArrayList persons = new ArrayList();

  public Person this [int index]
  {
    get { return ((Person)persons[index]); }
    set { persons[index] = value;         }
  }


  public void Add(Person person)
  { persons.Add(person); }

  public void Remove(Person person)
  { persons.Remove(person); }

  public int Count { get { return persons.Count; } }
}
```

Our Authors class is now much more useful. Instead of using a simple array of Person classes, we are now using an ArrayList of Person classes. The ArrayList object can be found in the System.Collections namespace. This ArrayList object inherently supports all of the functionality we need to make our Authors class work properly, so we are actually providing a strongly typed wrapper to the ArrayList object through an indexer. Our Authors class is strongly typed because an ArrayList object stores elements of type object. The Authors class is designed to accept and return values of type Person, which is why the indexer get accessor explicitly casts the ArrayList element as a Person.

> **Because ArrayList elements are of type Object, elements are implicitly boxed.**

To test the new Authors class, add the following client code:

```
public class SingleIndexer
{
    static void Main()
    {
        Authors authors = new Authors();
        authors.Add(new Person("James"));
        authors.Add(new Person("Roger"));
        authors.Add(new Person("Ben"));
        authors.Add(new Person("Richard"));
        authors.Add(new Person("Teun"));

        for(int i=0; i<authors.Count; i++)
            Console.WriteLine(authors[i].Name);
    }
}
```

The program will still produce the same results as the examples used earlier in this topic, even though we have significantly changed the implementation of the Authors class. The differences to note are:

❑   The Authors class contains a private ArrayList object, which is used to store each Person object.

❑   The Authors class Add() method is now used add a new Person to the Authors class instead of the indexer set accessor. The indexer set accessor still functions as a mechanism for updating Person objects through the Authors class.

❑   The indexer is being used within a for loop to provide the sequential output of the Name property of the Person class to the console window.

In this section we have used the `ArrayList` class to enhance the `Authors` class by providing the familiar `Add()`, `Remove()`, and `Count()` methods found in many of the .NET Framework classes. The `ArrayList` class itself provides this functionality so it makes sense to provide a strongly typed wrapper around the `ArrayList` as well as keeping the indexer property to support sequential read and update access.

Overloading Indexers

Sometimes it makes sense to index a collection on a value other than its ordinal value. The indexer used so far in this chapter is based on the ordinal value of a `Person` class within the `ArrayList`. However, we might want to index the collection based on the person's name for example. An indexer can be overloaded just like a method. The same rules for method overloading (discussed in Chapter 3) apply to overloading indexers, that is, multiple indexers may have the same name, as long as they have unique signatures.

To make this example possible, we need to expand the `Person` class to store some additional data. Our overloaded indexer will permit `Person` objects to be accessed by Name. An `Age` property will also be added to the `Person` object to demonstrate that the client code is working and the new indexer is finding the correct `Person`. The complete code listing can be found in `overloading_indexer.cs`:

```
using System;
using System.Collections;

public class Person
{
  string name;
  short age;

  public Person(string name, short age)
  {
    this.name = name;
    this.age = age;
  }

  public string Name
  {
    get { return name;  }
    set { name = value; }
  }

  public short Age
  {
    get { return age;  }
    set { age = value; }
  }
}

public class Authors
{
  private ArrayList persons = new ArrayList();

  public Person this [int index]
  { get { return ((Person)persons[index]); } }
```

We now provide an overload of the indexer that permits the client code to index based on the Name of the author (of type Person) as well as the ordinal value in the ArrayList.

```csharp
public Person this [string name]
{
  get
  {
    foreach(Person person in persons)
    {
      if (person.Name == name)
        return person;
    }
    return (Person)persons[0];
  }
}
```

The main difference between the new (overloaded) indexer and the first indexer is that the get accessor has to search for the correct Person class. This is done with a foreach loop. Note that this example only works because each person has a unique name. If the ArrayList contained more than one Person object with the same name, only the first Person would ever be found. Using the original indexer, which accesses the ArrayList by the ordinal value of the elements, would still permit access to other person objects with the same name.

> The ArrayList class also supports the methods BinarySearch and Contains which might provide an efficient search mechanism in the get accessors of your indexers.

```csharp
public void Add(Person person)
{ persons.Add(person); }

public void Remove(Person person)
{ persons.Remove(person); }

public int Count { get { return persons.Count; } }
}

public class OverloadedIndexer
{
  static void Main()
  {
    Authors authors = new Authors();
    authors.Add(new Person("James", 31));
    authors.Add(new Person("Roger", 21));
    authors.Add(new Person("Ben", 21));
    authors.Add(new Person("Richard", 21));
    authors.Add(new Person("Teun", 21));
```

```
        Person author = authors["James"];
        Console.WriteLine(author.Name + " - " + author.Age.ToString());
        author.Age = 21;
        author = authors["James"];
        Console.WriteLine(author.Name + " - " + author.Age.ToString());
    }
}
```

We have omitted the set accessors for both indexers, making the indexers read-only, because we would have to write some fairly awkward code, similar to the get accessor to search and then update the Person class. A much simpler solution is to provide set accessors within the Person class itself. Because the get accessors of both indexers actually return a reference to a Person type, we can channel all updates to an existing Person through a reference to the Person type.

> **When the internal array or collection contains lots of data, a more efficient search routine may be necessary so as not to degrade performance. Sequentially looping and comparing many objects within an ArrayList could be very inefficient if there are many elements. Consider using the BinarySearch or Contains methods instead.**

Indexer Summary

Indexers are used to make a class behave like an array by using the [] operator syntax. Indexer properties are actually a hidden default property called Item. This Item property is never referred to in C# code because it is the default type member. Because a class can only have one default type-member, there can only be one indexer in a class. However, an indexer can be overloaded to index a class on different internal data.

Although indexers can be used to index simple types such as strings or numbers, indexers are most effective when indexing more complex types such as custom classes like our Person class. To index a custom class, create a container class that exposes an indexer of the same type as the custom class that will be indexed. The container class should contain a private internal array or collection to store the indexed type, and have public methods to add, remove, and count the indexed type. The private ArrayList object already contains Add(), Remove(), and Count() members, so the container class then becomes a wrapper for the private ArrayList but with an indexer property to allow the client code to treat the custom class like an array.

We can provide overloaded indexers to index the custom class on one of its properties instead of its ordinal value within the ArrayList, by including specialized code to search for the required object in the ArrayList. To enable the search routines inside the indexer get accessor to deal with duplicate objects, a unique identifier can be used. The indexer is then used in a very similar way to relational database access.

Indexers actually work by overloading the [] operators to make a class behave like an array.

Operators in C#

Operators are the symbols and characters used to perform operations between one or more types. Consider the + operator, which can be used to add two numbers together and return the result. The + operator can also be used to add two strings together and return one concatenated string.

The behavior of an operator is defined at type level. This is called *operator overloading* because we are overloading an operator to exhibit specific behavior for a specific type.

The behavior of an operator on a type-by-type basis is contained within an operator overload method. Like all other types of method, this is an encapsulated section of code that performs a specific task. In the case of an operator overload method, however, the method contains the necessary logic and behavior that will be applied when an operator is used on a specific type. Operators can also therefore, be used to encapsulate expressions.

Operators are in Fact Expressions

The CLR has no knowledge of operators. When an operator is used, the C# language compiler actually generates the necessary MSIL code to perform the operation. Operators are treated and actually compiled into MSIL code as specialized methods. The MSIL code emitted by the C# compiler for operators will be examined later in this section.

Many types in the .NET Framework support operators; these types are typically primitive value types such as numbers and dates. For each of these types, decisions were made on which operators would be supported and what their behavior would be. When designing your own types, the same process must be followed. The class designer must consider which operators are relevant and what behavior each operator should exhibit for each custom type.

Operator overloading might be familiar to C++ developers; however, developers switching from Java and Visual Basic, including Visual Basic .NET might be new to operator overloading. This section will answer both how and when to use operator overloading.

In this chapter we will be looking at how operators can be defined for your own custom types. Although, these will primarily be classes, operators have an increased relevance with structures. We will examine the reasons for this within this section. The following table lists all of the operators that can be overloaded:

Type of Operator	Operators	Description
Unary Operators	+, -, !, ~, ++, -- , `true`, `false`	Unary operators take single arguments, for instance: `i++;`

Binary Operators	+, -, *, /, %, &, |, ^, <<, >>	Binary operators take two arguments, for instance:
		
		`int x = 7;`
		
		`int z = x + y;`

Comparison Operators	==, !=, <, >, <=, >=	Comparison operators always take two arguments and return a Boolean result, for instance:
		
		`int a = 7;`
		
		`int b = 10;`
		
		`if (a > b) {…}`
		
		Also note that comparison operators must be overloaded in pairs – for instance if > is overloaded < must be overloaded too.

Note that Conditional Logical Operators && and ||, Array indexing Operators [], Cast Operators (), Assignment Operators = and += and other operators such as new and typeof cannot be overloaded.

Before we launch into the details of operator overloading, consider the following:

❑ **New operators cannot be defined**. The list of operators available for overloading is finite and listed in the above table.

❑ **Operators have precedence**. When operators are used in expressions we have to remember that the multiply operator (*) has a higher precedence that the addition operator (+), and so on.

Operator Overloading Syntax

We will look at an example with an Employee type, which represents an Employee with Name and Salary attributes. We also have a Bonus type, which represents an annual bonus. This type has an Amount attribute. In our application, we need to award an Employee a Bonus by using this expression in our client code:

```
employee = employee + bonus;
```

We will study the implementation of these types later in this section. For now, an operator overload that permits such an expression can be declared as follows:

```
public static Employee operator+(Employee employee, Bonus bonus)
{
    employee.Salary = employee.Salary + bonus.Amount;
    return employee;
}
```

An operator overload is declared like a parameterized method. This operator is a static method and has public visibility. These directives within the method declaration are really there to make the code look consistent with other type members because all operator overloads must be public and static. The whole point of operators is to create simple, intuitive client-code expressions; the operator overload must be public to allow the operator to be used in client code. We generalize operator overloading because it enables us to use the operator for all instances of a type. We don't want an operator to be available for selected instances of a type; therefore, the operator overload must also be static.

The next part of the declaration is the return type of the operator. If we consider adding two integers together with the + operator, the return value (the sum) is also of type integer. In this example we will be returning an Employee type.

Next follow the parameters – an Employee type and a Bonus type. Examples for these types will follow shortly. The number and the order of parameters is important when creating operator overload methods:

Unary Operators	Must be declared to accept a single parameter and return a result. For instance, the ++ operator must accept a single parameter, and return the parameter incremented by 1.
Binary Operators	Must accept two parameters, representing the left and right sides of the expression. A binary operator overload then returns an appropriate result. For instance the * operator must accept the left and right side arguments and return their product.
Comparison Operators	Accept two parameters representing the left and right sides of the expression and return a boolean result. For instance the > operator must return true if the left-hand side parameter is greater than the right-hand side parameter.

Our example is based on the + operator which is a binary operator. The + operator accepts two parameters representing the left and right sides of the expression. Here is the desired client code expression:

```
employee = employee + bonus;
```

and here is the method signature:

```
(Employee employee, Bonus bonus)
```

As you can see, the operator overload method accepts an `Employee` parameter first as the left-hand side of the expression. The second parameter is of type `Bonus`; this is the right-hand side of the expression.

The method contains all of the necessary workings for how the + operator should behave while adding an `Employee` type with a `Bonus` type. In this example, we are using the + operator to calculate the salary of an `Employee` by adding the `Bonus.Amount` property to the `Employee.Salary` property.

Similarly, like methods and properties, operators can also be defined for structures and classes. This is an important consideration because unlike classes, structures tend to be better candidates for operator overloading.

Operators and Classes

To demonstrate just how powerful operators can be, let's contrast an example that has an operator overload with an equivalent example that does not use operators.

Here is a simple example that does not use operator overloading. The code can be found in `operators_no_operators.cs`:

```
using System;

class Bonus
{
    private int bonus;

    public int Amount
    {
        get { return bonus;  }
        set { bonus = value; }
    }
}

class Employee
{
    private string name;
    private int salary;

    public string Name
    {
        get { return name;  }
        set { name = value; }
    }
```

```
  public int Salary
  {
    get { return salary;  }
    set { salary = value; }
  }
}

class CalculateBonus
{
  static void Main()
  {
    Employee employee = new Employee();
    Bonus bonus = new Bonus();

    employee.Name = "James";
    employee.Salary = 8000;

    bonus.Amount = 1000;

    Console.WriteLine(employee.Name + " - " + employee.Salary);

    employee.Salary = employee.Salary + bonus.Amount;

    Console.WriteLine(employee.Name + " - " + employee.Salary);
  }
}
```

When you run the program the following should be displayed in the console window:

```
C:\Class Design\Ch 04>operators_no_operators.exe
James - 8000
James - 9000
```

There is nothing special about this example. All the techniques used have already been covered in this chapter. We are calculating an employee's new salary by adding a bonus amount. This is done in the client code with the following expression:

```
employee.Salary = employee.Salary + bonus.Amount;
```

Although this style of programming works in the functional sense, it has two minor disadvantages:

❏ It is not consistent with the way the rest of the .NET Framework works, and particularly when compared to primitive types. For example, to add two integers together we **would not** use an expression like this:

```
numberone.Value = numberone.Value + numbertwo.Value
```

❏ The business logic to calculate the new employee salary *is* the expression. It could be wrapped inside a method to provide encapsulation, but a method does not provide an equivalent level of abstraction to that which many developers take for granted when adding two numbers together.

155

Operator overloading allows us to use the simple expressions normally associated with primitive data types but for our own types. For example, by overloading the + operator in the Employee type example, we could write code like this:

```
employee = employee + bonus;
```

To achieve this, we need to create an operator overload method within the Employee class. Change the Employee class as follows. The complete code can be found in operators_overload.cs:

```
public static Employee operator+(Employee employee, Bonus bonus)
{
    employee.Salary = employee.Salary + bonus.Amount;
    return employee;
}
```

Here we have overloaded the + operator by using an operator overload method. As you know, operator overloads are really just specialized methods. They can change the parameters and return their values. These are typical characteristics of parameterized methods.

To test the operator overload, change the client code within Calculate Bonus as follows:

```
static void Main()
{
    Employee employee = new Employee();
    Bonus bonus = new Bonus();

    employee.Name = "James";
    employee.Salary = 8000;

    bonus.Amount = 1000;

    Console.WriteLine(employee.Name + " - " + employee.Salary);

    employee = employee + bonus;

    Console.WriteLine(employee.Name + " - " + employee.Salary);
}
```

When you run the program the following should be displayed in the Console window –

```
C:\Class Design\Ch 04>operators_overload.exe
James - 8000
James - 9000
```

Here the client code is now able to use a simple expression to calculate the employee bonus. This expression is semantically identical to an expression to add two numbers or concatenate two strings.

We have now made the client code simpler by permitting a simple expression through a + operator overload. The operator overload actually performs the original complex expression that we would have had to use without the + operator overload. All we have done is move the more complex expression from the client code to the Employee class. This should be considered good design because the calculation of the new Employee Salary is encapsulated within Employee class.

This example makes sense because the expression Employee = Employee + Bonus; is intuitive.

! It would not make sense, however, to overload an operator that permits an expression such as Employee = Employee + Employee; because adding two employees together does not make any sense.

> When considering operator overloading, it's best to think about what expressions make sense in the client code first. A good technique is to use pseudo code. Thinking about operator overloading in this way helps you create intuitive operator overloads that will make sense to the client code developers.

When used with forethought, operator overloading can lead to more intuitive programming with simpler client code expressions. But it is important to remember that the operator overload itself usually contains the expression that would have otherwise been used in the client code if the operator overload did not exist. It's worth considering how much effort you will save by creating operator overloads for your classes. If there are only one or two lines of client code that would otherwise use the more complex non-operator overloaded expression, it may not be worthwhile to go to the trouble of creating the operator overload in the first place.

Compiling Operators into MSIL

We will now examine the MSIL code emitted by the C# compiler for the operator overload. Run ildasm on the example operators_overload.exe. The following screen should be displayed after you have expanded the Bonus, CalculateBonus, and Employee nodes:

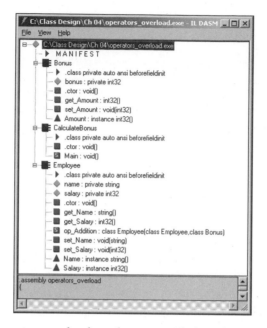

The `Employee` + operator overload can be seen with the other `Employee` class members. We can also see that it is a method by double clicking on:

op_Addition : class Employee(class Employee, class Bonus)

The following screen should be displayed:

```
Employee::op_Addition : class Employee(class Employee,class Bonus)
.method public hidebysig specialname static
        class Employee  op_Addition(class Employee employee,
                                    class Bonus bonus) cil managed
{
  // Code size       21 (0x15)
  .maxstack  4
  IL_0000:  ldarg.0
  IL_0001:  ldarg.0
  IL_0002:  callvirt    instance int32 Employee::get_Salary()
  IL_0007:  ldarg.1
  IL_0008:  callvirt    instance int32 Bonus::get_Amount()
  IL_000d:  add
  IL_000e:  callvirt    instance void Employee::set_Salary(int32)
  IL_0013:  ldarg.0
  IL_0014:  ret
} // end of method Employee::op_Addition
```

Actually the C# compiler emits this method, and it looks and behaves like any other parameterized method. The method receives arguments of type `Employee` and `Bonus`. We can see the `Employee` get_Salary() method being invoked, following by the `Bonus` get_Amount() method. The method then performs the addition and finally calls the `Employee` set_Salary() method. Remember here that the get() and set() methods are the accessors of a property and that properties are specialized methods.

In a nutshell, operator overloads are represented as parameterized methods in MSIL code.

Operator Overload and Cross-Language Support

We mentioned earlier that operator overloading might be new to Visual Basic and Java developers switching to C#. Developers switching from C++ might already be familiar with operator overloading. C# supports operator overloading but Visual Basic .NET does not. Given that programs authored in Visual Basic .NET cannot create types with operator overloads, this difference between the two .NET languages raises one very big question – How does Visual Basic .NET client code call C# classes with operator overloads?

The following Visual Basic .NET client program illustrates how to use an operator overload authored in a C# class but consumed in Visual Basic .NET client code. The following example can be found in operator_overload.vb:

```
//while compiling, use the /r: - reference switch for
//operators_overload.cs file. Remember to change the status of the
//Classes Employee and Bonus to public
Module CalculateBonus

    Sub Main()
        Dim emp As New Employee()
        Dim bonus As New Bonus()

        emp.Name = "James"
        emp.Salary = 8000

        bonus.Amount = 1000

        emp = Employee.op_Addition(emp, bonus)

        Console.WriteLine(emp.Name + " - " + emp.Salary.ToString())

    End Sub

End Module
```

Here we can see that Visual Basic .NET can still use a C# type with an operator overload, although in a non-intuitive way because we are invoking a method with an unfamiliar name. Also, this method is hidden from IntelliSense when accessing the C# class members. In Visual Basic .NET, we cannot use the operator overload expression in the same way as in a C# client program.

The operator overload is treated by Visual Basic .NET like all other parameterized methods; this ties in with the observations made when examining the MSIL code emitted by the C# compiler. Because Visual Basic .NET does not support the authoring of types with operator overloads, it doesn't support the customized expressions permissible in C# client code either.

If your C# classes are going to be consumed by non-C# client programs, it is a good idea to include a public method that exhibits the same behavior as the operator overload. This is better than invoking a hidden `op_Addition()` method (or other operator method) because a method intended for this purpose will be available in IntelliSense and can be named appropriately.

Symmetrical Operator Overloads

In the previous example we considered the following expression:

```
employee = employee + bonus;
```

This expression adds a `Bonus` type to an `Employee` type and returns an `Employee` type with the bonus added to the employee's salary. We created an operator overload for the + operator on the employee class to permit this client code expression.

However, we must also consider the following expression to be valid:

```
employee = bonus + employee;
```

By implication, these two expressions are the same and only differ by the order of the `Employee` and `Bonus` types. We would expect these two expressions to exhibit exactly the same behavior.

As operator overloads are really specialized methods, the order of the parameters passed to the method (which also equates to the order in which the expression should be used) is critical. The existing operator overload method will **not** support the alternative expression of :

```
employee = bonus + employee;
```

In these situations, we need to create a symmetrical operator overload, which is used to create a symmetrical expression when using a binary operator overload based on two different types. The symmetrical part comes from the requirement for an expression to be symmetrical; that is:

```
employee = employee + bonus;
```

is the same as:

```
employee = bonus + employee;
```

> **When considering binary operations on the same type, symmetrical operator overloads are not required.**

160

We can create a symmetrical operator overload by creating the first operator and overloading this with the new method to that performs the same calculation, but the parameters are the opposite way round. The details of method overloading are discussed in Chapter 3, but a method can be overloaded when the method signature differs. The following code (found in `operators_symmetrical.cs`), demonstrates how to overload operators to create symmetrical expressions. Add the following operator + overload method to the `Employee` class:

```
public static Employee operator+(Bonus bonus, Employee employee)
  {
    employee.Salary = employee.Salary + bonus.Amount;
    return employee;
  }
}
```

Now add the following to the `CalculateBonus` class:

```
    . . .
    employee = bonus + employee;

    Console.WriteLine(employee.Name + " - " + employee.Salary);
}
```

Type Comparison and Equality

When working with your own types, it is often necessary to compare two instances of the same type to see if they are the same. This is because the results of such a comparison do not necessarily depend on the values of the type members' variable assignments and comparisons differ in behavior between reference types such as classes and value types such as structures. The differences are exactly the same as when a reference type or a value type is passed as a method parameter. Passing arguments and using parameters is really the same as a variable assignment using the = operator.

Consider the following expression where `employee_one` and `employee_two` are of type `Employee` used in the earlier examples:

```
employee_one = employee_two;
```

Because the `Employee` type is a class and thus a reference type, the above assignment creates a shallow copy of the `Employee` object resulting in two references to the same instance. Comparisons between these two variables using either the == operator or `Equals()` method will always return `true` because they both point to the same instance. This is known as **referential equality** because the test for equality is based on the references stored in the two variables, which will always be the same for a reference type.

Comparisons between two **separate** instances of the `Employee` type will always return `false` even if they contain the same member data. This is because they do **not** have referential equality and the two variables point to different heap-based `Employee` instances. Again, no comparison made on the `Employee` type member data.

If we change the `Employee` type to a structure and therefore a value type, assignments create a deep copy of the structure thus creating two completely separate copies of the same structure. Changes made to one variable would not affect the other and comparisons will usually return `false` because the data in each of the structures is different.

We can see from the above rules that performing any kind of comparison will produce predictable results. If we have two references to the same object, referential equality works in our favor because both references point to the same heap-based object and the data will always be equal when a comparison is made between one reference and the other. When we have two separate instances of the same reference type we have to perform a member-by-member comparison to test for **value equality**.

> **Overloading the == operator provides a predictable approach to comparing two separate instances of the same reference type by providing value equality.**

To do this, we need to overload the `==` operator and the `!=` operator to provide your own customized comparisons. The `==` operator should return `true` when the member comparison is the same, and `!=` should return `false` if the member comparison is not the same. This is called testing for **value equality**. We can also compare two instances of a type using the `Equals()` method:

```
If (employee_one.Equals(employee_two))
{
    ...
}
```

The `Equals()` method is a member of `System.Object` and is therefore implicitly available on all types, reference or value. It must also be overridden along with the `==` and `!=` operator overloads to provide a complete and rounded comparison mechanism between two instances of the same reference type. In fact, the C# compiler forces you to override the `Equals` method when overloading the `==` and `!=` operators.

From Chapter 2 of this book, you should also be familiar with `GetHashCode()` method. This method allows a type to work correctly in a hash table by providing a unique hash value of the object. The `GetHashCode()` method should also be overridden to exhibit a customized hash value of the type.

The following code can be found in `operators_equality.cs`:

```
using System;

class Employee
{
  private string name;
  private int salary;

  public string Name
  {
    get { return name; }
    set { name = value; }
  }

  public int Salary
  {
    get { return salary; }
    set { salary = value; }
  }

  public static bool operator==(Employee left_employee,
                                Employee right_employee)
  {
    if (left_employee.Name == right_employee.Name)
      return true;
    else
      return false;
  }

  public static bool operator!=(Employee left_employee, Employee
right_employee)
  {
    if (left_employee.Name != right_employee.Name)
      return true;
    else
      return false;
  }

  public override bool Equals(object type)
  {
    if (!(type is Employee))
      return false;
    else
      return this ==(Employee)type;
  }

  public override int GetHashCode()
  {
    return this.Name.GetHashCode() + this.Salary.GetHashCode();
  }
}

  class CalculateBonus
  {
```

```
static void Main()
{
  Employee employee_one = new Employee();
  Employee employee_two = new Employee();
  Employee employee_three = new Employee();

  employee_one.Name = "James";
  employee_two.Name = "Steve";

  employee_three = employee_one;

  if (employee_one == employee_two)
    Console.WriteLine("Employee One is the same as Employee Two");
  else
    Console.WriteLine("Employee One is NOT the same as Employee
                      Two");

  if (employee_one == employee_three)
    Console.WriteLine("Employee One is the same as Employee
                      Three");
  else
    Console.WriteLine("Employee One is NOT the same as Employee
                      Three");

  employee_three.Name = "Steve";

  if (employee_two == employee_three)
    Console.WriteLine("Employee Two is the same as Employee
                      Three");
  else
    Console.WriteLine("Employee Two is NOT the same as Employee
                      Three");
  }
}
```

Running the program will produce the following results:

```
C:\Class Design\Ch 04>operators_equality.cs
Employee One is NOT the same as Employee Two
Employee One is the same as Employee Three
Employee Two is the same as Employee Three
```

Let's discuss the main points of interest in this program:

❑   The == operator has been overloaded to perform a **value equality**
     comparison (instead of referential equality) on the Employee Name
     property. Two separate instances of the Employee type are deemed to
     have value equality if their names are the same.

❑ The != operator has been overloaded to return false if the Employee Name property comparison is not the same. Overloading the != operator is mandatory when overloading the == operator because the operators == and != work as a pair.

❑ The Equals() method has been overridden to exhibit exactly the same behavior as the == operator. The Equals() method does not throw an exception if an invalid argument is passed. This is because if the argument is invalid, the comparison is always going to be false. The Equals() method therefore checks the type of the argument first before proceeding with the Employee type member comparison.

❑ GetHashCode() has been overridden to return the combined hash code of the Employee Name and Salary properties.

❑ Three new instances of the Employee class are created:

  • employee_one, Name property is assigned the value James.

  • employee_two, Name property is assigned the value Steve.

  • employee_three, Name property is left unassigned.

❑ A comparison is made between employee_one and employee_two. This returns false, because they have different names.

❑ employee_three is assigned to employee_one; employee_one and employee_three now hold separates references to the same Employee instance. The comparison returns true because they implicitly have the same Name property value.

❑ The Name property of employee_three Name is assigned the value Steve, when compared with employee_two, which is a separate instance of the Employee type, the comparison returns true, even through these two instances **do not** have referential equality. The == operator overload has deemed them the same because their Name property values are the same.

In short we can note the following points about type comparison and equality:

❑ Overloading the == and != operators can be used to test for value equality which overrides the default behavior of testing for referential equality. Normal behavior when comparing reference types is to check for referential equality and return true or false.

❑ When overloading the == and != operators, a type member comparison should be made between two instances of the same type. This can override the default behavior of testing for referential equality and return true if some or all of the type members are the same.

❑ In addition to overloading the == and != operators, you should also override the Equals() and GetHashCode() methods. The Equals() method is also used to test for equality and the GetHashCode() method is used to produce a hashed value of the type instance.

Operators and Structures

The examples we saw so far were based on a class representing an `Employee`. The benefits of providing operator overloads for classes similar to the `Employee` class are limited. This is because the number of operators we can overload is limited.

The golden rule we have established so far is – overload only those operators where the resulting client code expression 'makes sense'. In the previous code illustrations that were based on an `Employee` class, we used these examples:

❑ The expression `employee = employee + bonus;` makes sense because we can intuitively guess that the employee is being given a bonus.

❑ The expression `employee = bonus + employee;` also makes sense because this is a symmetrical expression to the above.

❑ The expression `employee_one == employee_two` makes sense because we know that this is a Boolean comparison between two instances of the same type.

❑ Expressions such as `employee = employee + employee;` do not make any sense, because an employee cannot be added to another employee.

When we consider some of the other operators we could overload for the `Employee` class, we can also see that these operators make either little or no sense if applied to an `Employee` class:

❑ `Employee++`

❑ `Employee * Employee`

❑ `Employee >= Employee`

❑ `Employee < Employee`

When we look at the way in which operators are used on primitive types, it is fair to say that operators have a broader appeal and increased value with simple values types. For instance, using operators such as `++`, `*`, `<`, `>`, `or >=` makes perfect sense with a number such as an integer.

> **As programmers, we instinctively recognize operators and intuitively know what behavior to expect when they are used with primitive and string types.**

Structures are ideal candidates for creating complex value types. If we think about the coordinates on a graph or an arithmetic fraction we can see that they are really more complex versions of existing primitive types. When representing entities like these in an application, value type structures (`struct`) are better choices than reference type classes because:

❑   They are comparatively lightweight

❑   They have a deterministic lifecycle and are not subject to garbage collection

We can see that structures are almost always better candidates for operator overloading than classes. To demonstrate the differences between structures and classes and the additional possibilities available for operator overloading, we will now create an application based on a fraction, which is a complex value type.

We have a number of operators that we can overload to create meaningful client code expressions with a fraction. To start with, we will create operators to handle subtractions and additions.

We can see these benefits in the following example, which can be found in operators_structs.cs:

```csharp
using System;

public struct Fraction
{

  private int numerator;
  private int denominator;

  public int Numerator
  {
    get { return numerator; }
    set { numerator = value; }
  }

  public int Denominator
  {
    get { return denominator; }
    set { denominator = value; }
  }

  private static int lcd(int x, int y)
  {
    int r, t = x * y;

    while (true)
    {
      r = x % y;
      if (r == 0) break;
      x = y; y = r;
    }

    return (t / y);
  }
```

```
  public static Fraction operator+(Fraction lh_fraction,
    Fraction rh_fraction)
  {
    Fraction result = new Fraction();
    result.Denominator = lcd(lh_fraction.Denominator,
      rh_fraction.Denominator);
    result.Numerator = lh_fraction.Numerator *
      (result.Denominator / lh_fraction.Denominator) +
      rh_fraction.Numerator *
      (result.Denominator / rh_fraction.Denominator);
    return result;
  }

  public static Fraction operator-(Fraction lh_fraction,
    Fraction rh_fraction)
  {
    Fraction result = new Fraction();
    result.Denominator = lcd(lh_fraction.Denominator,
      rh_fraction.Denominator);
    result.Numerator = lh_fraction.Numerator *
      (result.Denominator / lh_fraction.Denominator) -
      rh_fraction.Numerator *
      (result.Denominator / rh_fraction.Denominator);
    return result;
  }

  public override string ToString()
  { return (numerator.ToString() + "/" + denominator.ToString()); }
}

class FractionCalculator
{
  static void Main()
  {
    Fraction fraction1 = new Fraction();
    fraction1.Numerator = 2;
    fraction1.Denominator = 5;

    Fraction fraction2 = new Fraction();
    fraction2.Numerator = 1;
    fraction2.Denominator = 7;

    Console.WriteLine("Fraction 1 = " + fraction1.ToString());
    Console.WriteLine("Fraction 2 = " + fraction2.ToString());
    Console.WriteLine();

    Console.WriteLine("Fraction 1 + Fraction 2 = " + (fraction1 +
                      fraction2).ToString());
    Console.WriteLine("Fraction 1 - Fraction 2 = " + (fraction1 -
                      fraction2).ToString());
  }
}
```

When the program is executed you should see the following results:

```
C:\Class Design\Ch 04>operators_structs.exe
Fraction 1 = 2/5
Fraction 2 = 1/7

Fraction 1 + Fraction 2 = 19/35
Fraction 1 - Fraction 2 = 9/35
```

Lets go through the points of interest within this example:

❑ We have declared a Fraction type as a structure and not a class. It is therefore a value type.

❑ Value types are better candidates for operator overloading. The + and the – operators makes sense in the client code. We can also envisage other meaningful expressions using operators such as *, /, <, and >.

❑ The Fraction type overrides the ToString() method. This is to create a human-readable string representation of the Fraction which helps in our example.

❑ The Fraction structure includes a static method (lcd) to calculate the lowest common denominator using Euclid's algorithm.

Operator Overloading in Pairs

Some operators tend to be used in pairs. Consider the > and < operators. When overloading these operators, it makes sense to overload both operators and not just one of them. When working with types authored by somebody else, we would find it incredibly frustrating to find that only one half of a pair of operators had been overloaded for the type! Luckily, the C# compiler exercises some common sense and forces us to overload both of a pair of operators.

Extend the Fraction type by adding the code given below. This code is saved as operators_pairs.cs:

```
public static bool operator>(Fraction lh_fraction, Fraction
rh_fraction)
{
  int lowest;

  lowest = lcd(lh_fraction.Denominator,
    rh_fraction.Denominator);

  if (lh_fraction.Numerator *
    (lowest / lh_fraction.Denominator) >
    rh_fraction.Numerator *
    (lowest / rh_fraction.Denominator))
    return true;
```

```
    else
       return false;
    }

    public static bool operator<(Fraction lh_fraction, Fraction
    rh_fraction)
    {
       return !(lh_fraction > rh_fraction);
    }
```

Add the following lines to the client code in `FractionCalculator`:

```
    . . . . .
       Console.WriteLine();

       Console.WriteLine("Fraction 1 > Fraction 2? " + (fraction1 >
    fraction2).ToString());
       Console.WriteLine("Fraction 1 < Fraction 2? " + (fraction1 <
    fraction2).ToString());
       Console.WriteLine("Fraction 2 > Fraction 1? " + (fraction2 >
    fraction1).ToString());
       Console.WriteLine("Fraction 2 < Fraction 1? " + (fraction2 <
    fraction1).ToString());
    }
}
```

The program should now produce the following output:

```
C:\Class Design\Ch 04>operators_pairs
Fraction 1 = 2/5
Fraction 2 = 1/7

Fraction 1 + Fraction 2 = 19/35
Fraction 1 - Fraction 2 = 9/35

Fraction 1 > Fraction 2? True
Fraction 1 < Fraction 2? False
Fraction 2 > Fraction 1? False
Fraction 2 < Fraction 1? True
```

The `Fraction` example is now almost complete. We can perform additions, subtractions, and make greater than and less than comparisons. The client code expressions make sense. We could also go a stage further and implement the == and != operators already discussed and we could also implement the >= and <= operators which are obviously similar to the > and < operators.

When overloading operators you should always make the full complement of operators available. For instance, if the > and < operators have been overloaded, the >= and <= operators should be implemented as well.

170

Operator Overload Best Practice

We saw some examples on where and how to use operator overloading both for classes and structures. Operator overloading can sometimes be used in the wrong way. Here is a list of situations where operator overloading should not be used:

❑ Never create an operator overload when the resulting expression does not make sense. For example, `type_x = type_y + type_z;`.

❑ Structures, which tend to be used to represent complex value types, are inherently better choices for operator overloading than classes, which tend to be used for complex business entities. Try to limit the use of operators on your own types to structures used to represent complex value type data.

❑ Operators such as > and < ; == and !=; and >= and =< must be overloaded in pairs. The C# compiler will not let one half of a pair be overloaded on its own. When overloading in pairs consider implementing the comparison logic in the first operator then returning the opposite (NOT \ !) result of the first operator in the second operator.

❑ Overloading the == and != operators can be used to test for value equality between two instances of the same type. This can be especially useful when comparing two reference types, which would normally be compared by referential equality. When overloading these operators, remember to override the `Equals()` and `GetHashCode()` methods.

❑ When overloading binary operators such as + to add two different types, create an overload of the same operator but reverse the parameter sequence. This will permit symmetrical expressions in client code.

Operators Summary

Operators can be used to create simple meaningful expressions in the client code. These expressions should be intuitive to the client code developer and should make sense from the business purpose of the application. We also saw that operators are really just specialized methods, like scalar properties and indexers. The MSIL code emitted through the C# compiler confirms this.

Here are some final thoughts to remember when designing your own types with operator overloads:

❑ Consider operator overloads from the client-code perspective first. It can help to think in pseudo-code terms first to create the desired instinctive expression. This technique helps design operator overloads that are meaningful and intuitive.

❑ Operator overloads can be used to encapsulate expressions that are often used within an application. In fact, the operator overload usually contains the same expression that would have been used by the client code if the operator overload did not exist.

❑ Only use an operator overload if there are tangible benefits when developing the client code, not if only one or two lines of client code could be rewritten with the simplified expression.

❑ Because operator overloads are methods, they can be overloaded like any other method, provided we have different method signatures. Several overloads of the same operator for different types can make the overall client code more consistent. Overloading can also be used to create symmetrical expressions.

Summary

In this chapter, we've seen how to define scalar properties; we've discussed the tradeoff between properties, fields, and methods. We then saw how to define read/write, read-only, and write-only properties. We discussed guidelines and best practices for each of these techniques along the way. Indexers allow types to be represented as arrays.

Operators are symbols and characters used to perform operations on one or more types. They can be overloaded to encapsulate complex expressions. We also discussed how operator overloading works in C# and how it eases the readability of our code. We discussed the best practices of operator overloading and we saw how operators can be overloaded in a class as well as in a structure. We also discussed overloading the == and != operators to override the reference equality behavior in reference types. In the next chapter, we will discuss Constructors and their role in designing classes in C#.

C#

Class Design

Handbook

5

5

Constructors and the Object Lifecycle

Developers new to C# who have had experience in other object-oriented languages such as Java should not be surprised with the level of support for creating objects on the managed heap. Java developers have wallowed in the ideal that memory management is a function of the JVM and construction and destruction are managed processes that should be abstracted from the developer. The equivalent C++ developers, on the other hand, would have to manage memory themselves, which more often than not caused problems.

In C# we can use both managed and unmanaged code, which allows us to decide if we wish to create an object in managed code and not worry about the object's lifetime (because the CLR will take care of it for us), or create an object in unmanaged code and destroy it and reclaim the memory ourselves. In this chapter we will analyze all the ways of creating and destroying objects in C#; some are considered safe and others are considered unsafe. The hype surrounding the CLR is warranted in that the CLR memory allocation and de-allocation processes are far more efficient that we could ever hope to be ourselves.

In this chapter, we will look at the lifecycle of an object; specifically we will discuss the following:

❑   How objects are created on the managed heap and how to define and use constructors

❑   How objects are destroyed, including how to change the destruction pattern

❑   How to write efficient object construction code

❑   How to creating deep and shallow copies of objects

❑   How to use serialization and deserialization to construct and destroy objects

❑   Finally, we'll analyze the various Design Patterns used in object construction

The concept of automatic memory management is fundamental to the CLR, which will allocate memory on the heap for managed objects and use the Garbage Collector (GC) to deallocate the same memory for an object during Managed Execution of code – by Managed Execution we refer to the CLR's lifecycle management of an object (its creation and destruction) rather than our management of heap memory. When writing managed code, memory leaks (which were common with C++) disappear since we are no longer required to free up memory.

When managed code is executed, a managed heap is created so that memory can be allocated in order to create class instances (the managed heap is simply an area of memory managed by the CLR and GC). When faced with creating objects in C++, we generally have the choice of two areas. The first is the stack, in which each thread has its own limited quantity of fast memory. The second is the heap, and it is more practical to create an object on the heap. Unlike the stack space, the heap space doesn't have a size limitation defined as a fixed quantity by the OS; its amount is defined by the machine hardware and operational environment – other processes and memory consumption. However, object creation and destruction is slower than accessing memory on the stack.

The CLR is designed to optimize object creation by managing the heap address through the use of a pointer to the next available address after the object is created. The benefit of this is that the CLR will allocate memory based on the next available address space and increment a pointer, so that it knows where to allocate next. This system is much faster than the equivalent unmanaged heap and is supposedly nearly as fast as creating an object on the stack – this is due to the CLR not needing to search for a free block of memory to place an object in, since the managed heap pointer moves directly to the next block of memory after a new object has been created, thus cutting out the search time necessary to allocate an object with unmanaged code. The additional advantage is that since objects are stored contiguously, the application can locate objects far faster than it would by just having a pointer to a non-continuous area of memory.

The GC acts as an object manager by keeping an eye on object usage, by freeing up memory by deleting object space and marking it available for reuse. The GC will continually compact the managed heap so that space can be optimized and objects can be stored contiguously. Any references created to objects within code will be managed by the runtime, making the location of the object on the managed heap completely transparent to the developer. In C# and C++ .NET, this allocation and compaction of the heap can be a problem for objects that are created using *unsafe* code, which use direct access to memory, by returning pointers to heap memory for newly created objects. The runtime will be unable to update the references to the unmanaged object, and when compaction occurs we could end up with a pointer to an incorrect memory location. There are techniques that can be used to **fix** the object location so that the GC doesn't move it in memory and this process is called **pinning**. In the following example, the char* variable pre is pinned – this can be done with all unmanaged pointers. This file is called string.cs and has to be complied with an /unsafe switch:

```
using System;

class preString
{
  static unsafe string AddPreString(string s)
  {
    fixed(char* pre = "A")
    {
      return (s + *pre);
    }
  }

  [STAThread]
  static void Main()
  {
    Console.WriteLine(preString.AddPreString("PostString "));
  }
}
```

The following output is shown when we run the program:

```
C:\Class Design\Ch 05>string
PostString A
```

The compaction occurs when the runtime finds many objects with null references. These are objects that are not in use by the application and are considered *unreachable* by the GC. The GC is written to take advantage of the idea of generations, which enable it to free memory to the managed heap. The .NET Framework documentation defines the following three high-level rules, which make the idea of categorizing the managed heap into different generations optimal.

❑   The memory compaction processes functions quicker by compacting a subset of the managed heap rather than the entire heap. This is done since it will only act on a single generation of objects (the term generation with reference to the GC is explained in the section following).

❑   It has been shown that newer objects (objects which have been created at some point during execution but not right at the beginning) will have shorter lifetimes and older ones will likely have longer lifetimes.

❑   Newer objects tend to be related to each other generally, and this makes their storage contiguous and them likely to always be released in the lowest-level generation.

These rules are the fundamental reason for the generations idea of the GC. When we create an object, it will be created in generation 0, however, there will come a time when there will be no space on the managed heap to allocate any other objects within generation 0. At this stage, the GC will attempt to reclaim memory in generation 0 and probably compact enough memory to allow the application to continue creating objects. Those that survive the collection will be promoted to generation 1 and later generation 2 (these are just different areas of the managed heap) and are considered longer lasting objects so collection will occur on these generations less frequently. Despite the efficient memory deallocation process due to the GC, it is possible (though unlikely) that the GC will be unable to clean up the managed heap faster than objects are allocated to it. In this case, the GC will be unable to allocate memory for a new object and the application will throw an OutOfMemoryException.

Although the process is managed and we don't have any direct control of it, it is still useful to understand that there are things that we can do to aid the process. Any weaknesses actually lie within resources not managed by the GC, such as file handles and database connections. Later in this chapter, we shall look at the tools that are provided for us to write efficient code to release references to these types of unmanaged objects.

Object Creation

Object creation in C# is typically no different in code from how it is done for a variety of other languages. C++, Java, and VB developers have always used the new keyword to create a new object on the heap (C++ developers can use malloc(), heapalloc(), and so on, but these functions don't implicitly call the object constructor). Generally, all fields within an object are either assigned a value at creation time or are given an implicit value by the runtime if no assignment takes place (this is not the case with C++, which will generate both warnings and exceptions if there are no default values set). In C#, default assigned values depend on whether the field is a reference to a value type or a reference type. A reference type would by default initialize to null if no value was assigned to it. A value type such as int would initialize to 0 by default. The System.ValueType class (from which value types inherit) has a default constructor, which is invoked by the derived value type class (such as an int) and initializes the state for the class instance. Remember that System.String is not a value type and so it does not initialize to the empty string on construction.

The Employee class opposite demonstrates the issues involved with creating an object and initializing values. The field value is only assigned to the dept field; the others will be assigned default values, null for the string and 0 for the int. It is good practice to expose these private fields as property values as shown in the code. The following code file is called object_creation.cs:

```
using System;
class Employee
{
  private string name;
  private string dept = "IT";
  private int salary;

  public string Name { get {return name;} }
  public string Dept { get {return dept;} }
  public int Salary { get {return salary;} }
}

public class emp_class
{
  static void Main(string[] args)
  {
    Employee emp = new Employee();
    Console.WriteLine("Name: {0}\nDept: {1}\nSalary: {2}",
                      emp.Name, emp.Dept, emp.Salary);
  }
}
```

The above code will issue a warning stating that the Employee.name and Employee.salary fields are never assigned and are given default values of null and 0 respectively. On running the program the following output is seen:

```
C:\Class Design\Ch 05>object_creation
Name:
Dept: IT
Salary: 0
```

This idea of assigning default values to the fields helps us to avoid exceptions that can continually occur in code because the default values are outside the acceptable boundary values for application languages such as Java and VB, which will also compile without default assignments and generate null reference exceptions (or in the case of VB – Object variable or with block not set) if the fields are used without an additional assignment. It is always good practice to initialize field values irrespective of the default assignment since values assigned by the runtime may not conform to acceptable boundary values if the code fails to assign them at a later stage and uses them.

An important point here is that a class's field values are generally not known at design time and they may need to be initialized by the code that creates the class. For this reason C#, like virtually all other object-oriented languages, provides the ability to define class constructors. If this constructor exists, then it will be invoked when the object creation code uses the new keyword to create the object, the invocation of the constructor will then be part of the initialization process. C# supports that concept of overloading constructors which we will assess later in the chapter. The constructor is extremely important for initializing fields with values at run time – this is part of the object creation process so before a reference to the object is returned to the client code default field values can be set. Unlike a regular method, the constructor cannot be called explicitly; it will be called if it exists when the object is created and cannot have a return type. Every time we create an object, a constructor is called implicitly to initialize the state of the object.

In order to address some of the issues with initialization, we can create constructors with different signatures, that contain different lists and types of parameters, and only one of these will be called when the object is created (unless the others are called internally – this is a common practice, which we will review later in the chapter). The Employee class will need different types of constructor for different reasons. For example, we may need to populate all three fields when the object is created or we may only need to populate two fields since the default dept value is IT and the Employee we are creating belongs to the IT department. Additionally, we may not need to populate any of the object's field values, which could entail a single constructor without any parameters and provide some other form of initialization that doesn't involve the fields – this type of constructor may be useful when the object is responsible for its own field values that are initialized using other techniques, such as the combination of attributes and serialization. The code snippet shown below is constructor_parameters.cs:

```
public class Employee
{
  public Employee()
  {
    Console.WriteLine("Default constructor called with no params");
  }

  public Employee(string name, string dept, int salary)
  {
    this.name = name;
    this.dept = dept;
    this.salary = salary;
    Console.WriteLine("Constructor called with three params");
  }

  public Employee(string name, int salary)
  {
    this.name = name;
    this.salary = salary;
    Console.WriteLine("Constructor called with two params");
  }
}
```

We now need to add a Main() method. In the following example, the three Employee objects are created to take advantage of the new constructors. If we use breakpoints in Visual Studio .NET to check the order of execution, we will find that the fields are initialized (specifically the dept field) before the constructor is called. In this way we can always override the default field values using the constructor to allow us to specify default field values at design time and the final values at run time before a class instance is returned.

```
public class TestEmployee
{
  static void Main(string[] args)
```

```
{
    Employee emp1 = new Employee();
    Console.WriteLine("Name: {0}\nDept: {1}\nSalary: {2}",
                      emp1.Name, emp1.Dept, emp1.Salary);
    Console.WriteLine("---------------------");
    Employee emp2 = new Employee("Jones", "Operations", 30000);
    Console.WriteLine("Name: {0}\nDept: {1}\nSalary: {2}",
                      emp2.Name, emp2.Dept, emp2.Salary);
    Console.WriteLine("---------------------");
    Employee emp3 = new Employee("Smith", 35000);
    Console.WriteLine("Name: {0}\nDept: {1}\nSalary: {2}",
                      emp3.Name, emp3.Dept, emp3.Salary);
}
}
```

The output from this is shown below and matches our expectations. Calling the default constructor has not changed the initialization values of the fields:

```
C:\Class Design\Ch 05>emp_constructors
Default Constructor
Name:
Dept: IT
Salary: 0
---------------------
Constructor called with three params
Name: Jones
Dept: Operations
Salary: 30000
---------------------
Constructor called with two params
Name: Smith
Dept: IT
Salary: 35000
```

Destroying Objects

Part of the lifecycle of an object involves the object being destroyed by the runtime and the memory being reclaimed; although this process is automatic we still have a surprising level of control over this. The destruction of an object can be done explicitly by setting the object reference to null and taking care that there are no other references to the object, or it can be done implicitly by the runtime if the object becomes out-of-scope – in either case, the reference count will be amended and memory can be freed by the garbage collector when there are no more references.

The GC is smart enough to realize that it shouldn't be compacting and freeing memory at all if the object count within an application is so low that it doesn't need the GC to free memory, and new objects are created very infrequently. The object destruction process is carried out by the GC, and depends entirely on application memory availability and need.

There are mechanisms to make objects responsible for their own de-referencing of internal objects when they are destroyed, which is extremely useful for releasing handles to underlying resources that the CLR doesn't manage. Whenever the GC reclaims the memory occupied by an object it will invoke its `Finalize()` method, which should release any resources that are not managed by the CLR. You can think of this method as an interception by the runtime, which will stop the GC in its tracks and invoke code before the object is destroyed and memory de-allocated.

Java developers will be familiar with this syntax, as the same mechanism has been written into the Java language and the JVM since the JDK 1.0.

We can provide our own implementation of this method by overriding the implementation of the base class method from `System.Object`. For all .NET languages, we can generally use the `Finalize()` method by overriding the base class method of the same name and signature – except in C# and C++. The `Finalize()` method used to be used in place of destructors in C# throughout early beta releases of the .NET Framework SDK, but is now deprecated.

The concept of the `Finalize()` method is the same for C# and Managed C++, except we use a different syntax. C# uses a syntax known as a `destructor` to clean up resources – these resources should typically be unmanaged resources such as file handles and database connections. For example, in our `Employee` class, if we had created a database connection that we wanted closed and de-referenced when the `Employee` was garbage collected, we could simply create the a destructor, which would be called by the GC when destroying the object.

In the following example there is an unassigned member variable created. This will represent the file handle that we will use, which the destructor will later clean up.

```
using System;
using System.IO;

public class Employee
{
    FileStream fStream;
```

In the parameter-less constructor, add the following code to write to a file. We will not close or de-reference the `fStream` field at any stage during the object's lifetime.

```
public Employee()
{
    fStream = File.CreateText("C:\\temp.txt");
    StreamWriter sw = new StreamWriter(fStream);
    sw.Write("Default constructor called with no params");
}
```

In order to invoke this new constructor we will reuse the code shown earlier as part of the `Main()` method, which creates three employee objects. Terminating the application will invoke the destructor code three times sequentially for each of the employee objects, based on the order in which the GC attempts to free memory for each of the objects.

The following code for the destructor is wrapped in a `try...catch` block as, if the object was created using one of the other constructors, `fStream` would be set as `null` and so we need to catch the exception:

```
~Employee()
{
  try
  {
    fStream.Close();
    fStream = null;
  }
  catch {}
}
```

We have a modicum of control over whether we want this called for all three objects. For example, we don't really need to call the destructor for either of the objects that don't log anything to a file, as this will cause an exception that will terminate the execution of the destructor. In the parameterized constructor code, we can add the following line to ensure that the GC doesn't call the destructor for that particular object instance. However, in a production application the appropriate `null` reference checks should be applied within the destructor:

```
GC.SuppressFinalize(this);
```

There are occasions when a change is needed in this policy, so the GC provides an equivalent counter-method, which will allow the destructor to be called when collection occurs.

```
GC.ReRegisterForFinalize(this);
```

Although the GC knows when to collect all of the generations of objects on the managed heap, there may be occasions where the GC is not performing a necessary collection. An application may have few objects, but these objects contain many references to unmanaged resources. We can tell the GC to perform a collection to free more memory, which is otherwise not done. This is done by calling the `Collect()` method, although in most circumstances we would never need to do this as it generally has an adverse effect on the performance of an application. However there may be specific instances when not much memory is allocated on the managed heap where a few large objects that contain many references to unmanaged resources will not force a collection when memory needs to be reclaimed. In this instance we may wish to call `GC.Collect()` to possibly improve the performance of the application.

```
GC.Collect()
```

Using destructors is not recommended because it is costly to performance, although we will still need to clean up the resources used by the object before it is garbage collected. The GC builds a graph of all the objects that have yet to be de-referenced; that is, they have a reference count of greater than zero and so are still in use by the application code. All of the objects not graphed by the GC are destroyed as long as they don't have a destructor. If they do have a destructor they are moved to a special queue called the freachable (F-Reachable) queue, which is short for Finalization Reachable Queue, where a dedicated thread will manage all of the objects sequentially, calling their destructors before marking them as garbage. In this case, the memory of objects with destructors will not be reclaimed immediately as the object is not marked as garbage when the collection process begins. Therefore, a large number of destructors in an application will have an adverse effect on performance because a separate thread will be calling each destructor in sequence, and the memory will take longer to reclaim.

The preferred way to handle the disposal of objects is through the IDisposable interface. To use IDisposable, we have to implement the Dispose() method, which can act in the same way as the equivalent Finalize() or destructor method, except it doesn't interrupt the process of garbage collection or need to be queued and managed in the same way. In fact, the fundamental difference between the two methods of resource cleanup is that the Dispose() method can be called at any time by the calling code without incurring any performance cost to the application. It is encouraged that all resources are released on the Dispose() method and we should get used to implementing the IDisposable interface in classes that involve the release of unmanaged resources.

Dispose() is a convention and is generally used in objects that utilize many unmanaged resources such as calls to OLEDB libraries or file handles. Usually the Dispose() method is declared as virtual and is overridden in the derived class. In the derived class, the base class method is called to ensure that all resources derived from the base class are destroyed too.

The example following shortly defines a very simple inheritance hierarchy based on a shape. The important thing to identify here is the use of the Dispose() method. In the base class BasicShape, we implement the IDisposable interface and have to write an implementation for its one method, Dispose(). This will free the IO resources used by the class when called.

We don't create the BasicShape directly; instead we create a derived class called Square which will override both the GetCoords() and the Dispose() methods. With both of the derived class methods, GetCoords() and Dispose(), we should have a fuller class definition for the Square class including any code that is specific to the GetCoords() method in the derived class – possibly something using the example a and b fields (if x and y represent a single point then a and b represent the diagonal point forming the opposite corner of the square). The Dispose() method on the derived class can be used to clean-up any resources. The code snippet is contained within basic_shape.cs:

```csharp
using System;
using System.IO;

public abstract class BasicShape : IDisposable
{
  protected int x;
  protected int y;
  private FileStream fStream;

  public virtual void GetCoords()
  {
    //possibly open a file handle here
    try
    {
      StreamReader sr =
          new StreamReader((fStream = File.OpenRead("C:\\temp.txt")));
      int x = Convert.ToInt32(sr.ReadLine());
      int y = Convert.ToInt32(sr.ReadLine());
    }
    catch {}
  }

  public virtual void Dispose()
  {
    if(fStream!=null)
    {
      fStream.Close();
      fStream = null;
    }
  }
}

public class Square : BasicShape
{
  int a = 0;
  int b = 0;

  public override void GetCoords()
  {
    /** Do something associated with this class and then call the base
        class method which will change inherited fields **/
    base.GetCoords();
  }

  public override void Dispose()
  {
    //clean up any resources associated with this object
    base.Dispose();
  }
}
```

The object must never throw an exception when de-referencing the resources on the derived class as this would prevent every `Dispose()` method in the class hierarchy from being called. We must write any cleanup code for the `Square` class before calling the base method of the `BasicShape` class and where possible anticipate exceptions so that the entire process doesn't fail. With very large inheritance hierarchies it is important that the `Dispose()` method is called for each base class and if the chain of calling `Dispose()` is interrupted then there will be some resources that are not released as a result. Below is the code for testing this in a `Main()` method:

```
Square square = new Square();
square.GetCoords();
square.Dispose();
square = null;
```

Many of the examples given on MSDN combine both the destructor and the `IDisposable` interface that will ensure that the `Dispose()` method gets called (although in actuality using the destructor is not necessary). If we do the same, insert a `GC.SuppressFinalize(this);` line at the end of the base class's `Dispose()` method, and set the destructor to call `Dispose()`. In this case, if `Dispose()` is never called, then it will be called by the destructor. If it is, then the destructor will never be called and so the memory can be reclaimed immediately upon garbage collection.

The `Dispose()` method can be called by many other different techniques – for example we could write our own managed class called `GenericFile` which could implement `IDisposable`. We could use the `CreateFile` API to obtain file handles in unmanaged code using `P/Invoke` and implement a `Close()` method in the class which called `Dispose()`. `Dispose()` would use the `CloseHandle` API to release the unmanaged resources. As this is part of the lifecycle of a file anybody using the class will explicitly call `Close()` thus calling `Dispose()` and releasing all the resources. Virtually all classes in .NET Framework Class Libraries operate like this and automate the invocation of the `Dispose()` method.

Using Constructors

There are a variety of ways in which we can design classes to use constructors both minimizing the amount of code that we write and maximizing the functionality and ease of implementation of our class. We can explicitly write a constructor as we have seen to initialize fields although whether we initialize their values (or not) in the constructor, the runtime will initialize the fields with default values prior to invoking the constructor. We will see in this section that if we don't write a constructor for a class, the compiler will create a default constructor and the runtime will invoke it when we create a new object.

Chaining Constructors

There are standard ways to write constructor code, which can be used to minimize the amount of code written, make the code more readable, and avoid replicating similar code blocks within the same class. Chaining constructors is an effective way to build a very advanced interface with multiple overloaded constructors while providing and using an implementation for a single constructor.

The Manager class detailed shortly is a typical implementation of a class that uses constructor chaining to call one constructor from another. There are three Manager constructors; the last one contains two parameters and is the only constructor with an implementation. The first thing that each of the other constructors will do is to call the third constructor. This is done by using the this self-referential pointer to the current object. This syntax is new to C#; however C++, Jscript, and Java developers should be familiar with the use of this. The call to the two-parameter constructor will occur and it will populate the fields with the defaults specified and then any implementation code within the constructor code blocks will be invoked. There is extra code in the default parameter-less constructor so that we can ensure that it is logged every time we create a Manager class without a name (the entry is added to the event log). The file shown below is called chaining_const.cs:

```
using System;

public class Manager
{
   private int grade;
   private string name;

   public int Grade
   {
      get { return grade; }
      set { grade = value; }
   }

   public string Name
   {
      get { return name; }
      set{ name = value; }
   }

   public Manager() : this("N/A", 0)
   {
      Console.WriteLine("Manager created without name!");
   }

   public Manager(string name) : this(name, 0) {}

   public Manager(string name, int grade)
   {
```

```
      Name = name;
      Grade = grade;
   }

   public override string ToString()
   {
      return "Name: " + this.Name + ", Grade: " + this.Grade.ToString();
   }
}
```

Including the following `Main()` method will call the constructor with one parameter and passing the name `Jones` and a default grade of `0` to the implementation constructor.

```
public static void Main()
{
   Manager mgr_Jones = new Manager("Jones");
   Manager mgr_Blank = new Manager();
   Manager mgr_Name_Grade = new Manager("Jones", 4);
   Console.WriteLine(mgr_Jones.ToString());
   Console.WriteLine(mgr_Blank.ToString());
   Console.WriteLine(mgr_Name_Grade.ToString());
}
```

Calling a Base Class Constructor

Every deriving class invokes the base class constructor either implicitly or explicitly. In fact if we don't call the base class constructor the CLR will call it for us (the CLR will call the parameter-less constructor). The base class constructor can be called only from the derived class's constructor and it is the first thing that will be called followed by any implementation code within the derived class's constructor code block.

We could add two constructors to the abstract `BasicShape` class created earlier, marking them protected so that only a derived class can call them. We could also mark them public and it would make little difference, as the base class cannot be instantiated as it is abstract.

```
public abstract class BasicShape : IDisposable
{
   protected BasicShape()
   {
      x = 1;
      y = 1;
   }

   protected BasicShape(int x, int y)
   {
      this.x = x;
      this.y = y;
   }

   ...
```

In the derived class we can now add some code, which will call the base class's constructors. Each one of these methods calls the base class constructor as shown using the base keyword preceded by the colon. This constructor will be invoked before invocation of the derived class constructor occurs. As in the example below we don't always have to invoke a constructor on the base class with the same signature as a constructor on the derived class. We can see from the example that the Square() constructor with no arguments will invoke the base class constructor with two arguments.

```
public Square() : base(4, 4)
{
  this.a = 1;
  this.b = 1;
}

public Square(int a, int b) : base(4, 4)
{
  this.a = a;
  this.b = b;
}
```

Private Constructors

Private constructors at first seem purposeless, but they are in fact quite prolific within the .NET Framework classes. Generally, they are used within classes that contain many static methods that are supposed to be used as a library rather than an object; the constructor is added to ensure that the class cannot be created by anything external to it.

There are two reasons that are apparent for creating private constructors. There may be occasions when the class creation code should be prevented from using a public constructor. One case would be where it doesn't make sense to create an object without providing some initialization parameters, such as with a FileStream class.

The second reason is with creating certain object design patterns, like the factory pattern where a public static method on the class will call the private constructor and return an instance of the object to the object creation code, or the Singleton pattern, where the constructor should only be called once. We will delve into this later in the chapter.

In the example overleaf, the Teacher class is created using a public constructor and it throws an exception if a grade of less than 3 is passed to that constructor. Rather than using inline code or another method, it uses a private constructor to raise the exception. This example is greatly simplified, as in reality the private constructor would contain extra initialization code. In this example, any external code cannot create an instance of the Teacher class using a parameter-less constructor.

```
using System;

public class Teacher
{
  int grade = 0;

  public Teacher(int grade)
  {
    if(grade < 3)
      new Teacher();
    else
      throw new ArgumentException("Grade must be less than 3");
    this.grade= grade;
  }

  private Teacher()
  {
    // Initialization code
  }
}

public class TestTeacher
{
  static void Main()
  {
    Teacher teach = new Teacher(3)
  }
}
```

Earlier we saw that the derived class always calls the base class constructor whether specified or not. This effectively signifies that classes with private constructors cannot act as base classes as their constructor is not visible to the derived class.

There is one situation where the class containing the private constructor can be created by something other than itself. This occurs when another class is nested in the class with the private constructor. The nested constructor can always create an instance of its container class, whether the constructor is private or not.

The following NestedWorker class is nested within the Worker class. The former class has a public constructor and the latter a private constructor, to which the Worker class will create a reference and store it locally. We can therefore create and invoke the public constructor of the container class Worker from the nested class NestedWorker as shown in the Main() method, in the code below called nested_const.cs:

```
using System;

public class Worker
{
  public class NestedWorker
```

```
{
    Worker wk;
    public NestedWorker()
    {
        wk = new Worker();
    }
}

private Worker()
{
    Console.WriteLine("private constructor called!");
}

static void Main(string[] args)
{
    NestedWorker nw = new NestedWorker();
}
}
```

Static Constructors

Static constructors can be used in C# to initialize class data in the same way that instance constructors are used to initialize instance data. There are some differences in the rules governing static constructor use compared to instance constructor use. Unlike instance constructors they cannot be overloaded and so the only available static constructor is the default parameter-less constructor. Static constructors also cannot be invoked explicitly, and will not be inherited in a derived class, although they will be invoked when the base class type is created.

There are several guarantees made by .NET regarding the use of static constructors:

❏ They are invoked before a single instance of the class is created and hence before any instance constructors.

❏ They are invoked only once before the first instance of a class is created

❏ The static constructor is called before any static fields are referenced

To check the calling order of static constructors and instance constructors, we can add a static constructor and a public instance constructor to the Teacher class that was created in the previous example. We use the static keyword to define the static constructor and differentiate it from the instance constructors. This static constructor will allow us to initialize all the static members in the class. Java has an equivalent principle of static constructors, which are declared without referencing the class name as in C#, so a static constructor declaration is generally the word static followed by a code block. The following example is called static_const.cs:

```
. . .
public class Teacher
{
  public Teacher()
  {
    Console.WriteLine("Base class instance created");
  }

  static Teacher()
  {
    Console.WriteLine("Class loaded");
  }
  . . .
```

Then we create the SupplyTeacher class that derives from the Teacher class. This will result in the static constructor being invoked first before the base class instance constructor is invoked.

```
public class SupplyTeacher : Teacher
{
  public SupplyTeacher ()
  {
    Console.WriteLine("Derived class instance created");
  }
}

public class TestStaticConstructor
{
  static void Main(string[] args)
  {
    SupplyTeacher teach = new SupplyTeacher();
    SupplyTeacher teach1 = new SupplyTeacher();
  }
}
```

When an instance of the SupplyTeacher class is created the following output occurs confirming the order of invocation of each constructor type. In this example, two SupplyTeacher objects are created to demonstrate that the static constructor will only be invoked once even though the base class instance constructor is invoked twice with identical object creation patterns.

```
C:\Class Design\Ch 05>static_const
Class loaded
Base class instance created
Derived class instance created
Base class instance created
Derived class instance created
```

Conversion Operators

We have looked at the object lifecycle and different ways of creating and destroying objects, specifically defining ways of implementing constructors and destructors. There is yet another type of object construction we have to review. This section deals with conversion operators between different kinds of reference type and the effect that this has on the constructor invocation.

There exists a conversion mechanism between value types that allows an int to be converted into a long type or a short into an int type, and so on. Conversion operators can be used to convert between value and reference types this is either *implicit* or *explicit* depending on the type of conversion necessary. Implicit conversions differ from explicit conversions in that they don't have to use parenthesis to specify a cast from one type to another. The conversion below is implicit in that we use assignment to change the type from Bus to BigVehicle without specifying a cast directly in code.

```
Bus bus;
BigVehicle big = bus;
```

The converse scenario is an explicit conversion where the cast between two types has to be explicitly defined. In this example we change from a BigVehicle struct type to a Bus class type (both the class and struct will be shown at the end of this section).

```
BigVehicle big;
Bus bus = (Bus)big;
```

For the purposes of clarity the following examples will illustrate the use of both implicit and explicit conversion operators, although we will be more interested in the explicit conversion operator since we can effectively define a new type of object construction using this mechanism. Conversion operators can also be used to convert between class and struct values and vice versa.

To illustrate the use of conversion operators, we'll return to our Teacher class and add a simple struct called BigVehicle to supplement this, adding conversion operators so that we can cast implicitly and explicitly between these two types.

There are some new keywords that need be used for user-defined conversion, **implicit** and **explicit**. These methods must be created as static and must have the **operator** keyword to specify that we have overridden the behavior of the language operator. The implicit operator will create a new BigVehicle struct and copy the entire field values from the Bus class instance to the struct; it will use the bus parameter argument to do this. The explicit operator will use the big parameter to create a new instance of the Bus class by invoking the Bus class constructor and copying the BigVehicle value arguments to the Bus fields through the constructor initialization. The following code can be found in explicit_conversion.cs, and the conversion operators can be seen at the end of this listing:

```
using System;

public struct BigVehicle
{
  public string NumberPlate;
  public bool inService;
  public int seats;
}

public class Bus
{
  string numberPlate;
  bool inService;
  int seats;

  public string NumberPlate
  {
    get { return numberPlate;}
    set { numberPlate = value; }
  }

  public bool InService
  {
    get { return inService;}
    set { inService = value; }
  }

  public int Seats
  {
    get { return seats;}
    set { seats = value; }
  }

  public Bus(string numberPlate, int seats, bool inService)
  {
    this.numberPlate = numberPlate;
    this.seats = seats;
    this.inService = inService;
  }

  public static implicit operator BigVehicle(Bus bus)
  {
    BigVehicle big;
    big.inService = bus.NumberPlate;
    big.seats = bus.Seats;
    big.inService = bus.inService;
    return big;
  }

  public static explicit operator Bus(BigVehicle big)
  {
    return new Bus(big.NumberPlate, big.seats, big.inService);
  }
}
```

In order to convert between the Bus object and the BigVehicle struct value and invoke the implicit operator we can use the following code in a Main() method. The BigVehicle struct will be created in the code and populated with the property gets of the Bus object.

```
Bus bus1 = new Bus("Eazy Rider", 20, true);
BigVehicle big1 = bus1;
```

Similarly, we can invoke the explicit conversion operator by doing an explicit cast between BigVehicle and Bus. When the operator is invoked it will create a new instance of the Bus class and pass the BigVehicle value to the three parameter constructor (the values are extracted from the BigVehicle fields. Using the explicit operator in this way enables us to define the Bus constructor as private. This means that we can't explicitly create a new instance of the Bus but can provide a conversion interface so that the only way to create a new Bus object would be to convert a BigVehicle into a Bus (or any other type into a Bus that has a an explicit operator defined for it).

```
Bus bus2;
BigVehicle big2;
big2.inService = true;
big2.NumberPlate = "Eazy Rider";
big2.seats = 20;
bus2 = (Bus)big2;
```

The use of operators is fairly non-restrictive, which means that we can define a code block to convert from any value type to any reference type and vice versa. However we can only define one operator per type, as the compiler wouldn't be able to determine which operator we wanted to use for a particular conversion.

Being able to cast implicitly between structs and classes allows us to define value-type semantics for a reference type. One possibility would be if we wanted to define a Code type that takes the format of a letter followed by a number. We could use the following code to define such a type:

```
using System;

public class Code
{
  private string code = String.Empty;

  public Code(string code)
  {
    if(code!=null && code.Length == 2
      && char.IsLetter(code[0]) && char.IsNumber(code[1]))
      this.code = code.ToUpper();
    else
      throw new ArgumentException("Not a valid code");
  }
```

```
public static implicit operator Code(string address)
{
  return new Code(address);
}

public static explicit operator string(Code code)
{
  return code.code;
}

public override string ToString()
{
  return (string)this;
}
}
```

We could enter the code explicitly for this type (Code myCode = "C3";) and so if we used this type in a collection, for instance, we wouldn't have to perform any further validation to ensure that the codes were of the correct format, and by overriding the explicit string conversion operator and the ToString() method, it can behave exactly like a string when we want it to. Be wary of doing this, however, as if it behaves too much like a string, it may cause confusion to consumers of our code.

Conversion operators can also be used in a base class to convert between two types and similarly used in a derived class (as they are static they are not inherited, however, the derived class will not use the conversion operators of the base class). In the code below we can make the assumption that the BigBus class is derived from the Bus class but use a Bus type reference for it. Even though the BigBus class may have its own conversion operators it will use the Bus class conversion implicit operator.

```
Bus bus = new BigBus(40);
BigVehicle i = bus;
```

Cloning Objects

Cloning objects is required to facilitate working on copies of an object without affecting the original and its contents. Systems use cloning in many different ways but generally it will be used to initialize an object with a default state. This section will focus on the different ways we can clone an object and how it relates back to object construction.

Using the Copy Constructor

The need for cloning objects has led to the evolution of the copy constructor, which is a constructor that takes its own class type as a parameter. In this way, the class instance parameter can be used to populate the field values of the current instance of the object.

The Teacher class written below includes a copy constructor, where in every new instance of the class we can pass a single object reference that will initialize all new class instances of the Teacher class. There are many different approaches that can be taken here; either a class instance can be used to set initialization for all subsequent class instances, or in the case of the Teacher class we may want to create several class instances, one for each department and pass each one to the copy constructor of a subset of the Teacher objects we wish to create. We don't have to use the constructor as a template but can use it simply to copy certain aspects of a class, which are essential to initialization with default state for the particular object.

```
public class Teacher
{
  private int grade;
  private int salary;
  private string dept = String.Empty;

  public Teacher() {}

  public Teacher(int grade, int salary, string dept)
  {
    this.grade = grade;
    this.salary = salary;
    this.dept = dept;
  }
  public Teacher(Teacher teach)
  {
    grade = teach.grade;
    salary = teach.salary;
    dept = teach.dept;
  }
}
```

To invoke the copy constructor, we can use the following in a Main() method. The code file for this example is called copy_ctors.cs. This will first create a Teacher object with the default values that we intend to copy followed by passing the object reference to the copy constructor and using the values to populate the fields in the as-yet-not-initialized class instance.

```
Teacher teach1 = new Teacher(3, 23000, "IT");
Teacher teach2 = new Teacher(teach1);
```

With the introduction of reflection into the .NET Framework it is easy to conceive of developing generic copy constructors that can be used to reflect on a type and extract the values of a particular object by identifying the property values available in that type. We can use reflection to dynamically find everything out about the public interface of the type, and also to add the values to the current instance of the class. In order to use reflection we must either add public property values to the object or declare the fields as public. We have opted for the former in this case:

```
public int Grade { get { return grade; } set { grade = value; }}
public int Salary { get { return salary; } set { salary = value; }}
public string Dept { get { return dept; } set { dept = value; }}
```

The current implementation of the Teacher class copy constructor could be replaced by the following. This would enable a further abstraction allowing all the property values to be obtained from one instance of the class and used to populate the property values in the current instance. In this way the interface on the Teacher class can change (that is, we can add more properties to the class and not update any more code since the rest is relatively dynamic) with no updates to the copy constructor, as long as there are publicly accessible property or field values. The classes used below are available by referencing the System.Reflection namespace.

```
public Teacher(Teacher teach)
{
  PropertyInfo[] pInfoArray = teach.GetType().GetProperties();
  foreach(PropertyInfo pInfo in pInfoArray)
  {
    Type ty = pInfo.PropertyType;
    object myvalue =
        teach.GetType().InvokeMember(pInfo.Name,
                                BindingFlags.GetProperty, null,
                                teach, null);
    teach.GetType().InvokeMember(pInfo.Name,
                            BindingFlags.SetProperty, null,
                            this, new object[]{myvalue});
  }
}
```

Invoking the get property accessors on the new Teacher class instance will reveal that the values have been copied from one object to the other without specifically naming a field or property.

```
Console.WriteLine("Details:{0}, {1}, {2}",
        teach2.Grade, teach2.Dept, teach2.Salary);
```

The ICloneable Interface

Many classes within the .NET Framework implement the ICloneable interface, which can be used instead of a copy constructor to obtain a **clone** of an object. ICloneable provides a single Clone() method, which must be implemented. We can change the definition of the Teacher class by implementing the ICloneable class.

```
public class Teacher : ICloneable
```

We now have to implement the `Clone()` method to return a copied instance of the Teacher class. To comply with the `ICloneable` interface, the `Clone()` method must return an object type. Using `ICloneable` can prove very useful; since we understand the nature of the contract with `ICloneable` we can build classes that can test whether this supports cloning; that is, the `ICloneable` interface and then cast it in a generic manner. An object can then be returned by the application through a method that accepts any `ICloneable` interface type as opposed to a concrete class type.

```
public object Clone()
{
    return new Teacher(grade, salary, dept) as object;
}
```

Calling the `Clone()` method will return us a `Teacher` object of type object that we can cast back to a `Teacher`.

```
Teacher teach3 = (Teacher)teach2.Clone();
```

The above is an example of a *deep copy*. This is somewhat more expensive than an equivalent *shallow copy*. A deep copy will result in the copying of a fully populated object, which contains its own values of other reference and value types. A shallow copy, however, is a copy of all the references in one object, so in effect it's a copy of references to types that were created, initialized and used within another object. It doesn't have its own copy of these values and shares them through the references with all other objects that reference them. Each reference to a type will increase the reference count to that type by one, and hence overusing this will prohibit objects being destroyed by the GC. Every object inherits a method from `System.Object` called `MemberWiseClone()` that will return a shallow copy of the object. The main limitation with using a shallow copy of an object is that if any of the values are changed in the source object, then as the second copy references all the same values in memory, all of the changes are implicit and carried over to the cloned object. A member-wise clone causes a shallow copy but certain things are copied by value, like all the value types.

```
public object Clone()
{
    return this.MemberwiseClone();
}
```

Deep cloning can be a very expensive operation and should be avoided unless necessary, since a by-value copy of all the member fields will occur. On a grand scale this can be very expensive involving the creation of many objects, though in reality we may use combinations of the two types of cloning. Some objects that contain references to many other objects or object collection may function well with deep copies.

Serialization and Deserialization

Serialization is a concept that should be familiar to Java developers. It is used to create a representation of an object where the state of the object can be persisted and transported; the formatted representation of an object can be a stream of bytes, for example, or an XML document. There are many types of `Stream` members that we can serialize an object to, for example a `FileStream` or `NetworkStream`. Objects can be serialized and recovered later via a process called **deserialization**, which will use the formatted value and reconstruct it to form a .NET object. Formatters determine the rules for serialization so that we can specify what we want the serialized object to look like. In practice we will rarely need any other formatters except those that have been provided with the .NET Framework; these include a binary formatter, an XML formatter and a SOAP formatter. The binary formatter will serialize an object including all field values to a byte stream, which can be written to a file or network endpoint. The XML formatter will format the object to an XML document representation that can be written to any stream. The SOAP formatter will serialize an object to the Simple Object Access Protocol, which is an XML-based protocol (now a standard in v1.1), which is used to invoke a web service method.

Using deserialization, we can create several copies of the same object from a serialized source such as a file on disk or a network stream. Conceptually, an object is serialized to a stream to make the programming model simple and abstract, but this really excels when objects are transferred across the network. Using sockets, we can format an object using a binary formatter at the client, and recreate the same object at the server.

In this example, we'll serialize an object to a disk file and then reconstruct the object using deserialization. The following namespaces must be used to serialize objects. In order to have access to both files and streams we have to use the `System.IO` namespace as well. In this example we will cover the SOAP to illustrate what the output will look like when serialized but in practice we may wish to choose either one based on the circumstances. For example, the Binary Formatter will result in an object representation containing far fewer bytes, so we can use this for enhanced performance. Since the SOAP Formatted object is a standard it can be reconstructed by another programming language such as Java, which makes object serialization much more interoperable. The following was added to the `copy_ctors.cs` file. The new code file is called `serializable_deserializable.cs`:

```
using System.Runtime.Serialization;
/*we won't be using the Binary Formatter but if you need to use it you
must define the following using statement*/
using System.Runtime.Serialization.Formatters.Binary;
using System.Runtime.Serialization.Formatters.Soap;
```

Remember the teach reference created earlier when discussing member-wise cloning:

```
Teacher teach3 = (Teacher)teach2.Clone();
```

We can revise the definition of the Teacher class by adding the `Serializable` attribute to it, which specifies that the class can be serialized. This is necessary because the object will be checked for this attribute when we use a formatter to serialize it, and if it is not present a `SerializationException` will be thrown.

```
[Serializable()]
public class Teacher : ICloneable
```

The code below, which is included in the `Main()` method, will create a file `teacher.xml` if it doesn't already exist and return a `FileStream` object that can be used to serialize the `Teacher` object to disk. This process will be done using `SoapFormatter` object. The `Serialize()` method of the `SoapFormatter` class is invoked with the `FileStream` and the `Teacher` object as parameters.

```
FileStream fTeacher = File.Open("C:\\teacher.xml",
                                FileMode.OpenOrCreate,
                                FileAccess.ReadWrite);
SoapFormatter sfTeacher = new SoapFormatter();
sfTeacher.Serialize(fTeacher, teach3);
```

In this example the same stream is used to serialize and deserialize the object, which means that we have to ensure that the stream pointer is reset to the beginning, or else an exception will be thrown.

```
fTeacher.Position = 0;
```

The `Deserialize()` method is used with the open `FileStream` and will read everything from the stream and reconstitute it as a `Teacher` object. We can then check that this has been done correctly by printing out its field values.

```
Teacher teach4 = (Teacher)sfTeacher.Deserialize(fStream);
Console.WriteLine("Details:{0}, {1}, {2}",
    teach4.Grade, teach4.Dept, teach4.Salary);
```

This whole process can be used to reconstruct the `Teacher` object instance from the file on disk. From the code above we can see that we don't actually have to use the constructor to recreate the `Teacher` object; we call the `Deserialize()` method reading from the `FileStream` and then recast to a `Teacher` type. This technique is widely used to restore the state of an application, so that we take regular snapshots and save objects, as the idea behind the use of object databases to persist objects is gaining much ground in the development community, similar to the use of Java EJB Entity Beans, which are serializable. Using serialization is not just an alternative to cloning, it is complimentary – cloning can be used to replicate an object instance on the fly whereas serialization can be used to persist an object instance or transport it and have it reconstructed outside of the application boundaries.

We actually have just as much control over the serialization process as we have over the cloning process, and we can implement this in our serializable classes with ease. Field values can be marked as to whether they should be serialized or whether they should not be serialized. The mechanism is as simple as adding another attribute as depicted below to the fields that shouldn't be serialized.

```
[NonSerialized]
private string dept = String.Empty;
```

The Teacher object that has been serialized here is reproduced in serialized form. Much of the information enclosed in this is beyond the scope of the chapter and irrelevant to the understanding of serialization. It has been reproduced here to illustrate the effect of the NonSerialized attribute that was used above the dept field. We can see a tag in the SOAP XML below called a1:Teacher, and nested within this are two tags, grade and salary, which contain the values of these fields. Notice that the dept field hasn't been reproduced as it was marked NonSerialized. To generate this XML code, compile and run the serializable_deserializable.cs file, and type the following in the command prompt window:

```
C:\Class Design\Ch 05> type \teacher.xml
<SOAP-ENV:Envelope
    xmlns:xsi=http://www.w3.org/2001/XMLSchema-instance
    xmlns:xsd="http://www.w3.org/2001/XMLSchema"
    xmlns:SOAP-ENC=http://schemas.xmlsoap.org/soap/encoding/
    xmlns:SOAP-ENV=http://schemas.xmlsoap.org/soap/envelope/
    xmlns:clr="http://schemas.microsoft.com/soap/encoding/clr/1.0"

  SOAP-ENV:encodingStyle="http://schemas.xmlsoap.org/soap/encoding/">
  <SOAP-ENV:Body>
  <a1:Teacher id="ref-1"
      xmlns:a1=
                "http://schemas.microsoft.com/clr/nsassem/
                CloningAndSerialization/CloningAndSerialization
                %2C%20Version%3D1.0.1056.43019%2C%20Culture
                %3Dneutral%2C%20PublicKeyToken%3Dnull">
      <grade>3</grade>
      <salary>23000</salary>
    </a1:Teacher>
  </SOAP-ENV:Body>
</SOAP-ENV:Envelope>
```

In addition to this, the .NET Framework provides a rich XML serialization model, which can be used in a manner similar to the object serialization shown here.

The following is a very simple XML document that is saved to a file called computer.xml. From this document we can infer an XML Schema, which can be thought of as a template for the XML document. By analogy, we can suggest that the XML Schema's relationship to an XML document is reminiscent of a class's relationship to an object.

```
<COMPUTER>
 <HARDDRIVE>MAXTOR</HARDDRIVE>
 <GRAPHICSCARD>ATI</GRAPHICSCARD>
 <SOUNDCARD>CREATIVE LABS</SOUNDCARD>
</COMPUTER>
```

The .NET Framework provides a tool called xsd.exe that can be used to infer an XML schema, and then from that schema generate a C# class file:

```
C:\Class Design\Ch 05>xsd computer.xml
```

From the schema we can derive the C# class using the /c switch.

```
C:\Class Design\Ch 05>xsd /c computer.xsd
```

We have now created a class called COMPUTER that has been created in a file called computer.cs with the following auto-generated code. The attributes above the class declaration are synonymous with the Serializable attribute.

```csharp
using System.Xml.Serialization;

[System.Xml.Serialization.XmlTypeAttribute(
 Namespace="http://tempuri.org/computer.xsd")]
[System.Xml.Serialization.XmlRootAttribute(
 Namespace="http://tempuri.org/computer.xsd", IsNullable=false)]
public class COMPUTER
{
   public string HARDDRIVE;
   public string GRAPHICSCARD;
   public string SOUNDCARD;
}
```

To use the object stored in computer.xml, we can use the System.Xml.Serialization.XmlSerializer class to deserialize the contents of the file to an object of type COMPUTER. To check whether this process worked we can print out one of the field values as below.

```csharp
XmlSerializer xs = new XmlSerializer(typeof(COMPUTER));
COMPUTER cmp =
      (COMPUTER)xs.Deserialize(File.Open("computer.xml",
      FileMode.Open));
Console.WriteLine("Graphics card is: {0}", cmp.GRAPHICSCARD);
```

203

Design Patterns

We have seen the basic principles for object construction and how to vary the use of the object creation process to encompass the use of operators, constructor overloading, and chaining and static constructors to initialize a class constructor. Let's focus on a more abstract problem area now that we have the necessary understanding of object creation principles.

A design pattern is a reusable design that can template an object-oriented approach for solving a problem. These patterns can be applied to create an abstraction layer for design, and these design patterns are normally learned concurrently with OO development techniques to evolve good verses bad development principles.

Design patterns have been proposed by numerous individuals but they were originated by Erich Gamma, Richard Helm, Ralph Johnson, and John Vlissides, the so called Gang of Four. The Gang of Four's patterns are so widespread in computing that they are often known by the abbreviation 'Gof Patterns'. The Gang of Four created a series of reusable OO design patterns, which were adopted by the development community and used within most object-oriented projects. For more information refer to the Addison & Wesley book, *Design Patterns: Elements of Reusable Object-Oriented Software*, ISBN: 0-201-63361-2. Written by the Gang of Four, you'll often see it referred to as the GoF book. As we delve into several design patterns, which we can use in our own code, it will become apparent to all well versed in either the .NET Framework class libraries or Java class libraries that these design patterns are being used throughout the library code. The patterns in this section are described as *creational patterns* as they represent designs based on the creation of objects, as opposed to structural or behavior patterns, which represent acts of design based on class models or communication between objects.

Singleton

The Singleton is a design pattern that is used throughout most class libraries and OO models. The Singleton design pattern ensures that only a single instance of a class is available, and this is defined by a method that can be controlled by the use of static helper methods on the class. Singleton design patterns are prolific throughout the design of operating systems ensuring that when we request the use of a hardware device we use the single instance of the hardware device object rather than a newly created one.

The following example has a class called HeadTeacher that cannot be created directly by using the new keyword. This is made possible by specifying a private constructor, so only a nested class or a static method can create an instance of the HeadTeacher class. We have seen the nested class approach but we use a static method when defining a Singleton.

The static field headTeacher stores the HeadTeacher object instance. We control the creation of this through the static GetInstance() method, which will check to see if this is null. If it is null then this method will create and return a new instance of HeadTeacher, if not then it will return the static field reference. In this way only a single object of HeadTeacher can ever exist at one time, and all clients will have a reference to this instance.

```csharp
using System;

public class HeadTeacher
{
  private static HeadTeacher headTeacher;
  private int grade;
  private string name;

  private HeadTeacher() {}

  public static HeadTeacher GetInstance()
  {
    if(headTeacher == null)
    {
      Console.WriteLine("HeadTeacher instance created!");
      headTeacher = new HeadTeacher();
      return headTeacher;
    }
    else
    {
      Console.WriteLine("HeadTeacher instance already exists!");
      return headTeacher;
    }
  }

  public int Grade
  {
    get { return grade; }
    set { grade = value; }
  }

  public string Name
  {
    get { return name; }
    set { name = value; }
  }
}
```

A Main() method is used to check whether a single instance of the object is created. A single HeadTeacher object is created by invoking the GetInstance() method. We can set the Grade property to 10 and it will be identical for both object references because they reference the same object. The file containing all the source code is called singleton.cs:

```
public class mainHeadTeacher
{
  static void Main()
  {
    HeadTeacher ht1 = HeadTeacher.GetInstance();
    HeadTeacher ht2 = HeadTeacher.GetInstance();
    ht1.Grade = 10;

    Console.WriteLine("ht1 Grade:{0}", ht1.Grade);
    Console.WriteLine("ht2 Grade:{0}", ht2.Grade);
  }
}
```

The output from this will be.

```
C:\ Class Design\Ch 05> Singleton
HeadTeacher instance created!
HeadTeacher instance already exists!
ht1 Grade:10
ht2 Grade:10
```

By amending this, we can apply a second design pattern called the *Double-Checked Locking Pattern* to ensure that the Singleton class is threadsafe. To make anything threadsafe, we have to ensure that only one thread can enter the method at any one time. Consider the situation where a thread enters the GetInstance() method and another thread enters before the object is created, but after checking that the local variable containing the HeadTeacher object is null. Before control returns to the original thread, another thread has created the object. Assuming the calling code is multithreaded then h1 and h2 will reference different HeadTeacher objects!

We can use the native synchronization of .NET by using the following namespace.

```
using System.Runtime.CompilerServices;
```

We can now use the MethodImplOptions.Synchronized enumeration member on the MethodImpl attribute to ensure that this method is only ever called by one thread at a time. The new file is called locking_pattern.cs. Locks, Monitors, or Mutexes can also be used instead of this, but such threading topics are beyond the scope of this book.

```
[MethodImpl(MethodImplOptions.Synchronized)]
public static HeadTeacher getInstance()
{
  ...
}
```

The Abstract Factory Pattern

The Abstract Factory pattern, like the Singleton, is used throughout the .NET Framework class libraries. The Factory name should be familiar to Java developers where `Factory()` methods are present throughout the Java class libraries, and also COM developers may recognize the term from the `ClassFactory` objects used to create instances of COM classes.

To use the Abstract Factory pattern we don't need to create the class directly through a constructor; instead we simply expose a Factory, which will create the class on our behalf. We don't actually need to stipulate the concrete class; since the Factory knows the class it should return for us this can be also be extended to return a *default* class. Whenever the family of classes needs extending, the code can simply be changed in the Factory classes (which act as an abstraction) rather than changing any code in the `HospitalWorker` directly.

The best definition of an abstract factory is actually the definition given in the GoF book:

> '*The purpose of an abstract factory is to provide an interface for creating families of related objects without specifying their concrete classes.*'

In this example we create two types of hospital workers – doctors and nurses. The nurses and the doctors have certain traits in common, for example they are either qualified or students. To model this we create abstract base classes, `Doctor` and `Nurse`, which will contain a basic implementation of the underlying type of `HopitalWorkers` – the implementation does not matter to us in this case since we must use a separate class to create the doctor or nurse objects. As their properties are the same, however, we first create an abstract `MedicalStaff` class for the two abstract `Doctor` and `Nurse` classes to derive from.

```
public abstract class MedicalStaff
{
  protected int salary;
  protected int grade;
  protected string hospital;

  public int Pay
  {
    get { return this.salary; }
    set { this.salary = value; }
  }

  public int Grade
  {
    get { return this.grade; }
    set { this.grade = value; }
  }

  public string Hospital
  {
```

```
      get { return this.hospital; }
      set { this.hospital = value; }
   }
}

public abstract class Doctor : MedicalStaff {}
public abstract class Nurse : MedicalStaff {}
```

As there are two different types of nurses and doctors, both either qualified or students, we can derive new classes as a student or qualified representation of a nurse or a doctor. The implementation here is unimportant; the principle is all we need to understand the design pattern:

```
public class StudentNurse : Nurse {}
public class QualifiedNurse : Nurse {}
public class QualifiedDoctor : Doctor {}
public class StudentDoctor : Doctor {}
```

To continue with the design pattern we must create a base class to create the nurse or doctor, student or qualified. The base class is called `HospitalWorker` and has two methods that will return either a nurse or a doctor, which should be implemented in the derived classes.

```
public abstract class HospitalWorkerFactory
{
 public abstract Nurse GetNurse() {}
 public abstract Doctor GetDoctor() {}
}
```

The two derived classes are `StudentFactory` and `QualifiedFactory` respectively, which will return either a student doctor or nurse, or a qualified doctor or nurse depending on the method called.

```
public class StudentFactory : HospitalWorkerFactory
{
  public Nurse GetNurse()
  {
    return new StudentNurse();
  }

  public Doctor GetDoctor()
  {
    return new StudentDoctor();
  }
}

public class QualifiedFactory : HospitalWorkerFactory
{
  public Nurse GetNurse()
  {
```

```
        return new QualifiedNurse();
    }

    public Doctor GetDoctor()
    {
        return new QualifiedDoctor();
    }
}
```

The base class HospitalWorkerFactory is known as an Abstract Factory class after the pattern name simply because it is the interface that the creation code uses it is aFactory in the sense that it specifically creates and returns the object to us with a concrete name used. Each type of category, student or qualified, must have its own concrete implementation derived from the abstract factory.

In our creation code we can add another class called HospitalWorker, which will take the appropriate factory as a method parameter and return either a nurse or doctor. The fact that the HospitalWorkerFactory class is either of type StudentFactory or QualifiedFactory, thus enabling it to determine the appropriate class, determines the choice.

```
public class HospitalWorker
{
    public static Nurse GetNurse(HospitalWorkerFactory hwf)
    {
        return hwf.GetNurse();
    }

    public static Doctor GetDoctor(HospitalWorkerFactory hwf)
    {
        return hwf.GetDoctor();
    }
}
```

There are other types of Factory methods (the abstract factory method is only one of them), though they all intuitively use another class (a Factory class) to control the creation of a particular object. Here we made all types have the same properties, but in this example, we could have provided completely different properties and methods for the Doctor and Nurse abstract classes. The .NET Framework provides many examples of factories, like the WebRequest class, or the SymmetricAlgorithm class, rather than taking an abstract factory class argument, they normally use a string parameter that represents the literal name of the class for the static Create() method to return the appropriate class instance.

Lazy Initialization

The last two patterns are based on the abstraction of creation of objects, and they avoid the creation code directly. In the case of an Abstract Factory pattern we create the object we need without specifying the name of the concrete class directly, but deferring the creation through a factory method, and in the case of a Singleton we use a class to broker a single instance of the object, which either exists or needs to be created, using a static method. Lazy initialization ensures that the field values will only be set when they are first accessed by a piece of code; after this the same value is returned. Lazy Initialization is classed as a design pattern but can be conceived to be an optimization technique to avoid consumption of resources.

With the Doctors and Nurses in the previous section we could return a field value, which would currently be uninitialized. The lazy initialization model populates field values only when necessary, as they are seldom used by the implementation. For greater performance, do not allow this value to be set at construction in case it is time consuming. Lazy initialization specifies that get property accessors contain all the code necessary to retrieve information from a resource, and only when they are invoked is the underlying field value populated.

In the Lazy class below there are two fields, id and name. The number parameter is an integer value that is passed into the constructor when the object is first created and assigned to the id field. The name field is unassigned at object creation time and will use the id value when the Name get accessor is requested to populate the name field from the file so that it will effectively be initialized only if it is used.

```
public class Lazy
{
  private int id;
  private string name;

  public Lazy(int number)
  {
    this.id = number;
  }

  public int ID
  {
    get { return id; }
  }

  public string Name
  {
    get
    {
      if(this.name==null)
      {
        StreamReader sr;
        try
        {
```

```
        sr = new
            StreamReader("C:\\name"+id.ToString("0000")+".txt");
        name = sr.ReadToEnd();
      }
      finally
      {
        if(sr!=null)
            sr.Close();
      }
      return this.name;
    }
  }
 }
}
```

Copy-On-Write

Copy-on-write is an application of a general design pattern like the proxy pattern. It is relevant to the discussion of object construction since it relates directly to object construction through optimization in much the same way as Lazy Initialization does. Earlier in the chapter we discussed the notion that a deep copy was more expensive than a shallow copy so for the purposes of efficiency we may need to use a shallow copy in places. The problem here is that shallow copying relies on shared references to objects, which are fine for as long as the objects don't need to contain different field values; in practice they always will have to at some stage within an application.

Copy-on-write addresses this issue by determining when an object value is being written to, and if it is, it will take a copy of the referenced object and make the appropriate changes. In this way it is not as expensive as a deep copy since the second object reference may only need to apply read operations throughout the application and not a near identical copy. There are issues such as reference counting, and synchronization associated with copy-on-write, which make its implementation a little tougher in practice.

Copy-on-write can be built into classes and is inherent in some .NET objects. For example, if we look at the following code, we would say that the second variable world is a reference copy of the first hello. The world variable should change the underlying string so that both references when referenced and written to the screen should produce the expression Hello World!

This is not, however, what happens in this case as the string uses a copy-on-write technique of actually creating a by value copy of the string since the overloaded operator checks to see what the reference count on the string is. If the count is above 1 and the object value is being modified then a new copy will be created and a reference to the new copy altered stored in the second variable.

```
string hello = "Hello";
string world = hello;
world += " World!";
Console.WriteLine("{0}\{1}", hello, world);
```

This optimization can be done in objects using similar techniques of operator overloading. In the case of the string example above, every reference to the string could invoke an implicit conversion operator, which would return a reference to the current string and increment the reference count by one; when we use the += operator this would check to see if the reference count is greater than one, and if so copy the string by value and return a number string with the additional string argument appended, also setting the reference count to one. There is ample debate on the usefulness of the copy-on-write pattern since it requires synchronization and makes the reference counting and additional checks take more resources than an initial by-value copy.

Summary

This chapter has focused on the many techniques and principles we need to know to be able to create and destroy objects. This has included knowledge of the managed heap and garbage collector as well the semantics necessary to chain and overload constructors. Different forms of initialization and creation were covered including the use of object cloning, deserialization, and conversion operators. The chapter ended with a look at creational design demonstrating how it can be used to alter the object creation process making it more efficient and abstract and how object creation can be optimized for performance.

C#

Class Design

Handbook

6

Events and Delegates

Event-based programming is a cornerstone of the .NET Framework – it is fundamental to all .NET user-interface code, including Windows Forms and ASP.NET pages. Events can also be used effectively anywhere in applications to decouple the functionality of an object from other objects that depend on it. By exposing and firing events from within an object, we enable other objects to respond to its activities in ways that we did not necessarily anticipate when we coded the class. Therefore, events can be a powerful component in the interface of any C# type we code.

The event mechanism in the .NET Framework makes use of **delegates** (or callbacks). We introduced delegates briefly in Chapter 1 when we reviewed the .NET Framework Common Type System. A delegate encapsulates the signature of a function or subroutine. In C/C++, this would be similar to a function pointer. A function pointer is simply a memory address; the compiler has no knowledge of the signature of the method it points to. Therefore, function pointers are not type safe (you could pass a wrong type without the compiler noticing) and cannot be a part of a managed application. We define delegates to represent the signature of methods that we want to 'call back' in our application. We can then create an instance of a delegate and bind it to a particular method. We can use this delegate to invoke our chosen method. Because delegates can only point to a method of one specific signature, delegates can be type-safe.

In this chapter, we'll investigate the delegate mechanism in some detail. We'll see how delegates are compiled into MSIL code, which will help you understand how delegates work internally. Then we'll look at some advanced delegate issues, such as multi-cast delegates and asynchronous delegates.

Once we've seen how to use delegates, we'll examine the .NET Framework event model. Most programmers will be familiar with some sort of event model, but in the .NET Framework, events work differently from how they work in Visual Basic or Java. We'll describe how the event model makes use of delegates, and see how to use events in user-interface code. We'll also see how to use events as a general way of decoupling an event source object (which generates events) from event receiver objects (which receive event notifications).

Delegates

To understand how events work in C#, we must first describe how to use delegates. The event model uses delegates to identify event handler methods in our application. Delegates are also useful in their own right, above and beyond their role in the event mechanism.

A delegate is like a pointer to a method in an object in our application. As discussed earlier, the problem with function pointers as they are used in C and C++, is that they are not type-safe, because the compiler cannot know the signature of the function called. So, if the programmer makes a mistake, they could pass an argument of the wrong type to the function. The designers of Java resolved this issue by banning function pointers from their language specification.

For any programming problem that would normally be solved using a callback function (passing a pointer to the function), Java programmers resort to defining a specialized callback interface. The caller defines a type (either interface or class) that can be called. When writing code that must be called, you must implement this interface and your method must have the same name as defined by the caller. Like using delegates, this technique allows writing a calling object without knowing the object that will eventually be called. The called object, however, must contain considerable extra code implementing interfaces and must follow the design of the calling object. Delegates allow the developer the same flexibility as the unsafe function pointers, but with type safety.

The designers of the .NET Framework decided to overcome the problem of function pointers by wrapping them in a special kind of class, one per function signature. These classes are called delegate classes or delegates. We define a delegate class to specify the signature of methods we would like to call through the delegate. We can then create a delegate object and bind it to any method whose signature matches that of the delegate.

Delegates are useful in the following scenarios:

❏ **To register one of our object's methods as a callback method with another object**
When something important happens to that object, it can invoke our callback method. The object that invokes the delegate doesn't need to know anything about our object or its methods; the delegate contains all the information about which method to invoke on which object. Therefore, the object that invokes the delegate will continue to work correctly in the future even if we define new types of object with new method names.

216

❑ **To choose one of a series of methods (with the same signature) for use in an algorithm**
For example, in Chapter 1 we saw how to define a delegate to represent mathematical functions such as `Math.Sin`, `Math.Cos`, and `Math.Tan`.

❑ **To separate the selection of a method from its invocation**
We can create a delegate to indicate which method we want to call, but delay its execution until we are ready. For example, we can create a delegate to represent a method to call every ten seconds in a real-time application. We can then create a separate thread, and use the delegate to invoke the required method every ten seconds.

Creating and Using Simple Delegates

To use delegates in our application, and usingwe perform the following three steps:

❑ Declare the delegate type

❑ Create a delegate object, and bind it to a particular method

❑ Invoke the method by using the delegate object

We'll show an example of how to declare a delegate to draw different types of shape on a Windows form. As a fully visual example, we won't show all the form code here in the book. The source code for this example is located in the download code folder `DelegatesEvents\UsingDelegates.cs`.

The form will have the following appearance:

When the user clicks the Draw rectangle button, the application displays a rectangle with the specified position, size, and color. Likewise, when the user clicks the Draw ellipse button, the application displays an ellipse with the specified characteristics.

To achieve this functionality, we could write two completely separate button-click event handler methods to handle the Draw rectangle and Draw ellipse click events. However, this would result in a great deal of duplicate code, as both methods would need to perform the following tasks:

❑ Make sure all the textboxes have been filled in, to specify the position and size of the shape

❑ Make sure the shape fits in the drawing area on the screen

❑ Create a brush with the specified color

❑ Draw the required shape

To avoid duplication of code, we'll use a delegate to represent the drawing operation required. The delegate will either point to the `FillRectangle()` method or the `FillEllipse()` method, both of which are defined in the `Graphics` class in the .NET Framework class library. Then we'll write a generic method that takes this delegate as a parameter, and uses the delegate to invoke the appropriate drawing operation.

Let's look at a part of the supporting code for the application:

```
// omitted the delegate declaration here

public class UsingDelegates : System.Windows.Forms.Form
{
    //Declare a Rectangle field, to indicate available drawing area
    private Rectangle mRect;

    #region Windows Form Designer generated code
    // omitted for brevity. This region contains some event
    // related code as well. We will look at that later.
    #endregion

    //When the form receives a paint event,
    //color the available drawing area white
    private void UsingDelegates_Paint(object sender,
            System.Windows.Forms.PaintEventArgs e)
    {
      mRect = new Rectangle(0, 0, Width, Height / 2);
      e.Graphics.FillRectangle(new SolidBrush(Color.White), mRect);
    }

    private void btnColor_Click(object sender, System.EventArgs e)
    {
      ColorDialog dlgColor = new ColorDialog();
      dlgColor.ShowDialog(this);
      btnColor.BackColor = dlgColor.Color;
    }

    // Delegate-related code (see later)...
}
```

Note the following points in this code:

❏   We declare a `private` field named `mRect` to represent the drawing area on the form.

❏   We initialize the `mRect` field whenever the form paints itself, and paint the rectangle white.

❏   We've provided a click-event handler method for the Color button on our form. The method displays the standard color dialog box, so the user can choose a color for the next shape. To indicate which color has been selected, we repaint the Color button using the selected color. Note that it is not the name of the method that specifies that it handles the `Click` event from `btnColor`. The wiring of methods and events is done in the omitted Forms Designer code. We will look into this code in the second half of this chapter.

Now let's start looking at the delegate-specific code. Just before the start of the class definition, we placed a delegate definition. It looks like this:

```
//Define a Delegate type, to indicate signature of
//method to call
delegate void DrawShape(Brush aBrush , Rectangle aRect);
```

The delegate definition is like a class definition: it specifies a new type. It is a not part of the `UsingDelegates` class, but forms an independent class of its own. This delegate represents methods that return `void` and take two parameters:

❏   A `Brush` object, to specify the color of the shape

❏   A `Rectangle` object, to specify the position and size of the shape

This delegate corresponds with the signatures of the `FillRectangle()` and `FillEllipse()` methods in the `Graphics` class. The next step is to create an instance of the type, and bind it to a specific method on a particular object. Here is an example showing how to create a `DrawShape` instance and bind it to the `FillRectangle()` method on a `Graphics` object:

```
//Handle the Click event for the btnDrawRect button
private void btnDrawRect_Click(object sender, System.EventArgs e)
{
    // Create a Graphics object (we need its FillRectangle method)
    Graphics aGraphics = CreateGraphics();

    // Declare a DrawShape variable
    DrawShape DrawRectangleMethod;

    // Create a delegate object, and bind to the FillRectangle method
    DrawRectangleMethod = new DrawShape(aGraphics.FillRectangle);

    // Call MyDrawShape, and pass the delegate as a parameter
    MyDrawShape(DrawRectangleMethod);
}
```

Note the following points in the btnRectangle_Click() method above:

- ❑ We create a Graphics object because the drawing methods (such as FillRectangle() and FillEllipse()) are defined as instance methods in this class. Therefore, we need an instance of the Graphics class to enable us to call these methods. CreateGraphics() is an inherited method from the Control class (of which our form is a subclass).

- ❑ We declare a local variable of type DrawShape. This reinforces the fact that delegates are data types. Later in the chapter, we'll show the MSIL code for the DrawShape data type.

- ❑ We create an instance of the DrawShape type, and bind it to the FillRectangle() method on the Graphics object. Note that we pass the name of the method without parentheses. This syntax can only be used in constructors of delegates.

  It's also possible to bind delegates to static methods. To bind a delegate to a static method rather than an instance method, specify a class name before the method (for example, Math.Sin), rather than specifying an object name before the method (for example, aGraphics.FillRectangle).

- ❑ We pass the DrawShape instance into another method named MyDrawShape(). MyDrawShape() uses the delegate to invoke the specified drawing operation (aGraphics.FillRectangle).

Now we create a similar method for handling btnDrawEll. Often, delegate instances are created and immediately passed to a method. Using delegates in this code can be confusing. The code for btnDrawEll_Click() is functionally equivalent to btnDrawRect_Click(). Take your time to compare the two.

```
// Handle the Click event for the btnDrawEll button
private void btnDrawEll_Click(object sender, System.EventArgs e)
{
    // Use a shorter but more cryptic syntax.
    MyDrawShape(new DrawShape(CreateGraphics().FillEllipse));
}
```

Our final task is to use the delegate in the MyDrawShape() method, to invoke the required drawing operation. Here is the code for the MyDrawShape() method:

```
// MyDrawShape uses a delegate to indicate which method to call
private void MyDrawShape(DrawShape theDelegate )
{
    // Are any text fields blank?
    if (txtLeft.Text.Length == 0 || txtTop.Text.Length == 0 ||
        txtWidth.Text.Length == 0 || txtHeight.Text.Length == 0)
    {
```

```
    MessageBox.Show("Please fill in all text boxes", "Error",
                    MessageBoxButtons.OK,
                    MessageBoxIcon.Error);
    return;
}


// Get the coordinate values entered in the text fields
Rectangle aRect = new Rectangle(Int32.Parse(txtLeft.Text),
                               Int32.Parse(txtTop.Text),
                               Int32.Parse(txtWidth.Text),
                               Int32.Parse(txtHeight.Text));
// Make sure the coordinates are in range
if (mRect.Contains(aRect))
{
    // Get the color of the btnColor button
    Brush aBrush = new SolidBrush(btnColor.BackColor);
    // Call the delegate, to draw the specified shape
    theDelegate(aBrush, aRect);
}
else
{
    // Display error message, and return immediately
    MessageBox.Show("Coordinates are outside drawing area", "Error",
            MessageBoxButtons.OK, MessageBoxIcon.Error);
}
}
```

Note the following points in the MyDrawShape() method:

❑ MyDrawShape() takes a delegate of type DrawShape. The delegate object specifies the required drawing operation, and also specifies the Graphics object to use for the drawing operation. It's important to realize that MyDrawShape() has no idea what method is specified in the delegate. This makes it easier to extend the method in the future, for example if new kinds of drawing operation are introduced.

❑ MyDrawShape() performs various administrative tasks, such as getting the size, position, and color information entered by the user.

❑ MyDrawShape() uses the delegate to invoke the specified drawing method. Delegates can be called as if they were methods. As parameters, you must pass them the exact types specified in the delegate definition. For example, DrawShape takes a Brush parameter and a Rectangle parameter. If the target method has overloads with different parameters, these cannot be called using this delegate.

You can compile the application using the free command-line compiler or any graphical IDE, like Visual Studio .NET. To run the application, type the following command:

```
C:\Class Design\Ch 06> UsingDelegates.exe
```

The application runs, and we can then create rectangles and ellipses in any colors of our choice.

Fun though this is, it's perhaps useful to see how our application is compiled into MSIL code. Close the application, and type the following command at the command prompt (make sure ILDASM is in your system path):

```
C:\Class Design\Ch 06> ildasm UsingDelegates.exe
```

The MSIL Disassembler window displays the following information (we've expanded the nodes we're interested in this screenshot, to show the details for each of our types):

There's a great deal of information here, as you might expect in a Windows application. The important part as far as we are concerned is the MSIL code for DrawShape. Note the following points about DrawShape:

❑   DrawShape is a class. Whenever we define a new delegate type in our application, the compiler generates a class to encapsulate the information in the delegate's signature.

❑   The MSIL syntax extends [mscorlib]System.MulticastDelegate indicates that the generated class DrawShape inherits from a standard .NET Framework class named MulticastDelegate. We'll describe what we mean by **multicast delegates** later in this chapter. MulticastDelegate is logically located in the System namespace, and is physically located in the mscorlib assembly. We'll discuss inheritance in more detail in Chapter 7, and we'll investigate namespaces and assemblies in Chapter 8.

❑   DrawShape defines several methods in addition to those inherited from its super-class MulticastDelegate. First, it has methods named BeginInvoke() and EndInvoke(), which enable us to invoke methods asynchronously via the delegate, if required. In other words, we can use a delegate to invoke a method in a background thread; the main thread in the application can continue execution, without having to wait for the method to complete. We'll see an example of asynchronous delegates later in this chapter.

❑ DrawShape has another method named Invoke(), which enables us to invoke methods synchronously via the delegate. The compiler generated the Invoke() method from the signature we specified when we defined the DrawShape type. When we call the delegate, the compiler really generates IL code that calls the Invoke() method on our delegate instance. If you try to call the Invoke() method from your code, you'll see that the C# compiler raises an error, stating 'Invoke() cannot be called directly on a delegate'. In many other .NET languages, programmers have to call the Invoke() method themselves.

Creating and Using Multicast Delegates

The .NET Framework supports two distinct kinds of delegate:

❑ **Single-cast** delegates, which enable us to call a single method on a single object. We have seen how this works in the previous section.

❑ **Multicast** delegates, which enable us to call a series of methods on potentially different objects. Multicast delegates maintain an invocation list to remember which method to call on which object. When we call a multicast delegate, the delegate calls the specified methods on the designated objects, in sequence.

Actually, all delegates are multicast. Single-cast delegates are just delegates with only one method in their invocation list. But as the creation of a single-cast delegate (through the constructor) and a multicast delegate (by combining existing delegates) are so different, we treat them here as different entities.

Multicast delegates are useful if we need to perform the same operation on a collection of objects, or if we need to perform a series of operations on the same object, or any combination of these two cases. We can use multicast delegates implicitly to keep a collection of all the methods that need to be executed, and the objects upon which these methods are to be executed. Combining instances of the same delegate type creates multicast delegates.

To create and use a multicast delegate, we must follow these steps:

❑ Define a delegate type to represent the signature of the methods we want to call via the delegate. Multicast delegates can only be used to execute methods with the same signature, which is consistent with the general ethos of strong data typing with delegates.

❑ Write methods with the same signature as the delegate.

❑ Create a delegate object, and bind it to the first method we want to call via the delegate.

❑ Create another delegate object, and bind it to the next method we want to call.

❑ Call the Combine() method in the System.Delegate class to combine the two delegates into an integrated multicast delegate. The Combine() method returns a new delegate, whose invocation list contains both delegates.

❑ Repeat the previous two steps to create as many delegates as needed and combine them into an integrated multicast delegate.

❑ If we need to remove a delegate from a multicast delegate, call the Remove() method defined in the System.Delegate class. The Remove() method returns a new delegate, whose invocation list does not contain the removed delegate. If the delegate we just removed was the only delegate in the invocation list, the Remove() method returns null instead.

❑ When we are ready to invoke the methods specified by the multicast delegate, simply call the delegate as before. This invokes the methods in the order they appear in the invocation list, and returns only the result of the last method in the invocation list.

Besides the static methods Combine() and Remove() on the System.Delegate class, C# offers us another syntax to add or remove delegates to a multicast delegate: using the addition and subtraction operators (+ and -). You can just add two delegates together to create a new multicast delegate. The following two lines of code are equivalent:

```
// Combining DelegateA and DelegateB to CombinedDelegate
System.Delegate CombinedDelegate =
                System.Delegate.Combine(DelegateA, DelegateB);

// Idem
System.Delegate CombinedDelegate = DelegateA + DelegateB;
```

As always, these operators can be combined with the assignment operator to += and -=. This is actually the most common way to combine delegates in C#. The operator syntax often looks cleaner than using the Combine() and Remove() methods. The C# compiler translates the addition back to calls to the static methods (it is not an overloaded operator on the Delegate class).

To illustrate these concepts, and to show the C# syntax for multicast delegates, we'll work through a complete example that uses multicast delegates to paint any number of child forms in a Windows Forms application. The application has a main form that allows the user to create new child forms, and to change the color of all these forms at any time. The main form uses a multicast delegate to invoke a Repaint() method on each child form.

The source code for this example is located in the download folder DelegatesEvents\ MulticastDelegates. Before we look at the code, let's see how the application will work. The main form in the application appears as follows:

The user enters some screen coordinates, and then clicks Add Window to create the child form. At this stage in the application, we create a new delegate and bind it to the Repaint() method on the new child form. We combine this delegate into a multicast delegate in the main form, to keep track of all the open child forms.

The main form displays a message in its status bar to indicate the number of entries in the invocation list of the multicast delegate. This tells us how many child forms are currently open.

If the user clicks Add windows several times, we'll see several child forms on the screen. The multicast delegate keeps track of all these child forms. To be more precise, the invocation list in the multicast delegate holds the Repaint() method for each of the child forms:

When the user clicks Change Color to select a new color, we invoke the multicast delegate to repaint all the child forms. In other words, we call the multicast delegate, which invokes the Repaint() method on each child form. Each form repaints itself in the specified color:

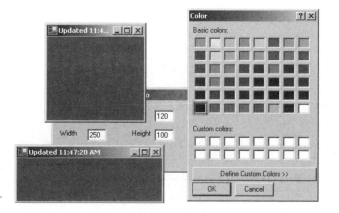

There is one more issue to consider. If the user closes a child form, we need to remove the corresponding delegate from the multicast delegate in the main form. To achieve this effect, the main form has a method named ChildFormClosing(), which the child form can call just before it closes. In the ChildFormClosing() method, we remove the child form's delegate from the multicast delegate, because we won't need to repaint the form in future.

❑ It is good practice to remove delegates from the invocation list when the objects they point to do not exist anymore. You may think an object is out of scope and will soon be garbage-collected, but the delegate is not only pointing to the method on the object, but also holds a reference to the object itself. Therefore, an object will remain in memory as long as the delegate is still in the invocation list.

Now that we've seen how the application works in principle, let's look at the code. The source code for the child form is fairly straightforward, because there is no delegate-related code in this class and child forms have no awareness of the other child forms in the application. The source code for the ChildForm class is provided in ChildForm.cs:

```
public class ChildForm : System.Windows.Forms.Form
{
    private System.ComponentModel.Container components = null;
    // omitted the constructor

    #region Windows Form Designer generated code
    // omitted for brevity
    #endregion

    private void ChildForm_Load(object sender, System.EventArgs e)
    {
        // Display the current time in the window's title bar
        this.Text = "Created " + DateTime.Now.ToLongTimeString();
    }

    // This method will be called via multicast delegate in main form
    public string Repaint(Color theColor)
    {
        // Set the color for this form, and update the caption bar
        this.BackColor = theColor;
        this.Text = "Updated " + DateTime.Now.ToLongTimeString();
        return this.Text;
    }

    // Handle the Cancel event for this form
    private void ChildForm_Closing(object sender,
                System.ComponentModel.CancelEventArgs e)
    {
        // Tell the main form we are closing, so the main form can
        // remove us from its multicast delegate
        Mainform MyOwner = (Mainform)this.Owner;
        MyOwner.ChildFormClosing(this);
    }

}
```

Note the following points in the ChildForm class:

❑ The ChildForm_Load() method displays the form's creation time on the caption bar.

❑ The Repaint() method has a Color parameter, to tell the form which color to repaint itself. The main form's multicast delegate calls this method whenever the user selects a new color.

❑ The ChildForm_Cancel() method informs the main form that this child form is about to close. We use the Owner property to get a reference to the main form, and then call its ChildFormClosing() method.

Now let's see the code for the main form in the application. This main form contains all the delegate-related processing. The first step is to define our delegate type, and to declare a field to refer to the multicast delegate object:

```
// define the Delegate type (and it's signature)
delegate string ChangeColorDelegate(Color aColor);

public class Mainform : System.Windows.Forms.Form
{
  // Declare a ChangeColorDelegate field,
  // to refer to the multicast delegate
  private ChangeColorDelegate mAllRepaintMethods;
}
```

Note the following points in the MainForm class definition above:

❑ ChangeColorDelegate defines the signature of the methods we want to call via this delegate type. As you'd expect, the delegate's signature matches that of the Repaint() method in the ChildForm class.

There is no difference in how we define single-cast delegate types and multicast delegate types in C#. In fact, every delegate type in C# is implicitly a multicast delegate. It's up to us whether we use the delegate to represent a single method or several methods.

❑ mAllRepaintMethods is a field that will point to the multicast delegate. In other words, mAllRepaintMethods will refer to a ChangeColorDelegate instance. Initially, mAllRepaintMethods is null because there are no child forms yet. When we create the first child form, we'll create a new ChangeColorDelegate instance and assign it to mAllRepaintMethods.

Now let's see how to create a new child form, and combine its Repaint() method into our multicast delegate:

```
// Handle the click event on the btnAddWindow button
// the registration of this method for the Click event is done
// elsewhere

private void btnAddWindow_Click(object sender, System.EventArgs e)
{
  // Are any text fields blank?
  if (txtLeft.Text.Length == 0 || txtTop.Text.Length == 0 ||
    txtWidth.Text.Length == 0 || txtHeight.Text.Length == 0)
  {
    MessageBox.Show("Please fill in all text boxes",
        "Error",
        MessageBoxButtons.OK,
        MessageBoxIcon.Error);
        return;
  }

    ChildForm aChildForm = new ChildForm();
    aChildForm.Owner = this;
    aChildForm.DesktopBounds = new Rectangle(
      Int32.Parse(txtLeft.Text),
      Int32.Parse(txtTop.Text),
      Int32.Parse(txtWidth.Text),
      Int32.Parse(txtHeight.Text));
    aChildForm.Show();

    // Create a new delegate for the child form's Repaint method
    ChangeColorDelegate newDelegate = new ChangeColorDelegate
                                    (aChildForm.Repaint);

    // Combine new delegate into the multicast delegate
    mAllRepaintMethods = (ChangeColorDelegate)System.Delegate.Combine(
                            mAllRepaintMethods, newDelegate);

    // Use multicast delegate to count the child forms
    sbStatus.Text = "Created child form " +
    mAllRepaintMethods.GetInvocationList().Length + ".";

}
```

Note the following points in the btnAddWindow_Click() method shown above:

❑   We begin by verifying if the user has entered numbers in all the text fields. If all is well, we create a new child form with the specified location and size, and display the form on the screen. We specify the main form as the Owner of the child form.

❑   We create a new ChangeColorDelegate instance, and bind it to the Repaint() method on the new child form.

❑   We use the static Combine() method on System.Delegate to add the newDelegate instance to the invocation list of the multicast delegate mAllRepaintMethods. The first time when mAllRepaintMethods is not yet initialized, the Combine() method returns the passed newDelegate instance.

❑ Delegates have a GetInvocationList() method, which returns an array of delegate objects representing all the entries in the multicast delegate. We can use the Length property to find the size of this array. In our example, this tells us how many child forms are currently open.

The line of code that performs the actual combination of the new delegate with the existing delegates into one new multicast delegate could also have been written like this:

```
mAllRepaintMethods += newDelegate;
```

In the resulting MSIL code, this would look identical. Once the user has created some child forms, they can click Change Color to change the color of these forms. The following code achieves this:

```
private void btnChangeColor_Click(object sender, System.EventArgs e)
{
  if(mAllRepaintMethods == null)
  {
    MessageBox.Show("There are no child forms to change.",
      "Error changing color",
      MessageBoxButtons.OK,
      MessageBoxIcon.Error);
  }
  else
  {
    // Ask user to choose a color
    ColorDialog dlgColor = new ColorDialog();
    dlgColor.ShowDialog();

    // Invoke multicast delegate, to repaint all the child forms
    mAllRepaintMethods (dlgColor.Color );

    // Use multicast delegate to count the child forms
    sbStatus.Text = "Updated " +
      mAllRepaintMethods.GetInvocationList().Length +
      " child form(s).";
  }
}
```

Note the following points in the btnColors_Click() method shown above:

❑ If mAllRepaintMethods is null, there are no child forms open, so we display an error message and return immediately. It is very easy to use the multicast delegate to keep track of the presence or absence of child forms.

❑ If mAllRepaintMethods is not null, we ask the user to choose a new color for the existing forms. We then call our multicast delegate, to invoke the Repaint() method on all the child forms. Again, it is convenient to use the multicast delegate to iterate through the child forms and repaint each one.

❑ We display a message in the status bar of the main form to indicate how many child forms have been repainted. As before, we get this information by calling GetInvocationList on the multicast delegate.

The final method we need to look at in the MainForm class is the ChildFormClosing() method. Child forms call this method just before they close, to enable the main form to keep track of its child forms. The code for the ChildFormClosing() method is shown below:

```
public void ChildFormClosing(ChildForm aChildForm )
{
  // Create a dummy delegate for the ChildForm that is closing
  ChangeColorDelegate unneededDelegate =
            new ChangeColorDelegate ( aChildForm.Repaint);

  // Remove the delegate from the multicast delegate
  mAllRepaintMethods = (ChangeColorDelegate)System.Delegate.Remove(
    mAllRepaintMethods, unneededDelegate);

  // If multicast delegate is Nothing, there are no child forms left
  if (mAllRepaintMethods == null)
  {
    sbStatus.Text = "Final child form has been closed.";
  }
  else
  {
    // Use multicast delegate to count the child forms
    sbStatus.Text = "Child form closed, " +
      mAllRepaintMethods.GetInvocationList().Length  +
      " form(s) remaining.";
  }
}
```

Note the following points in the ChildFormClosing() method shown above:

❑ The ChildFormClosing() method receives a ChildForm parameter, to indicate which child form is closing.

❑ We create a new delegate, and bind it to the Repaint() method on the soon-to-be-defunct child form. We then call the Remove() method in the System.Delegate class, to remove this delegate from the multicast delegate. The Remove() method returns one of two possible values:

• If we've just removed the final delegate from the multicast delegate, the multicast delegate no longer exists. In this case, the Remove() method returns null.

• Otherwise, the Remove() method returns a new multicast delegate that does not contain the removed delegate.

❑ Note that delegates exhibit value semantics; even though we have created a new delegate pointing to the method, we can use it to remove another delegate pointing to the same method. The two delegates are considered equivalent. If multiple delegates in the list point to the same method on the same object, only the first will be removed.

❑ We display an appropriate message in the status bar of the main form, to indicate how many child forms are left.

We could have written the code removing one of the delegates from the invocation list much shorter like this:

```
// Remove the delegate from the multicast delegate
mAllRepaintMethods -= unneededDelegate;
```

The code for the application is complete. To run the application, type the following command:

```
C:\Class Design\Ch 06> MainForm.exe
```

The application appears as follows, and enables us to open child windows and set their colors as previously advertised:

Multicast delegates make it easy to maintain a collection of objects that need to be notified in unison when something important happens. When we invoke the multicast delegate, it implicitly iterates through all the entries in its invocation list to call the specified method on each designated object.

Creating and Using Asynchronous Delegates

All of the examples we have seen so far have used delegates to invoke methods synchronously by calling the delegate directly. When we invoke a method synchronously, we have to wait for the method to return before we can continue processing.

We can also use delegates to invoke methods asynchronously. This means we can invoke the method in a background thread, and continue doing useful work in the main thread at the same time. This can be useful if we have lengthy tasks to perform.

To support asynchronous method calls via delegates, the C# compiler generates the following two methods in our delegate class (in addition to the Invoke() method, to support synchronous method calls):

❑ BeginInvoke()
We call BeginInvoke() to invoke the required method asynchronously, in a background thread.

❑   EndInvoke()
    After the specified method has completed execution, we can call
    EndInvoke() to get the return value from the method. EndInvoke() also
    allows us to access any output parameters from the method; for example, if
    the method takes parameters ByRef, and modifies these parameters during
    execution, we can use EndInvoke() to get the modified values for these
    parameters. If the method has not completed execution yet, the application
    will wait (and halt) until the return values are available, so be careful with
    calling EndInvoke().

There are several ways to use asynchronous delegates, depending on our needs. Here
are the possibilities, in order of increasing complexity:

❑   Invoke a method that does not return a result

❑   Invoke a method that returns a result, and wait a finite time for the result

❑   Invoke a method that returns a result, and define a callback method to
    receive the result whenever it arrives

To get a feel for the possibilities, we will have a look at a sample application that uses
all three possibilities and displays timing results for each. The source code for this
example is located in the download folder DelegatesEvents\AsyncDelegates.
Before we look at the code, let's see what the application will do. The application has
only one form. When you compile the application and run it, you will see this:

When you click any of the three buttons, the application will start downloading three
XML files from the Internet (you need a working network connection for testing this
example). They contain the top articles in three categories from the Slashdot website.
When a file is completely downloaded and parsed by the System.Xml.XmlDocument
class, we display the time in milliseconds since you clicked the button. So after
downloading the three files, the screen would look something like this:

As you can see, each of the downloads takes approximately 900 ms (in your
environment it may of course take longer or shorter, depending on your connection).
As the files are more or less of the same size and are served from the same server,
which is what we would expect.

First let's have a look at the synchronous code. It is called when the user clicks the
Load Synchronous button.

```
public class Mainform : System.Windows.Forms.Form
{
  private ArrayList mUrlList;

  private void Mainform_Load(object sender, System.EventArgs e)
  {
    // Initialising a list of three Urls containing valid Xml content
    mUrlList = new ArrayList();
    mUrlList.Add("http://slashdot.org/slashdot.rdf");
    mUrlList.Add("http://slashdot.org/science.rdf");
    mUrlList.Add("http:// slashdot.org/books.rdf");
  }

  private void btnSync_Click(object sender, System.EventArgs e)
  {
    // Clear the output
    ClearLog();
    // Initialise an array of XmlDocument objects
    XmlDocument[] Documents = new XmlDocument[mUrlList.Count];
    for (int i = 0; i<mUrlList.Count; i++)
    {
      Documents[i] = new XmlDocument();
      // Both the loading of the content over the network
      // and the parsing of this content happens in the next line.
      Documents[i].Load((string)mUrlList[i]);
      AppendLog("Loaded document from " + mUrlList[i]);
    }
  }
}
```

Note the following points:

❑   The `Mainform_Load()` method initializes the `ArrayList` of URLs we
     want to download; these URLs are hard coded.

❑   In the `btnSync_Click()` method, we use the methods `ClearLog()` and
     `AppendLog()`. The code of these methods is not printed here, but you can
     check them out in the code download. They manage the logging of timed
     milliseconds to the textbox on the form.

❑   `btnSync_Click()` itself is fairly straightforward: in a `for` loop, all of the URLs
     in `mUrlList` are used to load an `XmlDocument` object from the Internet. The
     `Load()` method on `XmlDocument` will wait until all of the remote resource has
     been downloaded and parsed and no errors have been encountered.

It doesn't matter if you have never worked with the classes in the `System.Xml`
namespace before because it is not relevant here. We just use the
`XmlDocument.Load()` method as an example of a long lasting operation.

Most of the 3 x 900ms, we are waiting for the network request, due to bandwidth and network delays. It would be much more efficient to make the three requests first (this takes hardly any bandwidth) and then wait for all requests at the same time. This traditionally required spawning additional threads and having each thread do a request and wait for its response. Multithreaded programming is hard to do well and errors are difficult to debug. Now with asynchronous calling of delegates, we can actually achieve a lot of the power of multithreaded programming without most of the pain. For a number of situations, the delegates actually do the multithreaded programming for us. These are:

❏   Calling a long-lasting operation without freezing the user interface.

❏   Calling multiple operations at the same time to use resources more efficiently

More complex multithreaded scenarios (like having a worker thread that monitors a resource) cannot be programmed with delegates. Check out the `System.Threading` namespace's documentation for more information. Be aware of the fact that your call creates a new thread that consumes resources. Calling a delegate asynchronously 10,000 times in a loop will slow down your system.

Now let's look at the code for the asynchronous approach. We start by defining a delegate suitable for calling the `Load()` method on `XmlDocument`:

```
delegate void DocumentLoad(string fileUrl);
```

Instead of calling the method directly, we can now create a delegate of type `DocumentLoad` and have the delegate call the method for us. To call it asynchronously, we would use the `BeginInvoke()` method on the delegate. The simplest way to use it would be like this:

```
private void btnAsync_Click(object sender, System.EventArgs e)
{
  ClearLog();
  XmlDocument[] Documents = new XmlDocument[mUrlList.Count];
  for (int i = 0; i<mUrlList.Count; i++)
  {
    XmlDocument Document[i] = new XmlDocument();
    DocumentLoad MyDelegate = new DocumentLoad(Document[i].Load);
    MyDelegate.BeginInvoke((string)mUrlList[i], null, null);
    AppendLog("Loaded document from " + mUrlList[i]);
  }
}
```

The two extra parameters that are passed to the delegate's `BeginInvoke()` method will be explained later. In this case, we just pass in `null`. If you work in Visual Studio .NET, you will notice that the IntelliSense support does not work on the `BeginInvoke()` and `EndInvoke()` methods.

This code will indeed call the Load() method for all three of the XmlDocuments. When BeginInvoke() is called, the method returns immediately, but on a different thread that was created by the delegate it is still busy loading the document. So when we call the AppendLog() method, we are not sure if the loading is completed yet (in fact we are quite sure that it is not).

In some cases, you don't really care when a method is finished, you just want to start it and go on with your main task. In these cases, calling BeginInvoke() like this may do the trick. But normally, you eventually need to know the results of the operation. In this case, you must hold on to the delegate and the return value from BeginInvoke().

You cannot get at a return value when the method calculating. It is still running on another thread. To get the return value from an asynchronous method call we use the EndInvoke() method. When you call this method, the delegate will hold the execution until the original call to the underlying method is completed. Be careful not to call EndInvoke() unless waiting for the completion of the method is OK. The EndInvoke() method returns the return value from the underlying method. The return type of the EndInvoke() method is always equal to the return value of the delegate itself.

If the method you call uses ref or out parameters, you can also get at the new values for these through EndInvoke(). We will not go into that here, but you can check the order of the parameters by looking into your delegate with ILDASM.exe.

EndInvoke() always expects an object implementing IAsyncResult as a parameter. For this parameter, you must use the return value you got from BeginInvoke(). This object is like a receipt for retrieving the return value through EndInvoke(). This mechanism is necessary because you can call the same delegate multiple times through BeginInvoke() (perhaps using different parameters). Now if you call EndInvoke(), the delegate must make sure exactly which call to BeginInvoke() you want to end. If you are not going to call EndInvoke anyway, you don't need the IAsyncResult object.

So, let's look at asynchronous downloading where we don't log the duration until the download is really complete:

```
private void btnAsync_Click(object sender, System.EventArgs e)
{
  ClearLog();
  // As we will now be working with several objects at the same time,
  // we declare arrays of XmlDocument, Delegate and the IAsyncResult
  XmlDocument[] Documents = new XmlDocument[mUrlList.Count];
  DocumentLoad[] Delegates = new DocumentLoad[mUrlList.Count];

  // VS.NET does not support arrays of interface type with
  // Intellisense, but this code is valid C# and compiles fine
  IAsyncResult[] Tickets = new IAsyncResult[mUrlList.Count];

  for (int i = 0; i<mUrlList.Count; i++)
```

```
{
    Documents[i] = new XmlDocument();
    Delegates[i] = new DocumentLoad(Documents[i].Load);
    // The next line starts the loading of the XmlDocument on a
    // different thread. We don't have to wait for its
    // completion now. The two null parameters at the end
    // are for use with callback functions.
    Tickets[i] = Delegates[i].BeginInvoke(
                (string)mUrlList[i], null, null);
    AppendLog("Started loading document from " + mUrlList[i]);
}
for (int i = 0; i<mUrlList.Count; i++)
{
    // Force to wait here until the call is completed. We
    // could have called BeginInvoke multiple times on the
    // same delegate instance, so we need the ticket (of
    // type IAsyncResult) to specify which call we mean exactly.
    Delegates[i].EndInvoke(Tickets[i]);
    AppendLog("Loaded document from " + mUrlList[i]);
}
}
```

First we loop through the list of URLs and for each URL create an XmlDocument instance and a DocumentLoad instance pointing at the Load() method of the XmlDocument object. Both the XmlDocument instances and the delegates pointing at them are stored in arrays. We need them again when we want to end the asynchronous operation. We then call BeginInvoke() on the delegate and store the returned object in a third array.

When all three delegates are started off, we could theoretically start doing some other processor-intensive work, as we have hundreds of milliseconds before the first response comes in. But as we don't have anything to do in this application, we just enter a second loop, where we wait for the three threads to finish. In the starting order, we call EndInvoke() on the delegate, passing it the appropriate ticket. Execution now halts until the method called by the delegate has completed. After completion, we log the time and go on to the next delegate.

What would we expect from the times logged for this situation? Well, for the first request, we would not expect much difference. Maybe a small delay caused by the creation of threads and the overhead of dealing with them. By clicking the second button, we get the following result:

Calling the EndInvoke() method as soon as you need the results is a good solution when you have an approximate idea of how long the operation will take. Sometimes waiting just isn't an option. Sometimes you want the application to start working without the results from the operation (you could gray out all functionality that needs the results to work properly and enable it as soon as the necessary information comes available). In these cases, callback functions are the solution. You must implement a method with a predefined signature and tell the delegate to call the callback method as soon as execution completes.

In our case, we would just use the callback method to create a line in the log, but you could also call EndInvoke() from the callback method and access the return value from the executed method. This is what the results might look like on screen:

Note that the order of starting the three downloads is not necessarily the same as the order of completing them. Let's look at the code:

```
private void btnCallback_Click(object sender, System.EventArgs e)
{
  ClearLog();

  XmlDocument[] Documents = new XmlDocument[mUrlList.Count];

  for (int i = 0; i<mUrlList.Count; i++)
  {
    Documents[i] = new XmlDocument();
    DocumentLoad TheDelegate = new DocumentLoad(Documents[i].Load);
    AsyncCallback CallbackDelegate = new
        AsyncCallback(this.ReadyLoading);

    // We start the loading of the XMLDocument, passing it
    // a delegate for calling the ReadyLoading method when
    // it is ready. A reference to the current XmlDocument
    // is also passed in. This will be passed to the callback
    // method as the AsyncState property of the IAsyncResult.

    TheDelegate.BeginInvoke((string)mUrlList[i],
        CallbackDelegate, Documents[i]);
    AppendLog("Started loading document from " + mUrlList[i]);
  }

}
```

```
private void ReadyLoading(IAsyncResult r)
{
  if (r.AsyncState is XmlDocument)
  {
    XmlDocument doc = (XmlDocument)r.AsyncState;
    AppendLog("Loaded " + doc.BaseURI);
  }
}
```

Starting at the bottom, we first see the actual callback function. It has the signature defined by the standard delegate `System.AsyncCallback`. If the `IAsyncResult.AsyncState` property of the passed object is of type `XmlDocument`, it adds a line to the log. The `AsyncState` property is filled by the code that initiates the asynchronous call.

If you look at the code starting the execution, you will see that we now actually use two delegates, one to point at the method to start executing and another one (of type `System.AsyncCallback`) to point at the callback method. This delegate is passed as the second parameter in `BeginInvoke()`. The third parameter is optional. Anything you pass there will be passed to the callback function as `IAsyncResult.AsyncState`. In this case we pass the `XmlDocument` instance itself. We use it in the callback method to log the URL of the loaded document.

So, we have seen three ways of calling a delegate instance:

❑   Synchronously, waiting for the method (or methods) to complete. This is by far the most common use of delegates.

❑   Asynchronously, waiting for the method to complete (by calling `EndInvoke()`), but only just before you need it to be completed.

❑   Asynchronously, registering a callback method to notify you as soon as execution completes.

Each is appropriate in different situations: it really depends on how hard you need the results from the method and how long the wait might take. Note that you cannot use asynchronous calling on multicast delegates. The delegate will throw an exception.

Events

In the first half of this chapter, we've seen how to use delegates to invoke methods on objects. We've seen how to use single-cast delegates to invoke single methods, and how to use multicast delegates to store multiple methods in an invocation list and call them in sequence. We've also seen that we can use delegates to invoke methods asynchronously, if required.

In the second half of this chapter, we turn our attention to events. The .NET Framework event model relies on delegates to indicate which methods to call when a particular event is raised. Events in the .NET Framework are implemented using delegates to store the subscribed event handling methods and to call them when the event is raised.

Most programmers will be familiar with the use of events in GUI applications. Interaction between user interface elements and application code is one of the most important uses of events, but events can be used in many other scenarios as well. Events in the .NET Framework are an implementation of the Observer design pattern. In this pattern, the object that can be observed exposes methods for registering and unregistering interested observer objects for notifications. When we program objects in C#, we can have most of this functionality created for us automatically.

Figure 1

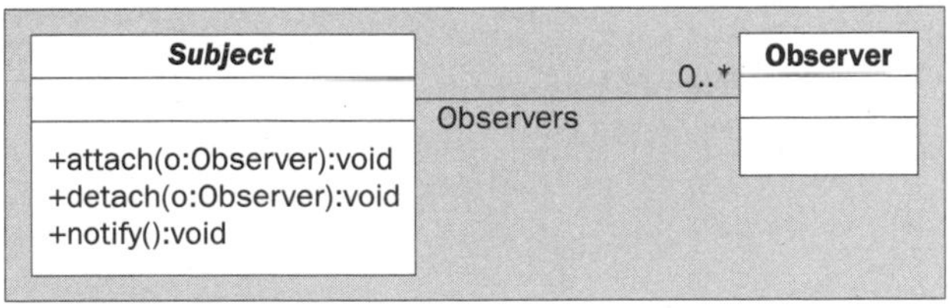

We'll examine the following issues in this section:

- ❏   What is the event architecture in the .NET Framework?

- ❏   How do we publish events?

- ❏   How do we subscribe to events?

- ❏   How do we raise events?

Event Architecture

Here is a brief summary of the event architecture in the .NET Framework. We've also provided a formal definition for some of the key terms associated with event processing in .NET:

An object that can raise events is known as an **event source**. For example, a Button object is an event source because it raises events such as Click and MouseEnter. The event source **publishes** the events it can raise; in C#, we use the event keyword to publish an event in a class definition. The type of an event is always a delegate type; the signature of this delegate type defines the signature of methods that can handle the event.

Objects that define event handler methods are known as **event receivers**. Event receivers **subscribe** to the events they wish to handle on the event source. An event receiver must provide an event-handler method with the correct signature for the event it is subscribing to. The event source uses a multicast delegate to keep track of these event-handler methods.

The event source **raises** events when something important happens. For example, `Button` objects raise the `Click` event when the user clicks the button control on the screen. When an event is raised, the event source automatically uses its multicast delegate to call the specified event-handler method on each event receiver.

The following diagram illustrates the relationship between an event-source object and event-receiver object(s):

Figure 2

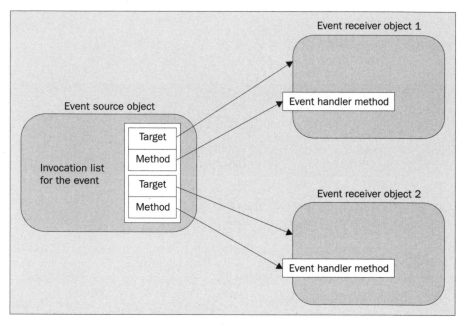

In this simple example, the event-source object only raises a single kind of event. The event-source object has an invocation list for this event, to keep track of the event-receiver objects that have subscribed to this event. Each entry in the invocation list stores two pieces of information:

❑   `Target` is a reference to an event-receiver object

❑   `Method` is a reference to the event-handler method on the event-receiver object

When the event source object raises an event, it uses the information in the invocation list to call each of the registered event-handler methods.

In the above figure, we've only shown the event-handler methods in the event-receiver objects. In reality, the event-receiver objects will have additional methods, properties, fields, and so on.

It should not come as a surprise that .NET uses a multicast delegate to provide the infrastructure for maintaining an invocation list of targets and methods.

So much for the theory, let's see how to use events in real C# code. We'll begin by seeing how to define events in a class.

Publishing and Subscribing to Events

To publish events in C#, we must declare event members in the event-source class. We must specify two pieces of information for each event:

❏ **The name of the event**
For example, the Button class publishes events named Click, MouseOver, and so on. We should declare event members for things that can happen to instances of our class, which might interest other objects.

❏ **The signature (parameter list) of the event**
When the event-source object raises the event, it will supply values for these parameters. These values will be passed to the event-handler method in the event-receiver object. This implies the event-handler methods must have the same signature as the event. The signature of an event is set by declaring the type of the event. This type must be a delegate.

For a simple example of a class exposing an event, have a look at the BankAccount class in the SimpleEvent project. You can find this project in the folder DelegatesEvents\SimpleEvent in the source code download.

Publishing our Event

First, we have a look at the structure of the code publishing the event in the BankAccount class:

```
using System;

public class BankAccount
{
  public BankAccount(string name)
  {
    mBalance = 0;
    mAccountName = name;
  }

  public event EventHandler Overdrawn;

  private double mBalance;
  private string mAccountName;

  public string Name{get{return mAccountName;}}
  public double Balance{get{return mBalance;}}

  public void Credit(double Amount)
  {
  }

  public void Debit(double Amount)
  {
  }
}
```

This class is fairly simple. It holds two private fields, `mBalance` and `mAccountName`. Both can be accessed through a read-only property. The account name can only be set through the constructor, while the balance can be changed by calling the methods `Debit()` and `Credit()`, but these have no implementation yet (we will see them implemented soon, when we deal with raising events). The only remarkable line is the one defining the event member.

We have used `System.EventHandler` as the type of our event. `System.EventHandler` is a built-in delegate, specially intended for use with simple events that do not need to pass any additional information to the event receiver. It is used by many events in the framework (for example the `Click` event in `Button`).

Events are members of the class, and can therefore have an access modifier. The default accessibility is `public`, because the nature of events is to broadcast information to other objects in the application. However, it is also possible to restrict event accessibility if appropriate:

- ❑ We can declare events as `private`, which means only methods in our own class can register as event-handler methods. We can use this technique to trigger behavior in our own class. For example, we might have a background thread that triggers a `Tick` event every second, and define event-handler methods in our class to perform tasks on each timer tick. Such a pattern is rare, but can lead to quite elegant code.

- ❑ We can declare events as `internal`, which means only methods in the same assembly can register as event-handler methods. We can use this technique in large applications that are spread over several assemblies. To reduce dependencies between assemblies, we can define class members with `internal` accessibility so that they cannot be accessed in other assemblies. This makes it easier to change the code inside one assembly, without adversely affecting the code in any other assembly. We investigate assemblies in detail in Chapter 8.

- ❑ We can declare events as `protected`, which means only methods in this class, or classes that inherit from this class, can register as event-handler methods.

The name of the event in this example is `Overdrawn`. Later in the chapter, we'll see how to raise this event when the customer tries to withdraw too much money from the account.

Events cannot have a return type. Events constitute a one-way flow of information from the event-source object to the event-receiver objects. It is an error to specify a return type in an event definition. As such, while events make use of delegates, it's clear there are ways we can use delegates that are not exposed by events. Ignoring the other capabilities of delegates and just using the event infrastructure would be a mistake.

The code looks deceivingly simple, but actually accomplishes several things:

- ❏ Publishes the event name and signature for event receivers
- ❏ Creates registration methods for registering and unregistering event receivers
- ❏ Keeps track of registered event receivers in an invocation list

By compiling the file as a .dll file and looking at the executable with ILDASM.exe, we can see these three pieces of the functionality appearing in our class.

```
C:\Class Design\Ch 06\DelegatesEvents\SimpleEvent>csc /t:library
BankAccount.cs
Microsoft (R) Visual C# .NET Compiler version 7.00.9466
for Microsoft (R) .NET Framework version 1.0.3705
Copyright (C) Microsoft Corporation 2001. All rights reserved.

C:\Class Design\Ch 06\DelegatesEvents\SimpleEvent>ildasm
BankAccount.dll
```

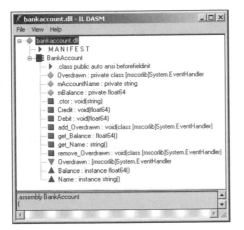

In the compiled MSIL code, we find four members related to our event declaration:

- ❏ **A private field of type EventHandler called OverDrawn**
  This field will hold an instance of System.EventHandler. It is used to store all of the registered event handlers as one multicast delegate. When the object is instantiated it is set to null. Note that this field is always private, even is the event itself is public.

- ❏ **A public method called add_OverDrawn()**
  The compiler generated this method to add a new event handler for the Overdrawn event. This method is called whenever another event-receiver subscribes to this event. Notice the add_Overdrawn() method receives a parameter of type EventHandler. This parameter is an instance of the EventHandler delegate type, and specifies a new event-receiver object and event-handler method for the Overdrawn event.

Open up the IL and take a look at statements IL_0002, IL_0007, and IL_0008. These statements combine the new delegate instance into the Overdrawn multicast delegate member in our BankAccount object. Notice the MSIL call to the method System.Delegate::Combine(), to combine the new delegate into the multicast delegate.

❑ **A public method called remove_OverDrawn()**
The compiler generated this method, to remove an existing event handler for the Overdrawn event. This method is called whenever an event receiver unsubscribes from this event. Looking at the MSIL, you'll find remove_Overdrawn() is similar to add_Overdrawn(), except that we now call the System.Delegate: :Remove() method to remove the specified delegate.

❑ **An event declaration called OverDrawn**
This member is only used during compilation of classes using this class, to identify the names of the methods for adding and removing event handlers for the Overdrawn event. It's similar in form to the property members we saw in Chapter 5, which pointed to the getter and setter methods. The MSIL code for this member is shown below:

```
BankAccount::Overdrawn : [mscorlib]System.EventHandler               _ | □ | x |
.event [mscorlib]System.EventHandler Overdrawn
{
  .addon instance void BankAccount::add_Overdrawn(class [mscorlib]System.EventHandler)
  .removeon instance void BankAccount::remove_Overdrawn(class [mscorlib]System.EventHandler)
} // end of event BankAccount::Overdrawn
```

So apparently, the C# compiler creates registration methods by just prefixing the name of the event with add_ and remove_. This means that you cannot use these names for your own methods. The following code cannot be compiled:

```
public event EventHandler Overdrawn;
public void add_Overdrawn(EventHandler e)
{
}
```

When you try to compile it, it will raise an exception: 'Class 'BankAccount' already defines a member called 'add_Overdrawn' with the same parameter types'.

Registering to a Published Event

Once we have a class publishing an event, we will try to register a method of ours as an event handler. To see how this works, have a look at the code for the BankAccountForm class in the same project.

Apart from the usual forms code, we find the following methods:

```
private BankAccount mBankAccount;
public BankAccountForm()
{
  //
  // Required for Windows Form Designer support
  //
  InitializeComponent();

  mBankAccount = new BankAccount("Teun Duynstee");
  RefreshTitle();
  mBankAccount.Overdrawn |= new
    EventHandler(this.OverdrawnHandlerMethod);
}

private void RefreshTitle()
{
  this.Text = String.Format("Account {0}, balance: {1}",
              mBankAccount.Name, mBankAccount.Balance );
}

private void btnCredit_Click(object sender, System.EventArgs e)
{
  mBankAccount.Credit(Double.Parse(txtAmount.Text));
  RefreshTitle();
}

private void btnDebit_Click(object sender, System.EventArgs e)
{
  mBankAccount.Debit(Double.Parse(txtAmount.Text));
  RefreshTitle();
}

private void OverdrawnHandlerMethod(object sender,
                   System.EventArgs e)
{
  MessageBox.Show("The bank account has been overdrawn. " +
    "The current balance is " + mBankAccount.Balance,
    "Overdrawn",
    MessageBoxButtons.OK,
    MessageBoxIcon.Information);
}
```

Note the following points:

❑ In the form's constructor, we create an instance of BankAccount and attach the method OverdrawnHandlerMethod() as a handler for the Overdrawn event. The syntax is rather verbose; we create a delegate of the type specified by the event. This delegate points at our handler method. Using the += operator, we add this delegate to the list of registered event receivers for this event. The += syntax is the only way in C# to connect a handler method to an event. In other .NET languages, the syntax may be quite different, but in the MSIL, the result should be identical. This guarantees us that programmers in other .NET languages can register for our event without problems or special considerations.

❑ The `OverdrawnHandlerMethod()` method just shows a message in a message box. The two parameters that are passed are not used. The first parameter is a reference to the object that raised the event. In our case, this is the `mBankAccount` object. We already have a reference to this object, so in this case we don't bother casting the sender parameter to `BankAccount`. The `System.EventArgs` object we get passed in the second parameter is rather useless. In more complex events, this object contains any additional information about the event. We will have a look at these event arguments later in this chapter.

❑ The `RefreshTitle`, `btnCredit_Click`, and `btnDebit_Click` methods don't do anything that would surprise you. They just use the available methods and properties on `BankAccount` to allow a user to perform operations on the `BankAccount` object.

Let's look at the part of the code marked Windows Form Designer generated code:

```
// A lot of other controls and properties have been omitted here
this.btnCredit = new System.Windows.Forms.Button();
this.btnDebit = new System.Windows.Forms.Button();

// btnCredit
this.btnCredit.Text = "Credit";
this.btnCredit.Click += new
                    System.EventHandler(this.btnCredit_Click);

// btnDebit
this.btnDebit.Text = "Debit";
this.btnDebit.Click += new System.EventHandler(this.btnDebit_Click);
```

Directly after instantiating the buttons and setting the properties, an `EventHandler` delegate instance is created, pointing to the methods in the form. Then the delegate instance is added to the `Click` event of the button.

When using a form's editor in a graphical development environment, you will normally have only one event handler method for each event on the form and any event handler method will normally handle only one event.

Raising the Event

For our simple example to work, we need the event to be raised. The obvious place to raise the `Overdrawn` event would be in the `Debit()` method of the `BankAccount` class. We had temporarily left the implementation of the `Debit()` and `Credit()` methods empty, but here is what they look like in the `BankAccount` class:

```
public void Credit(double Amount)
{
   mBalance += Amount;
}

public void Debit(double Amount)
{
```

```
mBalance -= Amount;
if (mBalance < 0)
{
  if (Overdrawn != null)
  {
    Overdrawn(this, new EventArgs());
  }
}
}
```

Both `Credit()` and `Debit()` make the appropriate changes to the `mBalance` field, but in `Debit()`, we also check if the result is lower than 0. If this is the case, we want to raise the `Overdrawn` event. As `Overdrawn` is implemented as a multicast delegate, raising the event comes down to calling the delegate. Two important points should be noted here:

❑ Before anyone has registered for the event, the `Overdrawn` field equals `null`. If you try to call `null`, a runtime exception will be thrown. When raising an event in C#, you must always first check if the delegate you call is not `null`.

❑ Like all predefined event handler classes, the signature of `System.EventHandler` returns `void` and has two parameters. In the first parameter, you must always pass a reference to the event-raising object (`this`). The second parameter must be an instance of `System.EventArgs`. `System.EventArgs` is like a dummy class. It can contain no information at all and is intended for use with events that pass no information anyway (like `Overdrawn`) and to serve as a base class for events that do.

The next section (*Creating Events that Pass Information*) will go into this. In our code, we created an instance of `System.EventArgs` by calling new `EventArgs()`, but `EventArgs()` also exposes a static property `Empty` that returns a new instance of the class as well. Some people prefer `EventArgs.Empty` to the new syntax.

The `Debit()` and `Credit()` methods should really also check for negative amounts and throw an exception whenever this happens, but that is beyond the scope of this example.

That completes our simple events example. We have created a `BankAccount` class exposing an `Overdrawn` event. On specific occasions (when the `Debit()` method is called and the resulting balance is lower than 0), the class raises the event. In our sample application, we have a main form using an instance of the class for performing bank transactions. On loading the form, it creates a new instance of `BankAccount` and registers for the event. When an event occurs, the form displays a message box informing us of the situation.

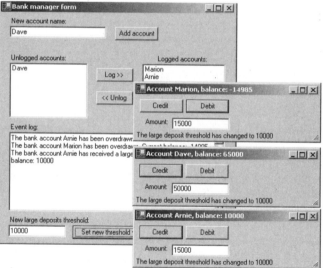

Creating Events that Pass Information

Leaving the really simple events behind us, we now move on to the next sample application: DelegatesEvents\AdvancedEvents. We will use this application to show several of the more advanced event features. Eventually, the application will consist of a large bank manager form, which can be used to create many small bank account forms (like the one in SimpleEvent). The bank manager can select for which of the active accounts to have the events logged to the event log screen. Besides the Overdrawn event, the bank accounts also raise an event for a large deposit (when the deposit is larger than the threshold value). When the manager changes the large deposit threshold, all of the bank account forms are notified of this fact.

When it is running, the application looks like this:

The first thing we will look into is defining events that pass information to their event destination. Most of the time, the notification alone is not enough. In our sample, we have an event called LargeDeposit. When some object is interested in the fact that a large deposit has just occurred on our BankAccount instance, they probably also want to know **how** large a deposit it was. The System.EventHandler type does not allow us to pass this amount to the event receiver, but we can of course define another delegate that does. In the first half of this chapter we have seen how this is done. Based on that experience, you might want to use the following code:

```
// Bad practice, do not do this
public event MyDelegate LargeDeposit;

public delegate void MyDelegate(BankAccount b, double Amount);
```

You could just declare a delegate that has a signature that includes not only the BankAccount that raised the event, but also a double containing the amount of the deposit. This would actually work just fine, but it does not follow the convention that Microsoft follows for both naming and signatures for events, delegates, and their arguments.

The name of the delegate type should follow the form XxxEventHandler. The signature is standardized; the return value should be void and there are two parameters:

❑ First parameter should refer to the object raising the event. It is often declared as an object, to allow any kind of object to use the event, but if you are sure that the event will only ever be raised by BankAccount() (in this case), you can also type it more specifically and prevent many unnecessary castings.

❑ The second parameter should hold an instance of a subclass of System.EventArgs. This class should be able to hold all of the information that must be passed to the event handler. The name of the class should be equal to the name of the delegate, but ending in EventArgs instead of EventHandler.

Following this convention, other programmers will understand your code more easily, but there are some direct advantages as well. Because the signatures of event handler methods follow the same form, you can use a method designed for handling events of type System.EventHandler for all other event types as well.

First let us have a look at the declaration as it should look following the event naming convention; we will explain the parts afterwards:

```
public delegate void BankTransactionEventHandler
                (BankAccount sender, BankTransactionEventArgs args);

public class BankTransactionEventArgs : EventArgs
{
  public BankTransactionEventArgs(double amount)
  {
    mAmount = amount;
  }
  private double mAmount;
  public double Amount
  {
    get{return mAmount;}
  }
}

public class BankAccount
```

```
{
    public event BankTransactionEventHandler LargeDeposit;
    // Many other members omitted
}
```

At the top you see the declaration of a delegate type. It is named
BankTransactionEventHandler.

Next comes the definition of the BankTransactionEventArgs class. It is a subclass
of EventArgs and defines one extra property, Amount, which is read-only and can
only be set through the constructor.

Last, we see how the LargeDeposit event in BankAccount is declared as type
BankTransactionEventHandler.

Now when an actual large deposit occurs, we need to raise this event. Let's have a
look at how that works.

```
private static double mThreshold = 10000;

public void Credit(double Amount)
{
    mBalance += Amount;
    if (Amount >= mThreshold)
    {
        if (LargeDeposit != null)
        {
            LargeDeposit(this, new BankTransactionEventArgs(Amount));
        }
    }
}
```

We have added two things:

❑   A private static field holding the threshold amount above which we consider
    a deposit a **large** deposit. This is obviously quite arbitrary, but it must at least
    be an equal value for all instances of BankAccount. Later we will add
    functionality for changing this value and for being notified of this change.

❑   We have added the code for calling the delegate holding the registered
    event handlers. Of course, we must check if the delegate is null. When
    we call it, we pass an instance of BankTransactionEventArgs. We
    instantiate it passing the amount of the deposit in the constructor. The
    event handlers will use this object to get at the size of the deposit. It is
    rather important to keep the EventArgs object immutable (keep the
    properties read-only), because the registered event handlers will all get the
    same instance passed sequentially. You never know who will register for
    the event and what they will try to do to the EventArgs instance.

250

By following this convention, you allow others to define event handlers that can handle **any** event. A method that can handle events of type `System.EventHandler` can effectively be used to handle all events (all events defined following the convention that is). The handling method expects two parameters, one of type `object` (you can pass any object there) and one of type `System.EventArgs`. As `BankTransactionEventArgs` is a subclass of `EventArgs`, the method accepts that type as well.

So following the convention for signatures of events makes them easier to use, because other programmers will understand from the naming what the classes are for, and more widely applicable, as they can be wired to standard event handlers.

Defining Static Events

We have seen events as instance members of objects, but it is also possible to define events as `static` (members of the type, not of the instance). Static events are much less common than instance events, for reasons that will become apparent when we look at how to subscribe to events in the next section.

First look into the `BankAccount` class of the `AdvancedEvents` sample. In the class you will find the following code:

```
public static event EventHandler ThresholdChanged;
private static double mThreshold = 10000;
public static double Threshold
{
  set
  {
    mThreshold = value;
    if (ThresholdChanged != null)
    {
      ThresholdChanged(null, EventArgs.Empty);
    }
  }
  get{return mThreshold;}
}
```

A new event has been defined, but apart from the added `static` keyword, it looks quite normal. We also defined a static property `Threshold` for exposing the `mThreshold` field. When a new value is set, the `ThresholdChanged` delegate is called (after checking if it's `null`).

Now if we look into the `BankAccountForm` class, which registers to the `ThresholdChanged` event, we see that registration does look a bit different. The constructor of the form contains this code:

```
mBankAccount = new BankAccount(accountName);
BankAccount.ThresholdChanged += new
              EventHandler(this.AlertThresholdChanged);
```

Note that the event registered to is not a member of the mBankAccount instance, but of the BankAccount itself. In fact, to register to this event, you don't even need an instance of the class.

In the bankmanagerform, we expose the functionality to change the threshold value through the static Threshold property on BankAccount:

```
private void btnSetThreshold_Click(object sender, System.EventArgs e)
{
  BankAccount.Threshold = Double.Parse(txtThreshold.Text);
}
```

As soon as the manager clicks the btnSetThreshold button, the static field in BankAccount changes value, changing the behavior of all instances of BankAccount. As soon as this has happened, all of the BankAccountForm instances will receive a notification of this event by way of a call to the AlertThresholdChanged() method. If you look at our executable in ildasm, you will see that a static event (just like a normal event) generates a private delegate field, two registration methods, and an event member. Only now all of these are marked static:

Dynamically Registering and Unregistering

Event handlers are registered at the time of creation of objects and remain valid during the whole lifetime of the object. This is always the case for event handlers for controls on forms when you use a forms builder to wire the events. However, this is by no means necessary; you can register and unregister your interest in receiving certain notifications during the run time of the program. For example, in the sample application we allow the bank manager to select which bank accounts to monitor through the log window. Only for these selected accounts will events like Overdrawn and LargeDeposit result in a line in the log textbox.

To achieve this, we have two methods in place, one for logging the Overdrawn event and one for logging the LargeDeposit event. When we create a BankAccountForm (which in turn creates a BankAccount object), we add the created BankAccount to the listbox lstUnlogged. Only when the user clicks the button Log >>, we start wiring the events on the selected BankAccount to the appropriate methods.

```
private void btnLog_Click(object sender, System.EventArgs e)
{
  if (lstUnlogged.SelectedItem is BankAccount)
  {
    BankAccount b = (BankAccount)lstUnlogged.SelectedItem;
    b.Overdrawn += new EventHandler(this.OverdrawnHandler);
    b.LargeDeposit += new
        BankTransactionEventHandler(this.LargeDepositHandler);
    lstLogged.Items.Add(b);
    lstUnlogged.Items.Remove(b);
  }
}
```

To prevent any runtime casting exceptions, we first test that the selected list item really is an instance of BankAccount (in this application, the only other thing that might be returned is null). If it is, we cast it to BankAccount and register the method OverdrawnHandler() to the Overdrawn event and the method LargeDepositHandler() to the event LargeDeposit. After that, we move the selected BankAccount from the list of items that are not logged to the list of items that are.

The reverse action is of course very much alike.

```
private void btnUnlog_Click(object sender, System.EventArgs e)
{
  if (lstLogged.SelectedItem is BankAccount)
  {
    BankAccount b = (BankAccount)lstLogged.SelectedItem ;
    b.Overdrawn -= new EventHandler(this.OverdrawnHandler);
    b.LargeDeposit -= new
            BankTransactionEventHandler(this.LargeDepositHandler);

    lstLogged.Items.Remove(b);
    lstUnlogged.Items.Add(b);
  }
}
```

You can probably imagine what happens in the two event handler methods, so we will not show them here. In the screenshot in the *Creating Events that Pass Information* section, you can see how three accounts have been created, but we see events appearing in the bank manager form only from two of the three accounts. The account named Dave is still in the list of unlogged accounts.

The beauty of the concept of events is very clear in this example: it is the object receiving the events that decides which events are interesting (or **when** they are interesting). Methods are implemented only for these events. The object raising the events does not have to worry about who should receive which notification, it can just call the event delegate and this will make sure that all registered event handlers will be called. The part that does the administration of event handlers is hidden from us in the two methods add_eventname() and remove_eventname().

Defining your own Registration Methods

Since the administration of registrations is hidden from us, we can prevent administrative mistakes. But you may need to change the generated MSIL, to be able to do things differently. To achieve this, you can define your own custom add and remove methods for your events.

C# offers us a special syntax, very much like the syntax for defining accessor methods on properties. Keep in mind though it is all or nothing. The event declaration generates both methods and a private field of a delegate type. If you choose to define custom accessor methods, you must define all of these: the add() method, the remove() method, and the storage of the invocation list (you could choose another implementation than a multicast delegate).

In the sample application DelegatesEvents\CustomAddRemove we show how to modify the registration methods. The application has two buttons, one to create a new event destination and register it to the event source and a second button to force the raising of the event from the event source. All of the objects have access to a textbox for logging.

❑   The event source logs a line just before it raises the event

❑   The event receiver logs a line when it receives an event notification

❑   The event source logs a line when it notices that a new event receiver has registered or unregistered. This is of course the functionality we want to demonstrate. We placed the logging code in the event registration methods.

The running application looks like this:

We will only show the code for the event declaration. You should be familiar with all of the other functionality by now.

```
private EventHandler mHappening;

public event EventHandler Happening
{
  add
  {
    mHappening = (EventHandler)Delegate.Combine(mHappening, value);
    mTextBox.Text += "A new handler has registered for
                                        Happening\r\n";

  }
  remove
  {
    mHappening = (EventHandler)Delegate.Remove(mHappening, value);
    mTextBox.Text += "A new handler has unregistered for
                                        Happening\r\n";

  }
}
```

Note how we declared two blocks of code within the event declaration. The code block after add will eventually be compiled into a method called add_Happening(), while the code behind remove will turn up in the remove_Happening() method in the MSIL. Apart from the lines adding some text to the logging textbox, the implementation as shown here is exactly identical to the default implementation. We declared a private field of type EventHandler to hold all of the event handler methods. The only thing we do for administering the methods is calling Delegate.Combine() in the add method and Delegate.Remove() in the remove methods. Both methods get an instance of EventHandler passed which can be accessed through the value keyword.

One other difference is in the naming. When we used the default implementation, the compiler generated a private field with a name identical to the name of the event (in this case, the private field would have been called Happening). This is fine in MSIL; an event and a private field can have the same name without problems. In C#, however, this is a naming conflict: the compiler would throw The class 'CustomAddRemove.EventGenerator' already contains a definition for 'Happening'. So we have to choose a different name for the field (we chose mHappening) and we must use this name when we want to raise the event as well:

```
public void SimulateEvent()
{
  mTextBox.Text += "EventGenerator is raising the event.\r\n";
  if (mHappening != null)
  {
    mHappening(this, EventArgs.Empty);
  }
}
```

Most developers will never need the ability to define custom registration methods and to ability to add some logging may not seem a very convincing application. Still, there are actually some real-world situations where this technique can make your code better and faster. In the framework library for example, most controls (both windows forms and ASP.NET) use custom registration methods.

The System.Windows.Forms.Control class is the base class for almost everything on a form: all of the controls, like buttons, labels checkboxes, and also the form itself. Control exposes 58 events. On an average form, there are many controls, most of which are very simple, and the large majority of the events are used only very seldom. Still, every instance of a control reserves some memory to hold the private delegate field (for keeping track of the event handlers). To keep controls lightweight, the implementers of the framework decided not to use a delegate instance per event, but to have one collection to store all of the event handlers of the control. When the control needs to raise a specific event, it knows how to retrieve the correct delegate from the collection and calls it. If no events are used at all, the control uses only the memory for the empty collection.

> *Actually, this approach is not implemented in* Control *itself, but in its base class* System.ComponentModel.Component. *This class exposes the protected* Events *property, which all of its subclasses can use to store seldom used events in.*

Role of Events in the Type Interfaces of the .NET Framework

Events in the .NET Framework are members just like properties and methods. A subclass inherits all of the events, including handler methods, from its base class. Even interfaces can contain events.

When we build a class that exposes an event, we tend to see the event and its implementation as one entity, one member. In MSIL though, the event, the private field to store the invocation list, and the registration methods are separate items. The event is just the published name and its references to the two registration methods. On the level of compiled .NET assemblies, the registration methods are methods like any other method. Also, the private field that holds the multicast delegate is a private field just like fields that have no relation with an event. The .NET runtime doesn't know it to be connected to the event. Keeping this in mind, we can explain the behavior of events in scenarios of inheritance and overriding.

If the event is declared virtual in the base class, you can override it. The declaration in the subclass would look like this (this code does not appear in the sample application):

```
// Valid code, but will not work as you would expect
public override event EventHandler Happening;
```

As you can see from the comment above it, this code will compile, but it will not work as you might expect. The override event will generate a new version of the event publication and a new version of the registration methods. These will all override the original implementation. It will also create a new private field for holding the multicast delegate. Now when some other class registers for an event, the event handler will be stored in the new private field in the subclass. However, if the base class tries to raise the event, it will call the delegate in the private field of the base class. This is because the default implementation of the event creates the field as private; the base class and subclass cannot refer to the same delegate. This makes this form of overriding pretty useless.

So to implement events that can be overridden will need custom implementation of the storage field. You can just keep the default implementation of the add() and remove() methods, but declare the delegate field as protected. Then in the subclass, you can effectively override the registration methods, but keep using the protected field for storage and for raising the event:

```
class BaseClass
{
  protected EventHandler mHappening;

  public virtual event EventHandler Happening
  {
    add
    {
      mHappening = (EventHandler)Delegate.Combine(mHappening, value);
    }
    remove
    {
      mHappening = (EventHandler)Delegate.Remove(mHappening, value);
    }
  }
}
class SubClass : BaseClass
{
  // No field declaration here
  public override event EventHandler Happening
  {
    add
    {
      mHappening = (EventHandler)Delegate.Combine(mHappening, value);
      mTextBox.Text += "A new handler has registered for
                        Happening\r\n";
    }
    remove
    {
      mHappening = (EventHandler)Delegate.Remove(mHappening, value);
      mTextBox.Text += "A new handler has unregistered for
                        Happening\r\n";
    }
  }
}
```

If the base class is using the default implementation, there is no way to implement a new registration method and still have access to the original field.

Summary

This has been a tough chapter, as you will have seen some new concepts and ways of programming. Still, a good understanding of how events work in the .NET Framework is essential for building even simple Windows Forms applications and ASP.NET Web Forms applications (commonly known as websites).

We've seen how to use delegates in general programming tasks, such as specifying which method to invoke but delaying its execution until we are ready or even having a task performed on a separate thread. Also, delegates can be used with or without the event mechanism.

Events in the .NET Framework make use of multicast delegates. We can define delegate types to specify the method signatures for our event-handler methods. The event mechanism implicitly creates delegate objects, and uses these delegate objects to keep track of the event handlers for each event.

We've seen many examples in this chapter, to illustrate recommended best practices for events and delegates in C#. We've also spent some time looking at MSIL code, to see how events and delegates work internally. This will help you decide how to use events and delegates effectively in your own applications.

C#

Class Design

Handbook

7

7

Inheritance and Polymorphism

Inheritance and polymorphism are two concepts that drive object-oriented design and development. Traditionally, all object-oriented languages support both of these concepts; for C# the syntax is similar to C++.

Inheritance allows class hierarchies to be formed. Class hierarchies are groups of classes that are related because they share certain things in common. For example, we could define a class hierarchy based on mammals where we could introduce human, monkey, and mouse as three different types of mammal. Each of these mammals is different but they are basically of the type 'mammal'. Hence, we can create a class hierarchy to model the behavior of mammals with a Mammal class at the top, which is referred to as the base class, and the other three classes as derived classes. The derived classes will not only inherit all the members of the base class (including its properties, fields, and methods, as long as these are not private to the base class) but will also have the ability to add to the behavior of the Mammal class that they have inherited from. For example, the Human class may have properties or methods that are unique to humans, like Job Title, or Telephone Number, and the Monkey class may have a Tree property that is unique to a monkey and specifies the location of the monkey's tree. In short, all of these classes would have the common elements attributed to all mammals, but specialized to include their own capabilities and attributes.

Inheritance avoids code duplication, and enables code reuse, which means that each class doesn't require its own copy of the Mammal class implementation. As a result we have also created a hierarchy of classes that can be used to illustrate class relationships in code. We can use inheritance and create categories of things and relationships and this enables us to break complex problems into more manageable chunks.

Polymorphism is enabled by inheritance. Because all of our derived classes inherit the basic functionality of the base class, we can treat instances of the derived classes as if they are an instance of the base class. This is the principle of substitutability – we can 'swap out' an instance of a base class, and substitute for it an instance of a derived class, and code will continue to work – to be able to call methods and access attributes of the instance that it would expect to access on the base class. The ability of an object of one type to be treated as if it were an instance of another type is called polymorphism.

One additional capability inheritance affords derived classes is that they can override the default base class implementation and provide their own implementation of properties or methods. In these cases, code that is designed to access functionality on a base class may find an instance of the base class 'substituted' with an instance of a different, derived class, and may then find that calling a method on the base class will cause code in the derived class to be executed. This is enabled in .NET by a technique called virtual method dispatching, and we'll look at how it works later on in the chapter. Sometimes, we may want to prevent derived classes from overriding functionality; other times, it may be crucial for them to do so. In this chapter, we'll see how we can control inheritance, and

In .NET, as in most object-oriented languages, we generally refer to the parent class as a base class and all of the child classes as derived classes. We can enable polymorphism in two ways – by defining an interface that is implemented by the derived class, or by inheritance and method overriding, which enables a new implementation of an inherited method. Other programming languages use different terminology for this, for example, Java often calls the base class a superclass and the derived class a subclass. Subclassing is a popular term among C++ developers to describe deriving from a base class and extending its operations and attributes.

> **Throughout this chapter we may use the terms operations and attributes interchangeably with the terms methods and fields; the former refer to the latter on a conceptual level and the latter are the terms we use to denote an implementation of these concepts in code.**

In the sections that follow we will describe some of the key concepts behind inheritance and polymorphism without using code, to enable a fuller understanding at a more conceptual level.

Inheritance

To explain our usage of inheritance and polymorphism, we will use **UML** (**Universal Modeling Language**) diagrams to explain class relationships.

A good general reference is *Instant UML* by Apress, ISBN 1-86100-087-1. For details on using UML with .NET, there is also the more recent *Professional UML with Visual Studio .NET*, ISBN 1-86100-795-7.

UML can be used to describe entire applications showing relationships between classes. There are two main kinds of relationship that we'll concern ourselves with here – either the *is a* or *has a* relationship concept of OO development. This is always the rule of thumb as to whether a class should derive from another class or should contain another class (this is the background of the `is` keyword used in C#, which we shall discuss later in the chapter).

These relationships can be best understood by describing them in terms of the `Mammal` class hierarchy we discussed earlier. We can say that a `Monkey` **is a** `Mammal` since it can do everything that a `Mammal` can do (and more). We also said earlier that a `Monkey` **has a** `Tree`. A `Monkey` can't do things a `Tree` can do, but we can access the functionality of a `Tree` by obtaining one from a `Monkey`.

The *is a* relationship is fundamental to polymorphism. If a `Monkey` is a `Mammal`, then any code we write that applies to `Mammal`s applies equally to `Monkey`s. So, we can substitute a `Mammal` with a `Monkey`, and polymorphism will apply. As we said before, polymorphism is provided through inheritance in .NET; it follows, therefore, that an *is a* relationship in .NET can generally be modeled with inheritance, and we should make our `Monkey` class inherit from `Mammal`.

The *has a* relationship has an impact on inheritance too. If a `Monkey` has a `Tree`, then we should expect any classes derived from `Monkey` to have a `Tree` also. Similarly, if we say that a `Mammal` has a `LatinName`, then it follows, because a `Monkey` is a `Mammal`, that a `Monkey` has a `LatinName`.

The following UML diagram represents the basic relationship between the `Mammal` and all of the classes that derive from the `Mammal` class. The arrow notation is all that we need to show the relationship of inheritance. In this example, the `Mammal` class is the base class and the derived classes are the `Human`, `Monkey`, and `Mouse`:

Figure 1

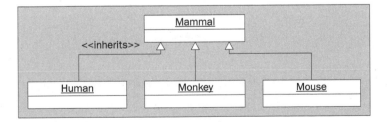

Inheritance Hierarchies

As there are different types of monkeys and humans, which may have different attributes from one another, we can extend the inheritance hierarchy by making the derived classes base classes to other classes. We could therefore extend this inheritance hierarchy to establish two distinct types of Monkey – either an Ape or a Chimpanzee. An ape or chimpanzee should have the characteristics of a monkey, such as a Climb() method, but not those of humans. We provide different operations and attributes for the two new types of monkey; for example, the ape being territorial, may have a Fight() method that a chimpanzee may lack, and the chimpanzee may have a Flee() method instead.

A revised model showing this new derived class relationship may be illustrated by the following figure, showing a second derived level.

Figure 2

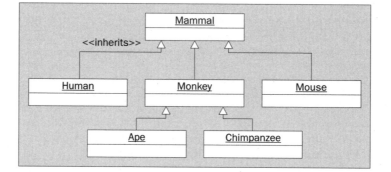

The Ape is a Mammal but it is a Monkey also, which has a different implementation from a Mammal. Note that this model still lacks the description necessary to tell us what each class can do over and above the base class. We can use the class symbol in UML to add more information such as operations and attributes about the class. The top section of the shape refers to the class name. The second section contains the names of class attributes. The final section contains operations.

Figure 3

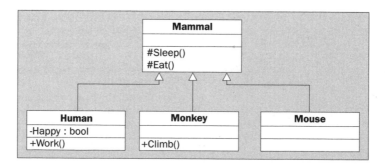

In the case of the Mammal class, the # symbol preceding the members means that both Sleep() and Eat() are protected members of the class, which means that they are accessible only to code contained in the class itself, and derived classes. The – symbol indicates a private member and the + symbol indicates a public member. In this diagram, we've added members to the Human class: a Work() operation, since humans are the only mammal which works, and an attribute to encompass the higher human emotions, which is a Boolean value to indicate whether the human is happy or sad. Similarly, the Monkey has a Climb() method as monkeys climb trees, while not all mammals normally climb trees, so we cannot implement it on the Mammal base class. There is no extra implementation of operations or attributes for a mouse since the mouse is a model mammal and will need very little more than sleeping or eating, although we could provide an extension for this class too, maybe in the form of a RunRoundWheel() method.

There is no need to redefine the extra operations or attributes pertaining to the base class since this is implicit in the UML model, as we have defined an inheritance association between the classes. By looking at this diagram we can assume that the human is capable of doing three operations:

❏   Sleep()

❏   Eat()

❏   Work()

and it has a single attribute:

❏   Happy

Overriding Base Class Operations

The base class exposes a series of operations (methods and properties) to the derived class, which can be overridden. We can allow derived classes to override the base class operations by making them virtual; this means that all these operations can have a new implementation in the derived class. Although methods marked as non-virtual cannot be overridden to provide a new implementation to the base class, we can define an operation with the same signature that will hide the respective base class operation. In the Mammal class hierarchy, the Sleep() operation should be virtual since each class will have a different implementation – for example, the mouse may need more sleep than the human or the monkey, and so on. So we can ascertain different methods for each of the derived classes based on how they differ from each other and whether they can inherit the base class implementation without changes. Defining an operation as virtual in the base class is represented in the UML class diagram by simply adding a method of the same name as the base class method to the derived class diagram.

If an operation is marked as virtual in the base class, it means that the derived class has the option to override the base class implementation. If it chooses to implement the operation, then it must use exactly the same signature as in the base class. We'll see how this is done using C# later in the chapter. However, each method signature that is overridden in the derived class must be marked to acknowledge that a new implementation is provided in the derived class.

Abstract Classes and Interfaces

An important concept in inheritance is the idea of the **concrete class**. The only classes we can instantiate are concrete classes. In order for an instance of a class to exist, it must have a fully defined implementation for every method in its interface. A class that meets these criteria is called a concrete class. Now, if all we could define were concrete classes, this distinction wouldn't be necessary, but there are two mechanisms we can use in .NET to define classes without defining implementations – **interfaces** and **abstract classes**.

An abstract class is a class that contains at least one abstract method. An abstract method is one that declares a signature, but no implementation. The implementation must be provided by creating a class derived from the abstract class, and adding an implementation there. If a class derived from an abstract class does not define an implementation for an abstract method, then the derived class is also abstract. An abstract class is the opposite of a concrete class. It cannot be instantiated, and it is used when generating class inheritance hierarchies to provide a more realistic inheritance model.

An interface is like a pure form of abstract class. While an abstract class may contain definitions for some methods, an interface contains only signature definitions. Because an interface cannot define implementations, they can be treated specially by the inheritance system, and we'll see how later.

Abstract classes are used as base classes providing implementation code where necessary, which will be inherited by all the classes. We could declare Mammal as an abstract class; it makes no sense to ever want to create an object of type Mammal that is not also of one of the subtypes of Mammal. It is considered good design to make an abstract class the base class in an inheritance model.

Each abstract operation that is declared in an abstract class is implicitly declared as virtual, because you have to either override this method, or declare it abstract in a derived class. This is not mandatory for non-abstract methods as the derived class can use the implementation of the abstract base class methods if necessary. To override the non-abstract methods declare them as virtual in the base class.

Both abstract classes and abstract methods are denoted in UML through the use of italics. Although the Mammal model contains a single method it is possible to have multiple abstract and non-abstract methods denoted by combinations of italic and non-italic text.

Figure 4

```
                        ┌──────────────┐
                        │   Mammal     │
                        ├──────────────┤
                        ├──────────────┤
                        │ #Sleep()     │
                        │ #Eat()       │
                        └──────────────┘
```

Human	Monkey	Mouse
-Happy : bool		
+Work()	+Climb()	

Types of Inheritance

There are two distinct approaches to inheritance – the first approach is implementation inheritance whereby the base class contains an implementation. This implementation can be overridden if operations are declared as `virtual` or must be overridden if operations are declared as `abstract`. This is the kind of inheritance we have considered so far. The second type is interface inheritance. Implementation inheritance requires interface inheritance; if we inherit the implementation of a method, we also inherit the method's signature, through which the implementation may be called. But as we say with abstract methods, we can inherit the obligation to provide an implementation, without inheriting an implementation. This is inheritance of interface. Using a pure interface type, you can declare a set of methods that a class must implement in order to inherit the interface. Every derived class must implement the operations specified on the interface.

In the diagram below the `Mouse` class implements the `ISmallAnimal` interface

Figure 5

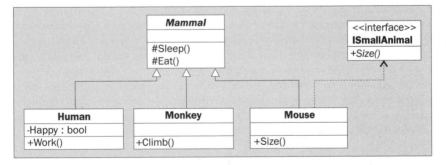

UML notation for interfaces is slightly different from that of classes. In the example above the use of <<interface>> specifies that `ISmallAnimal` is an interface not a class. An interface cannot contain any implementation, only operation signatures. For this reason interfaces will not have attributes declared. We can use dotted lines to encompass relationships between interfaces and other interfaces or classes. As you can see, the `Mouse` class provides an implementation of the `Size()` operation.

An interface provides a means of specifying the contracts of methods, but not their implementation. We use interface inheritance to provide different implementations of interface methods in a class. The collection classes in the Framework Class Library use interface inheritance to define their implementation for a variety of methods, such as Sort(), Reverse(), and Add(). An example using an ArrayList can be seen below, where an ArrayList is created, which implements ICollection, and hence is of type ICollection. We could use a Hashtable class instead of an ArrayList and our method won't differentiate between them because they both implement ICollection:

```
public static int ReturnCount(ICollection col)
{
  return col.Count;
}

public static void Main()
{
  ArrayList ar = new ArrayList();
  int count = ReturnCount(ar);
}
```

Multiple Inheritance

The CLS employed by the Microsoft CLR implementation requires that a class is only able to inherit from a single base class, and so cannot have two direct base classes. By avoiding the complexity inherent in multiple inheritance, .NET saves us a lot of headaches, and in those circumstances where we want to combine the capabilities of two classes into one, there are other mechanisms available. When we want to indicate that an instance of a class is more than one thing (has multiple *is a* relationships), we can do so with multiple interface inheritance, which we'll look at in a moment. The approach to multiple inheritance is very similar to the approach taken by the Java language designers but is different from that of C++. C++ does support multiple implementation inheritance but C# doesn't. Although it seems that multiple implementation inheritance can only make writing code easier consider Figure 6:

The class Human inherits from both Mammal and Species. Mammal itself is derived from Species. When all the links are resolved Human will effectively inherit the methods of Species twice. But on one side, what's to stop the Mammal class from overriding some of the methods in Species? In that case, how are we to resolve calls to methods on the Human class? It's actually much easier for us that this has been avoided in the CLR.

Figure 6

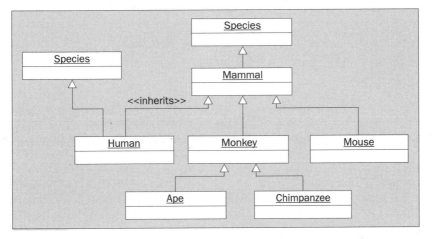

The same problems do not occur when the inheritance is only of interface, not implementation. As we said, inheriting an interface is inheriting an obligation to provide an implementation. You can inherit that obligation several times, and there will be no problem. You can inherit the same obligation from two different interfaces, and fulfilling it fulfils both interfaces. So, while multiple inheritance of implementation creates headaches, multiple inheritance of interface can help us solve many problems.

The following example of the use of the two techniques in conjunction within the .NET Framework Class libraries concerns the collection classes. For example, an ArrayList class implements the IList, ICollection, IEnumerable, and IClonable interfaces and therefore provides its own implementation for enumeration, cloning, and standard collection class methods such as Add(). The DomainUpDownItemsCollection that is used by the DomainUpDown Windows Forms Control derives from the ArrayList emphasizing the use of the implementation and interface inheritance in the same hierarchy. We can define the interfaces and a base class at the same level of the hierarchy, although the implementation below shows them at different levels.

Figure 7

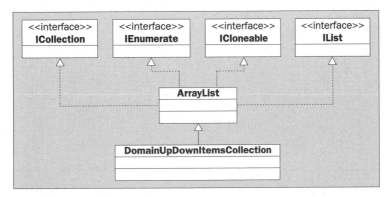

Creating a Class Hierarchy

In this section we'll look at some small examples to create a new class hierarchy, which encompasses many concepts that we have introduced in the UML section. This will include illustrating inheritance and polymorphism principles in code, creating abstract and concrete classes, and also creating implementation classes for multiple interface inheritance.

To illustrate, we can create two class types and one struct type. The Example1 class will not explicitly inherit from anything, but the Example2 class will inherit from the System.Object class. The Example3 struct will also not explicitly inherit from anything.

```
public class Example1
{//some code
}

public class Example2 : System.Object
{//some code
}
public struct Example3
{// some code
}
```

To find out the class inheritance structure, we can add code to the Main() method to return the type of the class and its base class; this will use reflection to get the type instance. Remember that each class implicitly inherits from System.Object, yet in Example2 we have explicitly inherited from System.Object.

It is important to understand that whether or not an object inherits from System.Object, the compiler will add this for us since it is implicit in each class definition in **all** .NET languages. The console will display the name of each class and also display that both Example1 and Example2 inherit from System.Object, as it is the ultimate base class of all .NET classes. The Example3 struct will inherit from System.ValueType – which will be displayed on the Console as the base class. The important point here, though, is that System.ValueType also inherits from System.Object and is simply used to provide an overridden implementation of the System.Object methods that is more relevant to a value type.

```
public class MainMethod
{
  static void Main()
  {
    Example1 example1 = new Example1();
    Console.WriteLine("Class type instance is {0}
             and derives from {1}", example1.GetType().Name,
             example1.GetType().BaseType);

    Example2 example2 = new Example2();
    Console.WriteLine("Class type instance is {0}
             and derives from {1}", example2.GetType().Name,
```

```
                 example2.GetType().BaseType);

    Example3 example3 = new Example3();
    Console.WriteLine("Class type instance is {0}
             and derives from {1}", example3.GetType().Name,
             example3.GetType().BaseType);
    }
}
```

The above code, called example_inheritance.cs, when executed will produce the following output:

```
C:\Class Design\Ch 07> example_inheritance
Class type instance is Example1 and derives from System.Object
Class type instance is Example2 and derives from System.Object
Class type instance is Example3 and derives from System.ValueType
```

The compiler will prevent you from creating your own value types by inheriting from System.ValueType. The CLR doesn't distinguish between classes and structs (that is, reference types and value types) directly. It uses the inheritance path to distinguish between the two enabling optimization of value types. The CLR can optimize how it handles value types since they are effectively sealed. Remember that a sealed class cannot be inherited from or derived from.

Class Definitions

Examining the MSIL output through the .NET Framework tool ILDASM allows us to check this correlation ensuring that the three types inherit from System.Object or System.ValueType respectively. An important point to draw attention to is that the struct value type Example3 has been marked sealed in the IL definition, meaning that we cannot use this type as a base class for anything. By default all value types contain this definition implying that we can't use any form of polymorphism with value types, which is all the CLR needs to know to optimize the behavior of memory allocation for a struct. An object instance will require a table of methods and the use of indirection to be able to support implementation inheritance and interface inheritance; effectively there is no need to engage in a lookup to find out what method to use, that is, the base class or overridden method, as the runtime knows that this can only have the one specified value, and this overhead can be avoided with a value type since it is effectively sealed.

```
Example1::.class public auto ansi beforefieldinit          _ □ x
.class public auto ansi beforefieldinit Example1
        extends [mscorlib]System.Object
{
} // end of class Example1
```

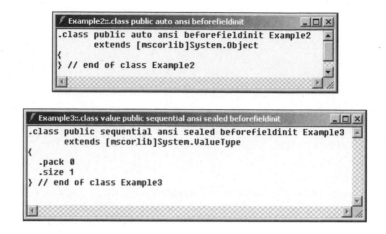

Designing a Base Class

We saw how to construct a class hierarchy with the Mammal as a base class and then derive classes, which inherit the methods of the mammal but provide definitions for new methods specific to the class. It is important to plan a class hierarchy from the outset, since any changes at source to the base class to the visible interface will result in changes to all of the classes that inherit from the base class.

The Teacher class hierarchy below defines two field values, Salary and Grade, and a single method CalculateDaysWorked(). The derived classes HeadTeacher, SupplyTeacher, and StaffTeacher are respectively the head school teacher, a supply teacher with a temporary post, and a staff teacher. We have the head teacher who will never teach, and a staff teacher and a supply teacher who will always teach.

Figure 8

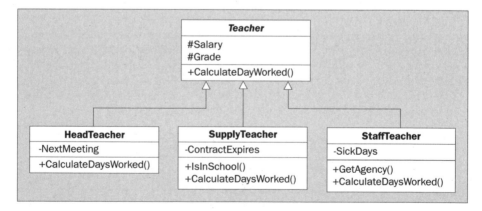

For example, the method CalculateDaysWorked() in the base-class Teacher, which will return the number of days that each teacher has worked so far in the year, has different implementations in each of the three concrete classes that derive from Teacher.

Suppose we want to accept another parameter and index to look up this value. Changing this method signature in the base class will affect all of the derived classes as they will still have to provide an implementation, which has to match the base class implementation. Having many derived classes means there will be a big rewrite. We can prevent this by using the `internal` modifier, which ensures that only classes within the same assembly will be able to see the classes that they wish to derive from. This is a way of ensuring that classes within our own assemblies can be inherited from but ensuring that other software developers cannot subclass our own classes from classes outside its assembly, ensuring that visible changes to the new base class will not break a software application.

Abstract vs. Concrete

Declare the base class `Teacher` as `abstract`, and declare all fields as `protected`, not private as they wouldn't be visible to the derived class. The derived class could provide a level of encapsulation by creating property accessors for the fields, or declare property accessors as `protected` in the base class and the underlying fields as `private`. In this way if the base class implementation changes the derived class will not be affected. By default, the methods are not considered abstract. The `IsWorking()` method can be overridden in derived classes as it is declared `virtual`; it will allow the value of the private `isWorking` variable to be changed.

```
using System;
public abstract class Teacher
{
    protected int salary;
    protected int grade;
    private bool isWorking = false;
    public abstract int CalculateDaysWorked ();
    public virtual void Work(bool isWorking)
    {
        //we could add some logging code here
        this.isWorking = isWorking;
    }
    protected bool IsWorking
    {
        get { return isWorking; }
    }
}
```

We could similarly define a constructor for this class but it would be better to mark it `protected` so that only our derived classes can access it. An alternative implementation of this class is exposing two property accessors, which write to private fields `Salary` and `Grade` in the base class. This will loosen the coupling between the base class and the derived class, since all the derived classes don't need to directly depend on the field types. Providing protected property accessors means that we can change the implementation in the base class to reflect a change in the field declaration. This means that the property accessor can always have the same method signature but the implementation code can change without any overhead to the derived class.

We could simply present a property accessor to the derived class that would get or set the value of the private `int` field. The property accessor would take a `long` argument and convert it into an `int` value (and vice versa).

```
protected Teacher(int Grade)
{
    this.grade = Grade;
}
protected long Grade
{
    set
    {this.grade = (int)value;
    }
    get
    {return (long)grade;
    }
}
```

Using Virtual Methods

We can add another generic `virtual` method that can be overridden only if necessary. We can also add a `CalculatePay()` method, which would calculate the monthly pay of a teacher based on their annual salary, including overtime. The `salary` field would contain the annual salary; if this is 0 the method will throw an exception; otherwise it will return the monthly salary plus the overtime. The overtime would be stored in the `overtime` field.

```
protected int overtime;
public virtual double CalculatePay()
{
    if(salary==0)
    {
    // throw new Exception("Unknown salary value");
    }
    return (salary / 12) + (overtime * (salary / (52 * 40)) * 1.5);
}

public class AbstractTeacherExample
{
    public static void Main(string[] args)
    {
    }
}
```

Occasionally you would need to override this method in derived classes, where we can have another implementation, returning a different value, for the `SupplyTeacher` class as it is based on a daily rate depending on the grade; a staff teacher's salary calculation is the same as the virtual method, and the head teacher has a similar calculation but with double time overtime and a yearly supplement based on their grade.

We have saved the file as `abstract_teacher.cs`. The MSIL shows the definition for the `Teacher` class and the `CalculateDaysWorked()` method. In the MSIL, the class is declared `abstract`, and the `CalculateDaysWorked()` method is set as `virtual`. We don't declare it `virtual` as all abstract methods are virtual by default.

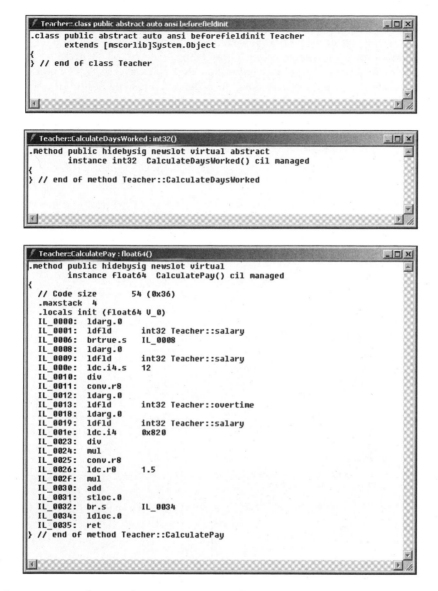

We have two new keywords – hidebysig and newslot. In conjunction with the virtual keyword hidebysig denotes that this method should be hidden in a derived class, if a method with the same signature exists, to avoid ambiguity when invoking methods.

The newslot keyword creates a new slot within a vtable (a virtual function table), which is a table of methods that each .NET object contains comprising all inherited methods and overridden as well as static methods. The vtable is the mechanism by which the CLR decides whether to invoke the virtual or overridden method on the derived class.

Sealing Classes

Another important concept that is enforced throughout the .NET Framework is the use of sealing classes or methods, to avoid classes from being inherited, or methods being overridden. While abstract classes ensure the class acts as a base class, sealed classes prohibit the class from being the base class. To make only one type of head teacher, which is defined by the HeadTeacher class you will create a definition for the HeadTeacher sealing the class to prevent it from being a base class to other classes. If you compiled the HeadTeacher class code now with the following sealed class definition, and chose to derive another class from it the C# compiler would generate an exception.

```
public sealed class HeadTeacher
```

Similarly, declaring a sealed method will prevent you from overriding it in a derived class. MSDN documentation specifies that sealed classes can also be used for classes that are not inherited. A sealed method cannot be first declared in a base class, it has to be overridden in a derived class and declared as sealed. Any class that then derives from this derived class will not be able to override the sealed method. The following code is saved as sealing_classes.cs:

```
public class SupplyTeacher : Teacher
{
  private int monthDays;
  public override sealed double CalculatePay()
  {
    if(monthDays==0)
       monthDays = GetMonthDays(DateTime.Now.Month,
                                 DateTime.Now.Year);
    return (100 + (this.Grade * 10)) * monthDays;
  }

  protected int MonthDays
  {
    set { monthDays = value; }
  }

  private int GetMonthDays(int month, int year)
  {      if(month==9||month==4||month==6||month==11)
    {
      return 30;
    }
    if(month==2&&(year%4==0))
    {
      return 29;
    }
    else if(month==2&&(year%4!=0))
    {
      return 28;
    }
    return 31;
  }
}
```

This section has reviewed some of the responsibilities of the base class and how it is used to affect behavior in any derived classes.

In the first two lines shown below, note that abstract, as an IL instruction is the converse of final (and by implication in C# also the converse of sealed) as the former ensures that the method must be overridden in the derived class, and the latter prevents the method from being overridden in the derived class.

```
SupplyTeacher::CalculatePay : float64()                                    _□×
.method public hidebysig final virtual instance float64
        CalculatePay() cil managed
{
    // Code size       71 (0x47)
    .maxstack  5
    .locals init (float64 V_0,
            valuetype [mscorlib]System.DateTime V_1)
    IL_0000:  ldarg.0
    IL_0001:  ldfld      int32 SupplyTeacher::monthDays
    IL_0006:  brtrue.s   IL_002e
    IL_0008:  ldarg.0
    IL_0009:  ldarg.0
    IL_000a:  call       valuetype [mscorlib]System.DateTime [mscorlib]System.DateTime
    IL_000f:  stloc.1
    IL_0010:  ldloca.s   V_1
    IL_0012:  call       instance int32 [mscorlib]System.DateTime::get_Month()
    IL_0017:  call       valuetype [mscorlib]System.DateTime [mscorlib]System.DateTime
    IL_001c:  stloc.1
    IL_001d:  ldloca.s   V_1
    IL_001f:  call       instance int32 [mscorlib]System.DateTime::get_Year()
    IL_0024:  call       instance int32 SupplyTeacher::GetMonthDays(int32,
                                                                    int32)
```

Deriving Classes

Returning to the Teacher model, we'll describe the three derived classes that we built into the model. When we create an instance of a derived class, the base class constructor will be invoked. The interesting point here is the order of precedence, since the base-class constructor will be invoked before that of the derived class. This top-down construction means that the System.Object constructor will be invoked first followed by all the derived class until the constructor of the ultimate derived class is invoked.

The SupplyTeacher class passes the int parameter into its constructor and then invokes the base-class constructor (Teacher) of the same signature. This will populate the grade field with a value other than the initial value of 0. We can then calculate a value for the salary field. The overridden method CalculatePay() is invoked to populate the salary field and a yearly salary is calculated. Note that if we place the CalculatePay() method invocation within the Teacher base class code block, even though the Teacher class has its own method CalculatePay(), the SupplyTeacher method CalculatePay() will still be invoked. This is because we are creating a derived-class type not a base-class type, and therefore the context of this object instantiation is known by the runtime along with the fact that the method has been overridden in the vtable.

```
public SupplyTeacher(int number) : base(number)
{
    salary = CalculatePay() * 12;
}
```

```
public abstract class Teacher
{
  protected Teacher(int Grade)
  {
    this.grade = Grade;
  }
  //all the other methods, properties and fields here
}
```

The use of initialization code is that, even though the derived class hasn't initialized, it still has access to the methods and properties of the base class. If we revert to the SupplyTeacher class, we can see that the syntax for inheritance is the colon (:) that specifies that SupplyTeacher inherits from Teacher. This syntax should be familiar to C++ developers; however, Java developers can associate this with the extends keyword, and the use of super instead of base to reference the base class. The code snippet shown below is a part of deriving_classes.cs:

```
public class SupplyTeacher : Teacher
{
  public SupplyTeacher(int number) : base(number)
  {
    Console.WriteLine(base.Salary);
    salary = CalculatePay() * 12;
  }
  //other methods and properties and fields here
}
```

Overriding and Shadowing Methods

The signature is as important as the name while specifying methods in the derived class. Let's create another method called CalculatePay() in the derived class StaffTeacher that will be used to add a monthly supplement to the monthly salary of the teacher; recall that the CalculatePay() method contained no arguments.

The standard model of defining virtual methods on the base class means creating an overloaded method for CalculatePay(), and expecting the derived class StaffTeacher to override it. However, this method overload will be visible to all other classes irrespective of whether they are overridden on any of the derived classes. Ideally, we don't want any derived classes except StaffTeacher to implement this overloaded method. This is impossible to implement by using a second overloaded virtual method – instead we create another method with the same name and return type but a different argument signature in the derived class StaffTeacher – this will appear as a single method with two overloads even though one is an overridden method and the other contains a completely new signature undefined in the base class.

We can use this with all the other derived classes to create overloaded methods with different signatures and hence have their own overloaded versions of these methods. This technique is called **shadowing**. In the example opposite, called overriding_and_shadowing.cs, we are allowed to declare all the extra overloaded methods with or without the new keyword, as the method doesn't hide an equivalent signature method in the base class.

```
public class StaffTeacher : Teacher
{
  public StaffTeacher(int code) : base(code)
  { }
  public override double CalculatePay()
  {
    return base.CalculatePay();
  }

  public double CalculatePay(int monthlySupplement)
  {
    if(monthlySupplement > 1000) throw new Exception("Supplement out
                                            of range exception");
    return base.CalculatePay() + monthlySupplement;
  }
}
```

If the CalculatePay() method is omitted, all method requests to the derived class matching this signature will be served by the virtual base class method of the same signature. The method itself can have its own implementation, which may include a call to the base class method, which will invoke the virtual base-class implementation of the method.

Virtual Method Dispatching

Virtual method dispatching embodies the idea of polymorphism. If you have a base-class reference to the derived class type instance, you can call any of the overridden methods of the derived class using the base-class reference. This enables you to substitute a base-class reference in code for a derived-class reference and remain ignorant of the derived type.

Even if you returned a reference to the Teacher class by creating a new instance of SupplyTeacher class, the code would see the interface (all of the public methods, properties and fields) of the Teacher class. This uses polymorphism to achieve implementation of code.

The following mechanism is known as virtual method dispatching, which helps you determine the type of class the variable is an instance of, by using the is or the as operator to check for a particular type.

```
Teacher st = new SupplyTeacher();
Console.WriteLine(st.CalculatePay());
//this will invoke the method on the derived class SupplyTeacher
```

Non-Virtual Method Dispatching

We can use non-virtual method dispatching to avoid the polymorphism that was used earlier. If you create a derived class instance exactly like the virtual method dispatching example above, you will not invoke derived class methods that don't override base class methods. Instead, you will invoke the base class method.

The compiler generates a warning message when we try to compile this code without the override keyword. The warning message says that the derived method has the same signature as the base class method and is therefore hiding it. We can get rid of this warning message by redefining the method in the derived class adding the new keyword. In the Teacher class we can declare the GetTaughtSubjectName() method.

```
protected string subject;
public virtual string GetTaughtSubjectName()
{
  return subject;
}
```

In the StaffTeacher class we can declare the equivalent method with the same public signature.

```
public string GetTaughtSubjectName()
{
  return this.subject;
}
```

Using the following code (nonvirtual_teacher.cs) to return the base class reference for a derived class instance and invoking a method using the reference will result in the base class method being invoked.

```
Teacher st = new SupplyTeacher();
Console.WriteLine(st.GetTaughtSubjectName());
//this will invoke the method on the base class Teacher
```

Polymorphism in Action

Another pronounced implementation of polymorphism is using the Teacher reference as an argument to a method, so that you don't have to know which derived class is being used, and you can treat it as a base class via a principle known as substitutability. In the method InvokeMemberOnTeacher() you pass in an object reference of type Teacher, which can refer to any kind of object whose type inherits from Teacher. As an instance of the derived class, SupplyTeacher is really being passed in the overridden method CalculatePay(). You return a string argument that contains the name of the type being passed in, so that the actual class instance is the derived type, which will be returned from this GetType invocation. Avoid using the is and as operators with polymorphism, as this defeats the principle of polymorphism, and with every derived class you add to the class hierarchy, you will have to update this method accordingly.

```
public class InvocationClass
{
public static int InvokeMemberOnTeacher(Teacher teach, out string
WhichTeacher)
{
```

```
        int pay = teach.CalculatePay();
        WhichTeacher = teach.GetType().Name;
        return pay;
    }
    static void Main()
    {
        Teacher st = new SupplyTeacher(6);
        string teacherString = String.Empty;
        Console.WriteLine("Teacher Pay: {0}",
                        InvocationClass.InvokeMemberOnTeacher
                                        (st, out teacherString));

        }
    }
```

The Main() method creates a SupplyTeacher class instance using a Teacher base-class reference. It will invoke the static method InvokeMemberOnTeacher() and display the output on the Console window. The output from the invocation is shown below.

```
C.\Class Design\Ch 07>polymorphism
Teacher Pay: 4960
```

MSIL code generated for the output of the CalculatePay() invocation contains an instruction callvirt, which is used only when calling virtual methods in place of the normally used call instruction. In contrast to callvirt, call simply uses the vtable of the current type reference, and can be used in our non-virtual method dispatching examples earlier. The callvirt gets information about the concrete type, and determines whether to invoke a virtual method on the type's base class, or the overridden method on the type. Note that the Teacher class hierarchy is in the Inheritance namespace.

The vtable simply contains a list of memory pointers to various methods owned by the class instance. It distinguishes between virtual and non-virtual methods by providing different areas for each. Method tables of the derived class and the base class will be similar in their structure, and the methods of the virtual method declarations will correspond to both of them. Both use a vtable that contains a series of pointers pointing to the positions in memory of each of the methods. Each virtual method adds the MSIL instruction newslot, which means adding another slot to the vtable. This addition only occurs in the virtual method section.

The newslot instruction adds a new entry at the end of the vtable, offset from where the last method pointer is encountered. Overriding the base class virtual method in the derived class will not add a newslot instruction, which prompts the CLR to check whether the method signature is the same in the base class and the derived class. If not, then it will be added to the end of the vtable, as the omission of the newslot instruction is just used to prompt the CLR to look at the base class's vtable.

If it is the same, it will replace the inherited vtable entry for that method, which will add the method pointer for the derived class's overridden method. The following MSIL code shows the StaffTeacher method CalculatePay() that omits the newslot instruction and is therefore treated as if it is supposed to replace the virtual method in the base class.

```
StaffTeacher::CalculatePay : float64()                          _ □ x
.method public hidebysig virtual instance float64
        CalculatePay() cil managed
{
  // Code size       11 (0xb)
  .maxstack  1
  .locals init (float64 V_0)
  IL_0000:  ldarg.0
  IL_0001:  call        instance float64 Teacher::CalculatePay()
  IL_0006:  stloc.0
  IL_0007:  br.s        IL_0009
  IL_0009:  ldloc.0
  IL_000a:  ret
} // end of method StaffTeacher::CalculatePay
```

The figure below shows a possible vtable layout for the StaffTeacher class instance.
It contains all the virtual methods in the top half of the object, and the non-virtual
methods in the lower half followed by all the instance and static methods.

Figure 9

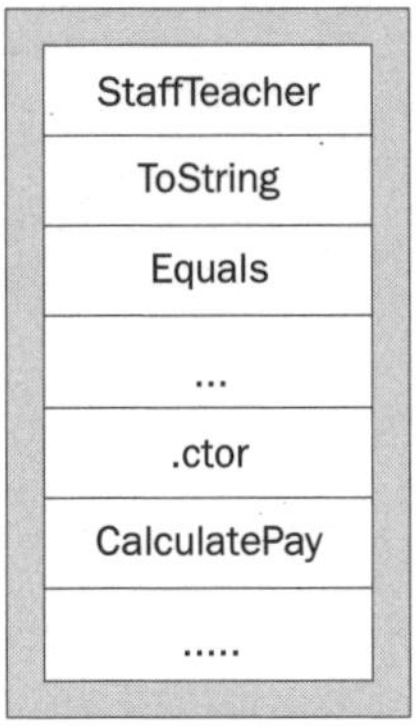

The following diagram shows a fuller description of the above diagram by including
support for distinction between inherited virtuals and additional virtuals. This is
necessary since the overridden methods will replace the equivalent method in the
inherited virtual method.

Figure 10

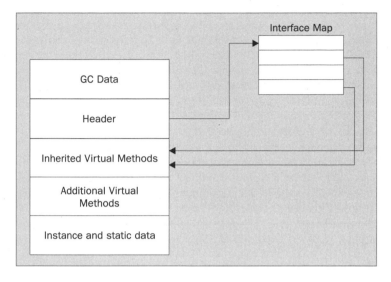

The garbage collector (GC) data section contains information that will be used for cleanup including whether an object has been marked for deletion, generation information, and so on. The `Header` contains a pointer to a memory interface map, which contains a set of pointers from supporting interfaces, back to the method table where the methods have been implemented. This enables any supported interfaces to find the methods being implemented in the implementation.

Finally, if we look at the class declaration in MSIL for the `StaffTeacher` class, we can see that the `extends` keyword is used to denote inheritance (syntactically similar to Java). If the class is not derived from another class then the default is for the MSIL to extend `System.Object`. So even when the class denotes that the `Teacher` class is the base class, the ultimate base class is always `System.Object`.

```
StaffTeacher::.class public auto ansi beforefieldinit           _ □ x
.class public auto ansi beforefieldinit StaffTeacher
        extends Teacher
{
} // end of class StaffTeacher
```

```
Teacher::.class public abstract auto ansi beforefieldinit       _ □ x
.class public abstract auto ansi beforefieldinit Teacher
        extends [mscorlib]System.Object
{
} // end of class Teacher
```

Interface-Based Programming

Now we focus on how to program interfaces in C# so that classes can implement the members of various interfaces. Implementation inheritance and interface inheritance can be combined as stipulated earlier in the chapter. There is an accepted format for declaring interfaces. You can extend the implementation of the SupplyTeacher class by defining two interfaces, which contain methods that the SupplyTeacher class must implement, as the interface declarations will only contain a method signature and no implementation.

The SupplyTeacher class inherits from Teacher and implements ITemporaryWorker and IPublicWorker interfaces. The interface names should always be preceded by I. This means that the SupplyTeacher class derives from the Teacher class, so it is really a type of Teacher with different features from a StaffTeacher. The ordering in the code generally begins with inheritance of the base class and is followed by a list of interfaces being implemented.

```
public class SupplyTeacher : Teacher, ITemporaryWorker, IPublicWorker
```

Interfaces can aid development tasks, as there is no limit to the number of interfaces that any of our classes can implement (unlike implementation inheritance). With interface inheritance we can decouple our concrete class from calling code so that there are no dependencies on the actual class in code. If the interface changes then the class implementation will change to insist that new implementations be revised in the concrete classes. A struct can implement an interface, but it cannot inherit implementation from a class.

The SupplyTeacher class supports two interfaces: ITemporaryWorker and IPublicWorker. By implementing these interfaces you can treat the class in the same manner by using substitutability. This is important since this class can be considered as a kind of ITemporaryWorker and IPublicWorker. This means that the SupplyTeacher class must implement all the methods specified on each of these interfaces, and can also be treated as each of these interfaces without actually needing to know the type of class. It must implement all the methods that each interface defines, since this is a contract between the class and the calling code, else the compiler will generate an exception.

In OO development the correct way to use multiple inheritance is to inherit multiple interfaces; this is the programming model supported by both .NET and Java. Interfaces can be used to complement the use of implementation inheritance. You may want to implement an interface on the Teacher class since a Teacher is a type of PublicSectorWorker and shares certain things in common with other public sector workers. By default all the derived classes would inherit the common interface that should be shared by all public sector workers, as each derived class could be treated as a type of PublicSectorWorker too. The following examples will extend the Teacher class model to enable the implementation of interfaces, which allow polymorphism to be used on the classes.

Defining an Interface

Creating a base class for all the public sector workers is not a good idea since it would fail the *is a* rule. Use interfaces to ensure that all the types of public services worker class implement the Load() method. We can define an interface called INonAdminPublicSectorEmployee that includes the Load() method in its definition. This means that all of the classes that implement this interface will have to implement the same signature method.

We define an interface below that supports two methods, the Load() method that takes a string argument and the GetItem() method, which takes a DateTime argument and returns a string. Note that there is no implementation in the definition. The interface cannot contain any implementation code, it can only contain signatures for methods, events, and properties (it cannot contain static members or instance members either!).

Each class must implement the two methods defined here in some way, else the C# compiler would generate an exception (unless the methods are abstract).

```
public interface INonAdminPublicSectorWorker
{
    void Load(string fileName);
    string GetItem(DateTime date);
}
```

Implementing the Interface

You can add a HospitalWorker class to the current class hierarchy for teachers, which will have a custom implementation of the INonAdminPublicSectorWorker interface methods. A simple implementation for the Load() method by the HospitalWorker() class is shown overleaf, which uses a comma-delimited file containing all of the date information for a particular day that relates to appointment entries. In this example, there is no prefix to the name of the method to register that it is an implementation of the interface signature since the compiler automatically knows that the method being implemented has the same signature as the one specified on the interface.

The runtime uses the interface map to determine the interfaces supported by the class and will check to see whether the supported method signature is present. The method table can check the interface map for interfaces supported by the class that will have knowledge of the class method positions in the vtable, which are stored sequentially per interface. This adds another level of indirection to using interfaces.

The Load() method will use the date and time values to create a DateTime object, which can be used as a key for the Hashtable, which will store all the relevant string values against the key. The second method GetItem() is also implemented, which takes a DateTime value using it as a key to the Hashtable and returns the appropriate value or returns an empty string if the DateTime() doesn't exist in the collection. Note that the implementation in the other implementation classes can take any form. The following code file is saved as implementing_interfaces.cs:

```
public class HospitalWorker : INonAdminPublicSectorWorker
{
    private Hashtable ht = new Hashtable();
    public void Load(string FileName)
    {
        try
        {
            FileStream stream = File.Open(FileName, FileMode.Open,
                                          FileAccess.Read);
            StreamReader reader = new StreamReader(stream);
            string fileContents = reader.ReadToEnd();
            foreach(string line in
                    fileContents.Split(Environment.NewLine.ToCharArray()))
            {
                string[] agenda = line.Split(new Char[] { ',' });
                ht.Add(DateTime.Parse(agenda[0]), agenda[1]);
            }
        }
        catch{}
        finally
        {
            if(reader!=null)
                {reader.Close();}
        }
    static void Main(string[] args)
    {
      HospitalWorker hw = new HospitalWorker();
      hw.Load("C:\\agenda.txt");
    }
    }
    public string GetItem(DateTime dt)
    {
        return ht[dt].ToString ();
    }
}
```

Polymorphism with Interfaces

We don't need to know whether the implementation class is a HospitalWorker, a Teacher, or any other class that implements the INonAdminPublicSectorWorker interface. We can change the class creation statement and the invocation. Then you simply need to know that the interface is an INonAdminPublicSectorWorker type. As a result, we have implemented the same level of abstraction in this example through polymorphism, as we did within the concrete base-class implementation, where the CLR automatically invoked the correct method on the derived class even though we used the more generic Teacher type in code.

```
INonAdminPublicSectorWorker hw = new HospitalWorker();
hw.Load("C:\\agenda.txt");
```

By using the interface with distinct types of classes we have an idea of the subset of functionality that each class offers; by using the INonAdminPublicSectorWorker interface in place of the class in the code example above we will only see the supporting methods that the interface supports as opposed to the class. This is the public signature between the classes, and the contract that binds the calling code and the concrete class.

As interfaces don't contain any implementation code, they cannot be instantiated like abstract classes, though they can be considered as a grouping mechanism for related classes. This is why polymorphism works with interfaces. For example, we could up-cast the HospitalWorker object to the interface type that it implements using the following code. When the class implements many interfaces it can be (up) cast to any one of those interfaces in code. Calling the Load() method on the inaps reference will invoke the required method on the HospitalWorker class instance as seen above.

```
HospitalWorker hw = new HospitalWorker();
INonAdminPublicSectorWorker inaps = (INonAdminPublicSectorWorker)hw;
inaps.Load("C:\\agenda.txt");
```

Be wary of using the interface type instead of the class type, as we can't invoke anything that is unsupported by the interface; this behavior is identical to the usage of the base-class type to invoke methods on the derived-class instance. For example, this would be illegal usage of interface-based programming since the INonAdminPublicSectorWorker doesn't support the ReturnEverything() method, which is a method supported by the HospitalWorker class:

```
inaps.ReturnEverything();
```

The way to get round this issue is to down-cast again to a HospitalWorker type, which has a different interface defined by the extra method ReturnEverything().

```
if(inaps is HospitalWorker) {
    HopsitalWorker hw = (HospitalWorker)inaps; }
```

We extend the model to define a method, which will use the interface type instead of the concrete type and invoke a method supported by that interface. This really emphasizes the benefits of using polymorphism in code providing a deep level of abstraction. We can write a static method using the base-derived class model passing in the interface type, instead of the concrete class and the filename of the agenda file, which would pass to the Load() method. It is irrelevant what concrete implementation class is used as long as it supports the correct interface.

```
public static void InvokeMemberOnNonAdmin(INonAdminPublicSectorWorker
inon, string fileName)
{
    try
    {
        inon.Load(fileName);
    }
```

```
  catch(Exception ex)
  {
    //log this exception to a file
  }
}
```

To invoke this we would use code similar to the earlier example. (Though try to avoid using such long method names in your code!)

```
INonAdminPublicSectorWorker hw = new HospitalWorker();
InvocationClass. InvokeMemberOnNonAdmin( hw, "C:\\agenda.txt");
```

We can have many interfaces implemented by the same class, and we can have many diverse classes that implement the same interface. This idea of having many interfaces being implemented by a single class is commonly known as multiple interface inheritance. When we talk implementation inheritance we normally say that we *inherit* from the base class whereas the equivalent usage of words for an interface suggests that we *implement* an interface.

This idea of a mix and match of interfaces can be used throughout our own class libraries, just as it has been with the .NET Framework; for example we could just as easily develop classes that implement common interfaces within the .NET Framework such as `IList`, `ICollection`, `ICloneable`, `IFormattable`, etc.

An example already seen is the implementation of a class that supports the `IComparer` interface. This class can be passed to the `Sort()` method of a collection class object, which will call the implemented `Compare()` method several times, to compare all the members of the collection. It allows us to use .NET Framework collection classes, rather than build our own, and specify the sort class that we want to use. The possibilities for multiple interface inheritance are evident because the same class can be used in a number of different ways using polymorphism with respect to many supported interfaces.

Multiple Interface Inheritance

The code below defines an `ILazyWorker` interface, which supports a single method called `WastedTime()` whose implementation is down to the implementation class. Interfaces can be declared as either public or internal, the default one being public.

```
interface ILazyWorker
{
    int WastedTime();
}
```

We can alter the definition of the `HospitalWorker` class to support both the `INonAdminPublicSectorWorker` interface and the new `ILazyWorker` interface. There is no limit to the number of interfaces that an object can support but most interfaces will support few methods to keep their footprint low.

```
public class HospitalWorker : INonAdminPublicSectorWorker, ILazyWorker
```

The HospitalWorker supporting the two interfaces listed above means that there is a contract between the code that creates instances of classes, and the classes themselves. The object creation code knows what the object should support. This enables us to assert what the object can do based on the definition of the interface rather than actually knowing what the type of object is. This is how polymorphism is enforced through the contractual obligations of the implementation class.

Figure 11

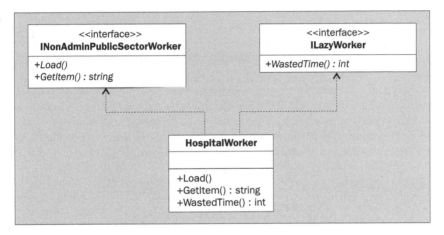

Interfaces in IL

Let's look at the MSIL for the ILazyWorker interface. The interface instruction allows an entry to be added to the interface map, and the abstract instruction specifies that the interface cannot be instantiated (just like abstract classes).

```
ILazyWorker::.class interface private abstract auto ansi

.class interface private abstract auto ansi ILazyWorker
{
} // end of class ILazyWorker
```

Viewing the MSIL we find that each method uses the newslot instruction, since there are no virtual implementations of this method in this interface. We are not overriding anything with this definition, and everything will be added to the virtual methods section of the interface. Each method is declared as abstract even though the definition is omitted from our C# code. We have defined a contract with the implementation of the interface exactly the same way as the implementation of an abstract method. The author of the implementing class must implement all the methods in an interface so every method on an interface is defined as abstract:

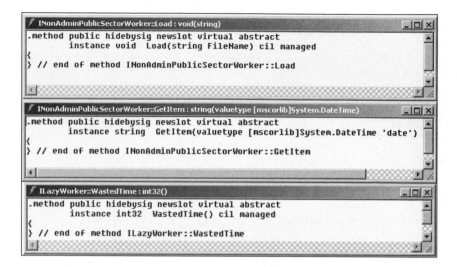

We assess the MSIL output of the implementation class `HospitalWorker`. Java programmers should be familiar with the syntax used to denote interface inheritance in MSIL – the `implements` instruction tells the CLR to add these interfaces to the interface map and check that the interface methods are being implemented by the concrete class.

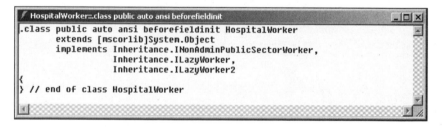

Two implemented methods of `INonAdminPublicSectorWorker` and `ILazyWorker` within the `HospitalWorker` class are shown opposite in MSIL. The MSIL instruction implementation shows that the method is declared using `newslot`, as there is no virtual implementation within the interface. Also note that this method is declared as `final` which means that we cannot override it in a derived class. We could circumvent this by declaring the method as `virtual` in the concrete class, which would remove the `final` instruction and allow it to be overridden in a derived class.

290

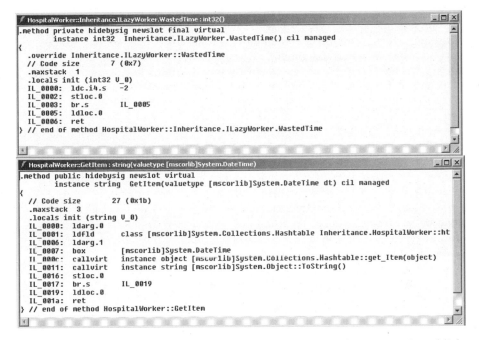

All methods implemented in the concrete HospitalWorker class are made publicly visible in the above code examples. The visibility can be varied by providing private definitions for the interface methods. Private members are invoked if we use an interface type reference, rather than the reference type of the concrete class.

Scoping Interface Methods

Let's reiterate the ILazyWorker interface. Notice how an access modifier is not used.

```
interface ILazyWorker
{
    int WastedTime();
}
```

The concrete implementation of this interface, the HospitalWorker class has a public method declared to implement the WastedTime() method of the ILazyWorker interface.

```
public int WastedTime()
{
    return -1;
}
```

We could also declare the ILazyWorker.WastedTime() method without an access modifier, which will automatically make the visibility of the method private, as all methods default to being privately visible in a class unless otherwise modified.

Thus, we can have methods for the concrete class and the interface, which would enable different methods to be invoked. The public method returns a strongly typed class instance, whereas the private method returns an object that will have to be (down) cast. Another use is that multiple interfaces can avoid method name and signature collision. This principle asserts that if two interfaces have a method with the same name and signature, their implementations will coexist in the same concrete class without any ambiguity.

This is achieved through the use of pointers, from the interface map back to the vtable, which will have either privately scoped, or public methods at the same offset in the method table for each contiguous interface method map. The determinant will be the type of reference used to invoke the method, which is determined from the RuntimeTypeHandle. If we had a reciprocal WastedTime() method on the INonAdminPublicWorker interface, then it would exist in isolation only visible through the interface reference. Try using this approach when implementing many interfaces against a single concrete class, as polymorphism through interface implementation avoids name collision.

```
int ILazyWorker.WastedTime()
{
    return -2;
}
```

We use the following code to obtain a concrete class type reference to the HospitalWorker class and invoke the WastedTime() method, and then reference the ILazyWorker interface.

```
HospitalWorker h = new HospitalWorker();
Console.WriteLine(h.WastedTime());
ILazyWorker ilw = new HospitalWorker();
Console.WriteLine(ilw.WastedTime());
```

The methods declared in the implementation class are stored within the method table, in the same way as virtual, overridden, or new methods are stored in a derived class (method table). The interface map is used by the CLR, and contains all the interfaces not just those supported by the current class. There are series of pointers in the table back to virtual methods, supported by each interface that the class implements.

Any cast to unsupported interfaces will not work, as there aren't any method table pointers for that method within the class. Looking up the interface map adds a second layer over and above the use of implementation inheritance, so it will result in a slightly slower implementation. Microsoft acknowledges that the JIT compiler can optimize this. The use of implementation inheritance involves a slight overhead, as the callvirt instruction is used instead of call, though the code maintainability, and the use of privately scoped interface methods compensate for this slight degradation in performance.

Casting to Different Interface Types

The idea behind polymorphism is that the class type is irrelevant to whether or not it supports the contract and can be substituted for an interface reference. The following example illustrates how to use multiple interfaces and cast them from the concrete type to the interface type. First we create a new `HopspitalWorker` class instance calling the `WastedTime()` method, which calls the public signature method since we are using the concrete class type reference. Then we cast the `HospitalWorker` to the supported interface `ILazyWorker`. We then cast the resultant `ilw` interface type reference field to the `INonAdminPublicSectorWorker` interface, since the underlying type is aware of the supported interfaces through the interface map. The compiler will filter out any unsupported interface casts from the concrete class to an interface type and generate an exception.

```
HospitalWorker worker = new HospitalWorker();
Console.WriteLine(worker.WastedTime());
ILazyWorker ilw = (ILazyWorker)h;
INonAdminPublicSectorWorker inaps2 = (INonAdminPublicSectorWorker)ilw;
Console.WriteLine(inaps2.GetItem(DateTime.Now));
Console.WriteLine(ilw.WastedTime());
```

The code would produce the following output as expected:

```
C:\Class Design\Ch 07>implementing_interfaces.cs
-1
-2
Not implemented!
```

Both interfaces invoke the corresponding interface methods rather than the public signature methods. The MSIL for this code section is recorded below – in all instances we can see the `callvirt` instruction being used for every method call whether the concrete reference or the interface reference is used. We can convert between supporting interfaces due to the presence of the `castclass` instruction, which uses the underlying base-class type to check if the interface is supported. If it is then the cast goes ahead – this is how we can cast between interfaces without using the concrete class reference directly.

```
InvocationClass::Main : void(string[])                                                                    _|□|x|
                                                                   string&)
IL_00c6:  pop
IL_00c7:  newobj     instance void Inheritance.HospitalWorker::.ctor()
IL_00cc:  stloc.s    V_6
IL_00ce:  ldloc.s    V_6
IL_00d0:  ldstr      "C:\\agenda.txt"
IL_00d5:  call       void Inheritance.InvocationClass::InvokeMemberOnINonAdminPublicSectorWorkerInterface(class Inheritan
                                                                                                          string)
IL_00da:  newobj     instance void Inheritance.HospitalWorker::.ctor()
IL_00df:  stloc.s    V_7
IL_00e1:  ldloc.s    V_7
IL_00e3:  stloc.s    V_8
IL_00e5:  ldloc.s    V_8
IL_00e7:  castclass  Inheritance.INonAdminPublicSectorWorker
IL_00ec:  stloc.s    V_9
IL_00ee:  ldloc.s    V_9
IL_00f0:  call       valuetype [mscorlib]System.DateTime [mscorlib]System.DateTime::get_Now()
IL_00f5:  callvirt   instance string Inheritance.INonAdminPublicSectorWorker::GetItem(valuetype [mscorlib]System.DateTime
IL_00fa:  call       void [mscorlib]System.Console::WriteLine(string)
IL_00ff:  ldloc.s    V_8
IL_0101:  callvirt   instance int32 Inheritance.ILazyWorker::WastedTime()
IL_0106:  call       void [mscorlib]System.Console::WriteLine(int32)
IL_010b:  call       int32 [mscorlib]System.Console::Read()
IL_0110:  pop
IL_0111:  ret
```

Name Ambiguity and Shadowing

We can declare a second interface that has the same method signature as the first, and there will be no name collision since we can only have one public signature on the concrete class. The `WastedTime()` method would therefore be the same for both interfaces publicly. Hence, the public contract would be fulfilled since both interfaces support this method.

```
interface ILazyWorker2
{
    int WastedTime();
}
```

To support shadowing between interfaces we can redefine the above interface with a slightly different method signature but the same method name. This enables us to introduce a new interface into the definition of the concrete class, which acts as if the `WastedTime()` method were overloaded on the public interface. Further, we can use this like an overloaded method and provide an implementation for the `WastedTime(int)` method, not the parameterless `WastedTime()` method. This allows the parameterless `WastedTime()` method to call the second method with a zero value, which doesn't affect the calculation. This is a good way of extending the implementation model while maintaining backward compatibility and providing a safe facility to overload methods in public concrete type interfaces.

```
interface ILazyWorker2
{
    int WastedTime(int time);
}
```

We can also use inheritance in the following way between interfaces. This will just act as a declaration that is identical in operation to using multiple interface inheritance of these two interfaces. In effect the implementation class will still have to implement both `ILazyWorker` and `ILazyWorker2`.

```
interface ILazyWorker : ILazyWorker2
{
    int WastedTime();
}
```

Summary

This chapter focused on the usage of inheritance in our code, that is, using implementation inheritance to write virtual methods in the base class, by using the `virtual` keyword declaration. Overriding virtual methods in the derived class by using the `override` keyword was discussed. We looked at the MSIL and discovered many keywords defining the implementation of inheritance, including `newslot` and `callvirt`.

We discussed the merits of using abstract base classes over concrete base classes. We also saw that the ultimate base class was the System.Object, which even structs (which derive from System.ValueType) have as their ultimate base class.

We saw virtual and non-virtual dispatching, including the use of the new keyword and emphasized hiding of inherited members. We saw how to register the expected behavior of the inherited classes using polymorphism by overriding methods in the derived class, or accessing base-class methods from a base-class reference to a derived-class object instance.

We also discussed the concept of shadowing and to how to add members to the class with the same method (or property) name as the inherited or overridden method, but with a different signature allowing us to specify a series of overloaded methods without changing the interface on the base class.

We discussed how each class had its own method table with contiguous regions for inherited virtuals and its own virtuals in vtables. This is used by an overridden method to overwrite the memory address of the inherited virtual method in the vtable.

We saw how to use interfaces and multiple interface inheritance and how the interface map identifies the interfaces that the concrete class supports. IL explains the operations and how C# code is compiled and supported by the CLR. We identified the use of multiple interface inheritance and saw how to avoid name collision by using scoping for the interface and method dispatching, depending on whether we were using the interface type reference or the concrete-class type reference.

C#

Class Design

Handbook

8

Code Organization and Metadata

This is the last chapter in the book, and it gives us a good opportunity to consider the larger issues that affect the logical and physical organization of our C# applications. In the first part of this chapter, we'll look at how applications may be logically structured during coding; then in the second part we'll see how this translates to a physical partitioning of files in preparation for deployment.

We'll discuss how to use **namespaces** to partition an application into groups of related types. Namespaces emphasize the logical structure of the application, and avoid clashes between type names. The .NET Framework class library highlights the importance of namespaces; the class library has been designed in a modular fashion, and namespaces reinforce the organization of the class library. We'll see how to define namespaces in C#, we'll see where this information is held in Visual Studio .NET, and we'll provide design guidelines that will help you use namespaces effectively. As an overview, in this chapter we:

- ❑ Discuss the definition of namespaces and how to create nested namespaces

- ❑ Investigate assemblies and metadata, which contain, among other things, versioning information, the files needed to run an application, and the various types defined

- ❑ Discover how to deploy applications in multi-assembly format

- ❑ Learn how to create shared assemblies and place them in the Global Assembly Cache (GAC) for easy discovery by the runtime

- ❑ See how to document code and how to furnish an assembly with information such as our company name, a copyright notice, and a description of the assembly

Parts of this chapter make use of Visual Studio .NET, rather than just the Framework SDK. We'll start with a discussion of namespaces.

Structuring Applications with Namespaces

All the types in a .NET application are logically defined in namespaces. The .NET Framework class library is itself logically organized into a hierarchical namespace structure. The following table describes some of the namespaces defined in the .NET Framework class library:

Namespace	Description
System	Contains fundamental classes, structures, interfaces, delegate types, and events that are used extensively in .NET applications. For example, the System namespace contains the Object class, from which all other types inherit. Object provides basic methods such as Equals, ToString, and Finalize.
System.Windows	Contains classes and other types for creating Windows-based GUIs.
System.Web	Contains classes and other types for creating ASP.NET pages and server controls.
System.Data	Contains basic ADO.NET classes and types for querying, updating, and managing databases.
System.Xml	Contains classes and types for creating and processing XML documents.

If we create a new C# project, Visual Studio .NET assigns a default namespace for the project. To illustrate this, open Visual Studio .NET and create a new project (for example, a Windows application). Now, if you right-click on the project icon in the Solution Explorer, and select Properties from the Shortcut menu, then the Property Pages dialog box appears as follows:

Our project has the default namespace SimpleWindowsApplication. By default, this is the same as the project name, but we can change this namespace if we want a different one. For example, if we create several different projects and we want them all to inhabit the same namespace, we can change the default namespace in each project to what is required. This will ensure that any classes we add using the Visual Studio .NET wizards will be placed in the correct namespace. The wizards achieve this by inserting a namespace declaration into any files they generate. The namespace name for these directives is obtained from this property. Changing the value here won't change the namespace of any classes that already exist in the project, however. Also, make sure you don't delete the default namespace entry in the project properties dialog; if you do, rather than leaving out a namespace directive, Visual Studio .NET will add a blank namespace around any classes you add with the wizard, and this will result in a compilation error unless you fill in a namespace yourself.

> *If you come across Visual Basic .NET code, you may be surprised to find no namespace declarations in the code itself, yet discover that the compiled types all belong to namespaces. VB.NET has a similar project-level namespace property, but rather than using it to insert default namespace declarations, it uses it at compile-time to wrap all the types in the specified namespace. So by default, all VB.NET types belong to a namespace with the same name as the project in which they are declared.*

It's also possible to write namespace statements explicitly into our code ourselves. For example, we can edit Form1.cs in our simple application and add an additional namespace declaration around the Form1 class as follows:

```
namespace SimpleWindowsApplication
{
  namespace MyNamespace
  {
```

```
    public class Form1 : System.Windows.Forms.Form
    {
    ...
    }
  }
}
```

So it's possible to define a nested namespace. In this example, the namespace declaration for MyNamespace is now nested within the declaration of another namespace called SimpleWindowsApplication. Therefore, the fully qualified name of the Form1 class is SimpleWindowsApplication.MyNamespace.Form1.

You can build the application directly from Visual Studio .NET, but if you want to compile this application on the command line, then the minimum code needed to create a simple form is shown below, and is contained in the download material for this book, in the file Form1.cs:

```
// form1.cs
using System;
using System.Windows.Forms;

namespace SimpleWindowsApplication
{
  namespace MyNamespace
  {
    public class Form1 : System.Windows.Forms.Form
    {
      static void Main()
      {
        Application.Run(new Form1());
      }
    }
  }
}
```

If you look at the resulting IL in the MSIL Disassembler window, it appears as follows. The window confirms that the Form1 class is defined in the namespace SimpleWindowsApplication.MyNamespace:

Designing and Implementing Namespaces

We can learn a lot about namespaces by looking at the .NET Framework. There are thousands of classes and other types in the .NET Framework class library, and Microsoft has organized these classes and types into a hierarchical namespace structure as follows:

❑ Namespaces that start with the word System contain classes and types that are common to all .NET languages. For example: System.Data contains ADO.NET types; System.Drawing contains graphical types; System.Security contains security-related types; and so on.

❑ Namespaces that start with the word Microsoft contain classes and types that are specific to Microsoft. These include namespaces for all of the .NET languages. For example, Microsoft.CSharp contains classes that support compilation and code generation for C#. Similarly, Microsoft.VisualBasic contains the Visual Basic .NET runtime, plus classes and other types that support compilation and code generation for Visual Basic .NET.

You should start thinking about namespaces during the design phase of any project, because they provide an excellent way of partitioning a large system into discrete sub-systems.

Many organizations use the Unified Modeling Language (UML) to model their object-oriented systems. For more information about UML, see *Instant UML* 1-86100-087-1 published by Wrox Press. UML includes graphical notation for **packages**, which contain groups of related classes and types in the system being modeled. During object-oriented design, we identify which classes are dependent on each other, and put these classes into the same package. Packages provide a way to compartmentalize dependent classes into a cohesive unit of logic and functionality, which provides an ancillary benefit of presenting a system which is easier to understand.

Example of Designing Namespaces

Imagine a system that allows people to borrow books from a library. The system might have classes such as Member, Book, and so on. The following diagram shows a simplified UML-like object model for this system:

Figure 1

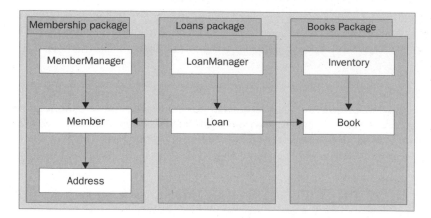

There are three packages in this model:

❑ The Membership package contains all the classes and types to implement the membership rules for the library. The MemberManager object has a collection of Member objects, and each Member has an Address.

❑ The Loans package contains all the classes and types to implement the rules for loaning and returning books. The LoanManager object has a collection of Loan objects. Each Loan object has a reference to a Member object and a Book object, to indicate which member has borrowed which book.

❑ The Books package contains all the classes and types to implement the rules for maintaining the library's inventory. Each Book object holds information about a book, such as its title and author.

Clearly, this is a simplified object model, and we've ignored many details that would be present in a real library system. Nevertheless, we can already see how packages help us to view the system as a collection of loosely coupled sub-systems.

In object-oriented design, we aim to minimize the dependencies between the classes in different packages. This makes it easier to change the implementation details within a package, without adversely affecting the other packages in the system.

Example of Implementing Namespaces

When we start writing code for our system, following the most logical mapping from UML to code, each package should be represented with a separate namespace. The C# application for our library system will therefore consist of three namespaces:

Namespace	Classes in this namespace
Membership	MemberManager, Member, and Address
Loans	LoanManager and Loan
Books	Inventory and Book

By mapping UML packages to namespaces in our code, we achieve continuity between the design phase and the construction phase of the project. In addition, it will help maintenance programmers understand how the application is structured when they have to fix bugs, or add new features, in the future.

Namespaces define the logical grouping of types in our system. They do not specify where we should write these namespaces in C# source files. Here are some options:

- ❑ Write all the types in all the namespaces in a single C# source file. This is only feasible if the namespaces are small and the types few in number. Otherwise, if the size of the source file grows unacceptably large, because there are so many classes and types in it, it will make the code difficult to navigate. This also more or less prevents a team collaborating on different parts of the code at the same time.

- ❑ Write each type in a separate source file. This gives maximum flexibility for collaboration, but disconnects the development of related functionality in different types. When working on a type in this system, it is as easy to reference a type in a different namespace as it is to reference one in the same namespace, so we run the risk of crossing the boundaries between namespaces more often than we would like.

- ❑ Put groups of related types in the same source file, ignoring namespace boundaries. We could, for instance, put all of our 'entity' classes – Member, Book, and Loan in our example – in one source file, because we may write them all at the same time. But this blurs the logical boundaries we set up in our UML analysis. Nonetheless, sometimes it makes sense to put two types from different namespaces in the same file, where they are very closely related, perhaps because they form the interface between the two subsystems in the two namespaces.

- ❑ Put all of the types in a namespace into the same source file. This most closely follows the logical structure of the application. Again, it will only be practical if number of types in each namespace is small, and generally you will want to split the namespace into several groups of related types. Our example, however, has few types in each namespace, and they are closely related in every case. This pattern makes sense in this situation.

We'll take the last approach, and create a C# application that consists of four files:

Filename	Description
membership.cs	Implements all the types in the Membership namespace
books.cs	Implements all the types in the Books namespace
loans.cs	Implements all the types in the Loans namespace
library_app.cs	Contains the Main method for our application

Writing the Membership Namespace

Here is the full source code for the Membership namespace. The code is defined in membership.cs. We'll discuss the salient design issues after the code listing; one thing to notice at the outset, though, is that the Membership namespace has no dependencies on any of the other namespaces in our application – it only uses system namespaces.

```
using System;
using System.Collections;

namespace Membership
{
  public class MemberManager
  {
    private static MemberManager mInstance;
    private Hashtable mLibraryMembers;

    private MemberManager()
    {
      mLibraryMembers = new Hashtable();
    }

    public static MemberManager Instance
    {
      get
      {
        if (mInstance == null)
          mInstance = new MemberManager();
        return mInstance;
      }
    }

    public Member CreateMember(string name, string street,
                               string city)
    {
      Member newMem = new Member(name, street, city);
      mLibraryMembers[name] = newMem;
      return newMem;
    }
```

```
      public Member this [string name]
      {
        get { return (Member)mLibraryMembers[name]; }
      }
    }

    // ... more to follow
  }
```

The `MemberManager` class is a singleton class, which means there will only ever be a single instance of this class. To achieve this effect, we define the constructor as `private`. We also provide a `static` property named `Instance`, which returns the single instance of `MemberManager`. This property uses lazy initialization; it only creates the `MemberManager` instance when it is first requested.

The `MemberManager` class uses a `Hashtable` to keep a collection of `Member` objects. `Member` objects are created and added to the collection using the `CreateMember` factory method. To allow us to retrieve `Member` objects from the collection, using the member name as a key, we have created a read-only indexer. Note that this simplified implementation assumes that member names will be unique.

The file `membership.cs` also contains the definition of the `Member` class:

```
public class Member
{
  private string mName;
  private Address mAddress;

  public Member(string name, string street, string city)
  {
    mName = name;
    mAddress = new Address(street, city);
  }

  public override string ToString()
  {
    return mName + ", address: " + mAddress.ToString();
  }
}
```

The `Member` class holds the name and address of a member. The address is encapsulated in the `Address` class. We have provided `ToString` methods in each class, to retrieve the information in text format. The `Address` class, which completes the `Membership` namespace, is shown below:

```
public class Address
{
  private string mStreet;
  private string mCity;
```

```
    public Address(string street, string city)
      {
        mStreet = street;
        mCity = city;
      }

    public override string ToString()
    {
      return mStreet + ", " + mCity;
    }
  }
}
```

This source code illustrates several important issues that we have discussed in this chapter and in earlier chapters. Most importantly, it represents a generic membership framework that could be used in another member-based application.

Writing the Books Namespace

Now let's look at the source code for the Books namespace. The code is defined in books.cs:

```
using System;
using System.Collections;

namespace Books
{
  public class Inventory
  {
    private static Inventory mInstance;
    private Hashtable mLibraryBooks;

    private Inventory()
    {
      mLibraryBooks = new Hashtable();
    }

    public static Inventory Instance
    {
      get
      {
        if (mInstance == null)
          mInstance = new Inventory();
        return mInstance;
      }
    }

    public Book CreateBook(string title, string author,
                           string isbn)
    {
```

```csharp
      Book newBook = new Book(title, author, isbn);
      mLibraryBooks[isbn] = newBook;
      return newBook;
    }

    public Book this [string ISBN]
    {
      get { return (Book)mLibraryBooks[ISBN]; }
    }
  }

  public class Book
  {
    private string mTitle;
    private string mAuthor;
    private string mISBN;

    public Book(string title, string author, string isbn)
    {
      mTitle = title;
      mAuthor = author;
      mISBN = isbn;
    }

    public override string ToString()
    {
      return mTitle + " (ISBN: " + mISBN + "), by: " + mAuthor;
    }
  }
}
```

There are many noticeable similarities between the Inventory class and the MemberManager class. Both classes are singleton classes, and both use a Hashtable to hold a collection of other objects (Inventory holds a list of Book objects, and MemberManager holds a collection of Member objects).

Another similarity is the way Inventory and MemberManager provide access to the objects in their collections. Both classes provide a factory method to create objects and add them to the collection, and an indexer to retrieve the items. In this simplified example, Books are indexed using a string representation of their ISBN. (Although the N in ISBN is for number, an ISBN doesn't just consist of numbers; it can also end with the character X).

Notice again that the Books namespace has no dependency whatsoever on any of the other namespaces in our application. This illustrates the design goal of loose coupling between namespaces.

Writing the Loans Namespace

The Loans namespace contains the LoanManager and Loan classes. Every time a
member borrows a book, the LoanManager creates a new Loan object to identify the
book and the borrower. The LoanManager also allows books to be returned, which is
an important business rule for the library.

The code for the Loans namespace is defined in loans.cs. We'll discuss the design
issues after the code listing:

```
using System;
using System.Collections;
using Membership;
using Books;

namespace Loans
{
  public class LoanManager
  {
    private static LoanManager mInstance;
    private Hashtable mLoans;

    private LoanManager()
    {
      mLoans = new Hashtable();
    }

    public static LoanManager Instance
    {
      get
      {
        if (mInstance == null)
          mInstance = new LoanManager();
        return mInstance;
      }
    }

    public void BorrowBook(string isbn, string member)
    {
      Inventory inv = Inventory.Instance;
      MemberManager mem = MemberManager.Instance;

      Book theBook = inv[isbn];
      Member theMember = mem[member];

      if (theBook != null && theMember != null)
      {
        Loan theLoan = new Loan(theBook, theMember);
        mLoans[isbn] = theLoan;
        Console.WriteLine(theLoan.ToString());
      }
```

```
        else
           Console.WriteLine("Cannot borrow book");
      }

      public void ReturnBook(string isbn)
      {
         if (mLoans.ContainsKey(isbn))
         {
            mLoans.Remove(isbn);
            Console.WriteLine("Book {0} has been returned", isbn);
         }
         else
            Console.WriteLine("Cannot return book");
      }
   }

   public class Loan
   {
      private Book mTheBook;
      private Member mTheMember;

      public Loan(Book TheBook, Member TheMember)
      {
         mTheBook = TheBook;
         mTheMember = TheMember;
      }

      public override string ToString()
      {
         return "Book: " + mTheBook.ToString() +
            "\nBorrowed by: " + mTheMember.ToString() + "\n";
      }
   }
}
```

Note the following points in this source file:

❑ We import the Membership and Books namespaces. This enables us to access the classes defined in these namespaces, without needing to use fully qualified class names such as Membership.MemberManager.

This is the one occasion where dependencies with other namespaces cannot be avoided. Some degree of coupling is inevitable; the important thing is to identify where this coupling occurs, and to minimize it as much as possible.

❑ LoanManager is a singleton class, because there is only one LoanManager in our library system.

❑ The BorrowBook method enables books to be borrowed by members. The book and member are identified by unique identifiers. In this simple example, we use the book's ISBN as a lookup key in Inventory to get a reference to the Book object with this ISBN. Likewise, we use the member name as a lookup key in MemberManager to get a reference to the Member object with this name. Obviously, in a real-world application, we would need to be more careful in selecting unique identifiers as these would probably represent a primary key in a database table. While this example uses Hashtables internally, we could easily change the Inventory and/or MemberManager classes to use a different storage technique without needing to change any other classes.

If the Book and Member objects can be located, we create a new Loan object to remember which member has borrowed which book. We store the Loan object in a Hashtable, using the book's ISBN as the lookup key. In our simple example, this is a reasonable choice for a lookup key, because each book can only be on loan to one member at a time.

❑ The ReturnBook method enables books to be returned to the library. The only information we need when a book is returned is the book's ISBN (it doesn't matter who returns the book – not in our model, anyway).

If the book's ISBN can be located in the loans Hashtable, it means the book is indeed on loan. In this case, we remove the Loan from the Hashtable to indicate that the book is no longer on loan.

❑ The Loan class has a reference to a Book object, and a reference to a Member object. In UML terms, Loan is an **association object**; it defines an association between a Book and a Member.

Writing the Main() Method for the Application

Now that we've seen how to implement the core namespaces in our application, all that remains is to write a Main method to use these namespaces. The code for the Main method is shown below, and is located in the file library_app.cs:

```
using System;
using Membership;
using Books;
using Loans;

namespace LibraryApp
{
    public class LibraryApp
    {
     public static void Main()
     {
        Inventory inv = Inventory.Instance;
        inv.CreateBook("Professional C#", "Robinson",
                       "1-86100-704-3");
        inv.CreateBook("Instant UML", "Muller", "1-86100-087-1");
```

```
MemberManager mem = MemberManager.Instance;
mem.CreateMember("Georgia", "5th Avenue", "New York");
mem.CreateMember("William", "Park Lane", "London");

LoanManager loanmgr = LoanManager.Instance;
loanmgr.BorrowBook("1-86100-704-3", "Georgia");
loanmgr.BorrowBook("1-86100-087-1", "William");

loanmgr.ReturnBook("1-86100-704-3");
loanmgr.ReturnBook("1-86100-087-1");
    }
  }
}
```

Note the following, regarding this code:

❑   We import the Membership, Books, and Loans namespaces. We use classes from all these namespaces in this application.

❑   In Main, we get a reference to the Inventory object, and create two books in the inventory. We also get a reference to the MemberManager object, and create two members.

❑   We get a reference to the LoanManager object, and call BorrowBook twice to borrow two books from the library. Then we call ReturnBook twice, to return these books to the library. In all these cases, we identify the books and members by their ISBNs and names respectively.

Building and Running the Application

One way to build this application is to open a .NET Framework Command Prompt window and type the following command:

```
C:\> csc library_app.cs membership.cs books.cs loans.cs
```

This command compiles the four C# source files in this application, and creates a single assembly named library_app.exe. The assembly is named after the first source file in the list of files to be compiled; to create a different name for the assembly, use the /out:filename compiler switch. Another option would be to compile each of the namespaces into a separate DLL. Then we could just use the /r switch as necessary to link to these DLLs. Visual Studio .NET can also provide a number of different options for compilation, and you can choose whichever method is most appropriate. We'll look at these physical options later on.

When we run the application, it displays the following output on the console window:

Book: Professional C# (ISBN: 1-86100-704-3), by: Robinson
Borrowed by: Georgia, address: 5th Avenue, New York

Book: Instant UML (ISBN: 1-86100-087-1), by: Muller
Borrowed by: William, address: Park Lane, London

Book 1-86100-704-3 has been returned
Book 1-86100-087-1 has been returned

Nested Namespaces

Nested namespaces allow us to define a layered architecture, which offers different levels of abstraction in our application. This helps us grasp the overall shape of the system, while at the same time offering enough detail to model extremely large or complex systems in an organized and comprehensible manner.

The .NET Framework class library is a good example of a layered namespace design:

❑   The top-level namespaces System and Microsoft differentiate system-wide classes (in the System namespace) from vendor-specific classes (in the Microsoft namespace).

❑   Nested namespaces, such as System.Data and System.Drawing, partition the system-wide classes into logical groups. Each namespace exhibits the desirable characteristics of high cohesion (everything that belongs together, *is* together), and loose coupling (there are very few dependencies between classes in different namespaces).

❑   A further level of nesting provides still more granularity. For example, the following table describes the nested namespaces beneath System.Data.

Namespace	Description
System.Data.SqlClient	Contains ADO.NET classes and types for accessing SQL Server 7.0 (and later) databases.
System.Data.OleDb	Contains ADO.NET classes and types for accessing SQL Server 6.5 (and earlier) databases, and other databases such as Oracle and Microsoft Access.
System.Data.Common	Contains common ADO.NET classes and types that are used to access any kind of database. For example, this namespace includes the DataSet class, which represents an in-memory cache of data in a disconnected application.
System.Data.SqlTypes	Contains types to represent native SQL Server data types.

Defining Nested Namespaces

There are two different ways to define nested namespaces in our code. The following example illustrates both techniques. The source code for this example is located in the download folder; the following file is named nested_namespaces.cs:

```
namespace MyNamespace1
{
  public class MyClassA
  {
    // members
  }

  namespace MyNestedNamespace1
  {
    public class MyClassB
    {
      // members
    }
  }
}

namespace MyNamespace2.MyNestedNamespace2
{
  public class MyClassC
  {
    // members
  }
}
```

Note the following points:

❑ MyNamespace1 is an outer namespace, and contains a class called MyClassA. The fully qualified name of this class is MyNamespace1.MyClassA.

❑ MyNestedNamespace1 is defined inside MyNamespace1. This creates a nested namespace called MyNamespace1.MyNestedNamespace1. This namespace contains a class called MyClassB; the fully qualified name of this class is MyNamespace1.MyNestedNamespace1.MyClassB.

❑ MyNamespace2.MyNestedNamespace2 is a nested namespace. This again illustrates how to use the 'dot' syntax in a Namespace statement, to create a nested namespace. This namespace contains a class called MyClassC; the fully qualified name of this class is MyNamespace2.MyNestedNamespace2.MyClassC.

Using Nested Namespaces

If we want to use the classes defined in nested namespaces, we can use fully qualified class names as follows. The source code below is located in the file named use_fully_qualified.cs.

```
public class UseFullyQualified
{
  public static void Main()
  {
    MyNamespace1.MyClassA a = new MyNamespace1.MyClassA();
    MyNamespace1.MyNestedNamespace1.MyClassB b =
      new MyNamespace1.MyNestedNamespace1.MyClassB();
    MyNamespace2.MyNestedNamespace2.MyClassC c =
      new MyNamespace2.MyNestedNamespace2.MyClassC();
  }
}
```

Compile these files into an assembly by opening a .NET Framework Command Prompt window and typing the command given below:

```
C:\> csc use_fully_qualified.cs nested_namespaces.cs
```

Then open this assembly in the MSIL Disassembler to see what the compiler has made of our namespaces and classes. The MSIL Disassembler window displays the following information:

The MSIL Disassembler shows there are three namespaces in our assembly.

Using fully qualified class names can be tiresome if we use the same classes several times in our code. To save some keystrokes, as you already know, we can import the required namespaces as follows. The source code opposite is located in the file named use_shortnames.cs:

```
using MyNamespace1;
using MyNamespace1.MyNestedNamespace1;
using MyNamespace2.MyNestedNamespace2;

public class UseShortnames
{
  public static void Main()
  {
      MyClassA a = new MyClassA();
    MyClassB b = new MyClassB();
    MyClassC c = new MyClassC();
  }
}
```

Compile this code along with nested_namespaces.cs, and if you open this assembly in the MSIL Disassembler, you will we see the same classes and namespaces as in the previous example. Note that we need to specify each namespace separately in a using statement, even nested namespaces. The using statement will not search recursively through nested namespaces to resolve type names.

Understanding Assemblies

Now that we've seen how to organize our code into a logical grouping of namespaces and/or source files during the design phase, we can turn our attention to the way we translate this into a physical set of files for deployment. To do this, we need to understand assemblies.

What Is An Assembly?

An **assembly** is a term coined by Microsoft to describe a set of one or more logically-related files containing type definitions and/or resources. Strictly speaking, each physical file in an assembly is known as a **module**, and may have been compiled from one or more of your source files.

Single-File Assemblies

If you are using Visual Studio .NET, then you will only ever produce single-file (isingle-module) assemblies. In this scenario, each *project* in a solution will produce *exactly one assembly* as its main output – which (leaving aside ASP.NET for one moment) will be an .exe or a .dll. In a Visual Studio .NET solution, all of these assemblies – which may be a combination of .exe's and .dll's – form an application.

Each assembly includes an **assembly manifest**, which contains versioning and security information. For this reason, an assembly is the smallest unit of reuse.

Multi-File Assemblies

If you are not using Visual Studio .NET, it is possible to produce a multi-file assembly, which is a collection of modules, each in its own file. Also, each module may have been produced by a different .NET language compiler.

In this scenario, only one of the modules in the assembly holds the **assembly manifest**, which in this case also lists the other files (modules) that make up the assembly. The module that holds the manifest will typically have an `.exe` or `.dll` extension, while the remaining modules will (by default) have the extension `.netmodule`. We'll see an example of exactly how to do this later.

Logical vs. Physical Organization

Whichever way you choose to compile your code, all of the above files – `.exe`'s, `.dll`'s, and `.netmodule`'s – must be deployed on the end-user's machine when you distribute your application.

Note also that there is absolutely no relationship between the logical structure of your source code and the physical structure of your deployed application. Multiple source files may be compiled into one module, which may or may not form part of a larger assembly. Namespaces may span multiple assemblies and a module may contain multiple namespaces, each with a number of types. You could (although it certainly wouldn't be recommended) compile the same source file into more than one module, perhaps with different conditional compilation options, then combine them into a single assembly!

This is probably immediately confusing. Apart from the familiar file extensions, there's really no parallels in terms of other development tools. Coming from a C++ background you might think that `.netmodule`'s are similar to `.obj` files – except that a module can be built from more than one source file! But, there's more to come.

Metadata

Every assembly – whether single-file or multi-file – contains **metadata**. Metadata is generated by all of the .NET language compilers and describes the types and members defined in our code. This is what replaces C++ header files, Interface Definition Language (IDL), and type libraries, which have kept COM developers occupied for a decade. This information is all held in the compiled `.exe` or `.dll`. The metadata also lists the types and members that we reference in our code, but that are defined in other assemblies.

Metadata gives the Common Language Runtime all the information it needs to load types and invoke methods at run time. The CLR also uses metadata to help it enforce security. The security system uses permissions to deny code access to resources that it does not have authority to access.

In this section, we'll see how to view all the available metadata for a single-file assembly. Then we'll see how to create a multi-file assembly, and how it is useful.

Viewing Metadata in a Single-File Assembly

The easiest way to view metadata is by using the MSIL Disassembler tool, `ildasm.exe`. We've used this tool a lot already, and we'll use it much more throughout this chapter.

Let's look at the metadata for a simple assembly, for a simple console application. The source code for this example is located in `simple_console.cs`:

```
using System;

namespace MetadataSimpleApp
{
  class SimpleConsole
  {
    public static void Main()
    {
      Console.WriteLine("Wrox Rocks!");
    }
  }
}
```

Build this application, giving it a namespace of `MetadataSimpleApp` as shown, and open the MSIL Disassembler tool using the `/adv` or `/advanced` command line switch as follows:

```
C:\> ildasm /adv simple_console.exe
```

The MSIL Disassembler tells us the following:

- ❑ The MANIFEST entry provides manifest information. As we'll see later in this chapter, the manifest lists the files and types in our assembly, plus the types used from other assemblies.

- ❑ Our assembly has a namespace called `MetadataSimpleApp`.

- ❑ The `MetadataSimpleApp` namespace has a class called `SimpleConsole`.

- ❑ `SimpleConsole` has a compiler-generated constructor, plus a `Main` method that we wrote ourselves.

This is just a small part of the information available in the MSIL Disassembler tool. Because we used the `/adv` switch, we have access to advanced information including full metadata for our assembly. To view this metadata, click on View, select MetaInfo, and then select Show!. A window appears, showing comprehensive metadata for our assembly:

Let's look at the important parts of this metadata:

❑ Metadata about this .NET module.

❑ Metadata about this assembly. At this moment, the assembly only contains one .NET module.

❑ Metadata about the types defined in this assembly.

❑ Metadata about referenced types that reside in other assemblies.

❑ Metadata about other referenced assemblies.

Metadata about this .NET Module

The first two lines in the metadata listing give us information about this **.NET module**. As we mentioned earlier, a .NET module is a **Portable Executable** (**PE**) format file, such as an .exe or .dll file, or a stand alone module with the file extension .netmodule. All the C# examples we've seen so far have been single-module assemblies, which means the assembly only comprises a single file. Later in this chapter we'll see how to create an assembly that comprises multiple .NET modules; we'll also discuss why this might be a useful thing to do.

Getting back to our discussion on .NET module metadata, the following module metadata is available:

```
ScopeName : simple_console.exe
MVID     : {9271A944-5B7E-4F7B-BA3C-97EDA8302130}
```

Note the following points in the .NET module metadata:

❑ ScopeName is the name of the .NET module, excluding the path.

❑ MVID is the module version ID, which is a Globally Unique ID (GUID) for the .NET module generated by the compiler. The compiler generates a different MVID every time we build the module.

Metadata about this Assembly

Near the end of the metadata listing, we find the following metadata about this assembly (we've abbreviated this information slightly, by removing metadata about custom attributes):

```
Assembly
-------------------------------------------------------
  Token: 0x20000001
  Name : simple_console
  Public Key  :
  Hash Algorithm : 0x00008004
  Major Version: 0x00000000
```

```
Minor Version: 0x00000000
Build Number: 0x00000000
Revision Number: 0x00000000
Locale: <null>
Flags : [SideBySideCompatible]   (00000000)
```

Here is a selective description of some of the assembly metadata:

❑ Token is a 4-byte metadata token. Each item of metadata is uniquely identified by a different token. The top byte of the token indicates what kind of metadata this is: for example, 0x20 denotes an assembly definition, 0x23 denotes an assembly reference, 0x02 denotes a type definition, and so on. For a full list of token types, open the C++ header file CorHdr.h (located in the FrameworkSDK\include sub-folder) and find the CorTokenType enumerated type.

❑ Name is the name of the assembly, excluding the path and extension.

❑ PublicKey indicates the public key that was used to sign the assembly. It's blank here because we haven't signed the assembly. We'll see how to sign an assembly later in the chapter, when we discuss how to install shared assemblies into the **Global Assembly Cache** (**GAC**) on the computer.

❑ Major Version, Minor Version, Build Number, and Revision Number identify the precise version of this assembly. This four-part version number differentiates this assembly from other versions of the assembly, and enables other .NET applications to specify precisely which version of the assembly they want to use.

Each piece of the four-part version number has a particular meaning to the CLR, so that it can decide which version of an assembly to load. Imagine an assembly A references a particular version number of another assembly B. The runtime uses the following rules to load an appropriate version of assembly B:

1. If there is a version of B with exactly the same version number as requested by A, the runtime will load this version of B.

2. If there is a version of B with a different Build Number, this indicates a compatible change to the assembly (such as a security fix). The runtime will load this version of B, in the absence of an exact match.

3. If there is a version of B with a different Revision Number, this indicates an incremental change to the assembly (such as a Service Pack). The runtime considers this assembly is probably compatible with the version requested by A, so the runtime will load this version of B in the absence of a better match.

4. If there is a version of B with a different Major Version or Minor Version, this indicates a major difference to previous versions of the assembly (such as major new product release). The runtime will not load this version of B.

Metadata about the Types Defined in this Assembly

When we define types (such as classes and structures) in an assembly, the assembly will contain metadata for each of these types. Our simple C# application defines a single type, which is a `class` called `SimpleConsole`. Therefore, the assembly's metadata contains a single type definition as follows:

```
TypeDef #1
----------------------------------------------------------------
    TypDefName: MetadataSimpleApp.SimpleConsole   (02000002)
    Flags    : [NotPublic] [AutoLayout] [Class] [AnsiClass] (00100000)
    Extends   : 01000001 [TypeRef] System.Object
    Method #1 [ENTRYPOINT]
    -----------------------------------------------------------
    MethodName: Main (06000001)
    Flags    : [Public] [Static] [HideBySig] [ReuseSlot] (00000096)
    RVA      : 0x00002050
    ImplFlags : [IL] [Managed]   (00000000)
    CallCnvntn: [DEFAULT]
    ReturnType: Void
    No arguments.
```

Note the following points in this metadata:

❑ `TypeDefName` is the name of the type. The name of this type is `MetadataSimpleApp.SimpleConsole`. The value in parentheses is the metadata token for this piece of metadata (remember, the value `0x02` in the top byte indicates this is a *type definition*).

❑ `Flags` provides more information about `MetadataSimpleApp.MyModule`. Here's a brief synopsis: `[NotPublic]` indicates `MyModule` is not a public type; `[AutoLayout]` indicates the layout of its members is handled automatically by the CLR; `[Class]` indicates this is a class; and `[AnsiClass]` indicates `LPTSTR` string types will be treated as ANSI strings (rather than Unicode strings).

❑ `Extends` indicates that our type inherits from `System.Object`.

❑ `Method #1` provides metadata about the first method in our type. This metadata indicates the name of the method (`Main`), its arguments (none), its return type (`void`), and other information such as the fact it's a `public` and `static` method. As we only defined one method, the only other method you'll find listed in the metadata is the compiler-generated constructor.

Metadata about Other Referenced Assemblies

Our assembly contains metadata about all the other assemblies referenced by our assembly. This information is clearly needed by the CLR, so that it can load these assemblies when needed. Our assembly references several assemblies, for example:

```
AssemblyRef #1
-----------------------------------------------------------
    Token: 0x23000001
    Public Key or Token: b7 7a 5c 56 19 34 e0 89
    Name: mscorlib
    Major Version: 0x00000001
    Minor Version: 0x00000000
    Build Number: 0x00000ce4
    Revision Number: 0x00000000
    Locale: <null>
    HashValue Blob:
    Flags: [none] (00000000)
```

Note the following points in the metadata for the referenced assembly:

❑   Public Key or Token indicates the public key that was used to sign the referenced assembly.

❑   Name indicates that the name of the referenced assembly is mscorlib.

❑   Major Version, Minor Version, Build Number, and Revision Number identify precisely which version of the assembly we want to reference. This ensures we always reference the correct version of the assembly, even if later versions of the assembly are subsequently installed on the computer.

❑   Locale facilitates localization of assemblies. It's possible to have several assemblies that contain copies of the same data in different languages (such as English and French). We can assign a different locale to each assembly. The Locale metadata in our assembly indicates which locale-specific assembly we want to reference.

Metadata about Types Used in Referenced Assemblies

As well as the details of the assemblies referenced, we also have details of the types in those assemblies that are used by our code. For example:

```
TypeRef #4 (01000004)
-----------------------------------------------------------
Token:         0x01000004
ResolutionScope:    0x23000001
TypeRefName:     System.Console
  MemberRef #1
  -----------------------------------------------------------
    Member: (0a000003) WriteLine:
    CallCnvntn: [DEFAULT]
    ReturnType: Void
    1 Arguments
      Argument #1:  String
```

This indicates that we not only reference the type System.Console, but that we also reference a particular overload of this type's WriteLine method. In a more comprehensive application, we could see from the metadata exactly which types and type members are used from other assemblies.

Creating Multi-File Assemblies

All the examples we have presented in this book so far have used single-file assemblies. A single-file assembly comprises a single PE file (or .NET module). The PE file is typically a .dll or .exe file, with a manifest and with metadata that describes the types in the assembly.

It is also possible to create an assembly that comprises multiple .NET modules (hence the name, 'assembly'). When we compile each .NET module, we get a separate PE file that contains MSIL code and metadata for that module. One of the .NET modules in the assembly must be identified as the 'main' module. This .NET module will also have a manifest that identifies all of the other .NET modules in the assembly. The main module will normally have an .exe or .dll extension and the remaining modules will have a .netmodule extension.

There are several reasons for implementing an assembly as a collection of separate .NET modules:

❑   We can write each module in a different .NET programming language. This might be useful for companies that use a variety of languages and/or people to implement different parts of the system.

❑   We can organize our types into separate modules, to optimize how our code is loaded into the Common Language Runtime. We can place related types into the same module, so that they are loaded together when the module is loaded into the runtime. Seldom-used types can be placed in a separate module; the runtime will only load this module when these types are required in the application. This way, we can minimize the footprint of our application and reduce load time too.

❑   We can include data-only modules that contain resources such as images, XML documents, music clips, and so on. The .NET Framework SDK includes a tool called the **Assembly Linker** (AL.exe) to link these non-MSIL modules into our assembly.

Example of a Multi-File Assembly

In this section, we'll see how to create an assembly containing three separate modules. The modules will be written in different .NET programming languages, and will then be linked together to create a single logical assembly. This is a typical reason for creating an assembly out of separate modules (rather than creating an assembly from just one module).

Here's a description of the three modules in this example:

❑   The first module will be called CSMod, and will be written in Visual C#. This module will have a class named DistanceConverter, to convert distances between miles and kilometers.

❑ The second module will be called VBMod, and will be written in Visual Basic .NET. This module will have a class named TempConverter, to convert temperatures between Celsius and Fahrenheit.

❑ The third module will be called MainMod, and will be written in Visual C#. We're going to make this the main module in the assembly, which means the file will contain a manifest that identifies all the other modules in the assembly.

This is how the modules will work together to form a multi-file assembly:

Figure 2

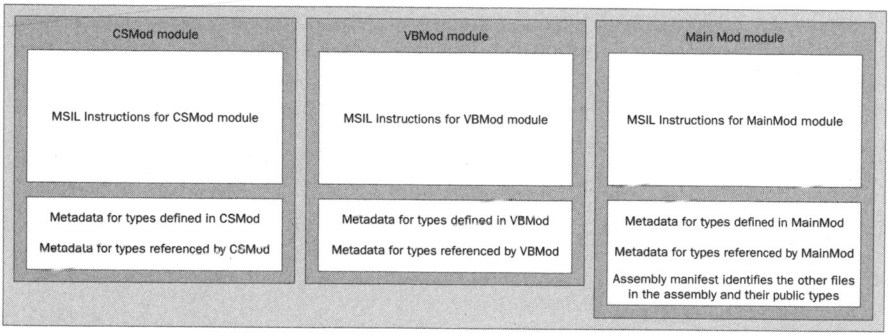

Each module in the assembly contains MSIL instructions and metadata; the metadata describes the types defined in and referenced by the module. The main module in the assembly is MainMod; this module will contain the manifest for the assembly. The manifest identifies all the other modules in the assembly (CSMod and VBMod), and the public types defined in these modules. We'll see what this metadata looks like as we work through the example.

This manifest information is required by the CLR, so that it can load the appropriate module when one of these types is used in the application.

Let's see how to implement what we've just described. There are three steps:

❑ Write the source code for CSMod.cs, and compile it into a .NET module.

❑ Write the source code for VBMod.vb, and compile it into another .NET module.

❑ Write the source code for MainMod.cs, and compile it into the main .NET module in the assembly. At this stage, we'll need to specify which other modules we want in the assembly (that is, CSMod and VBMod).

Creating the CSMod Module

Here is the C# source code for CSMod.cs. The source code for this module (and all the other modules we're going to see in this example) is located in the download folder MultiFileAssembly.

```
public class DistanceConverter
{
  public static double MileToKm(double miles)
  {
    return (miles * 1.6093);
  }

  public static double KmToMile(double km)
  {
    return (km / 1.6093);
  }
}
```

To compile this file into a module (as opposed to a standalone assembly), we must use the Visual C# .NET command-line compiler. We can't use Visual Studio .NET to create a .NET module; Visual Studio .NET always creates a standalone assembly for our project (the exception to this rule is for Managed Extensions for C++ projects, where we can set the /NOASSEMBLY option to create a module rather than an assembly).

Open a .NET Framework Command Prompt window and compile the code as follows:

```
C:\> csc /target:module CSMod.cs
```

The /target:module compiler switch tells the compiler to generate a module (in this case CSMod.netmodule) rather than an assembly. The module contains the compiled MSIL instructions for our code, and contains metadata to describe the types defined and referenced in our code. Later, we'll link this module to other modules to create a multi-file assembly.

The /target compiler switch can be abbreviated to /t.

Creating the VBMod Module

Here is the Visual Basic .NET source code for VBMod.vb:

```
Public Class TempConverter
  Public Shared Function CelsiusToFahr(ByVal C As Double) As Double
  Return (C * 9.0 / 5.0) + 32
  End Function

  Public Shared Function FahrToCelsius(ByVal F As Double) As Double
  Return (F - 32) * 5.0 / 9.0
  End Function
End Class
```

To compile this file into a separate module, run the Visual Basic .NET compiler as follows:

```
C:\> vbc /target:module VBMod.vb
```

This generates a .NET module named VBMod.netmodule. Note that at this stage, there is no linkage whatsoever between this module and the one we created earlier (CSMod.netmodule).

Creating the Main Module in the Assembly

Here is the source code for MainMod.cs. Notice that this source code uses the types defined in the other two modules:

```csharp
using System;

public class MyClass
{
  public static void Main()
  {
    Console.WriteLine("Select an option: ");
    Console.WriteLine("  1  C to F");
    Console.WriteLine("  2  F to C");
    Console.WriteLine("  3  Miles to Km");
    Console.WriteLine("  4  Km to Miles");
    Console.Write("=>");

    string input = Console.ReadLine();
    int opt = Int32.Parse(input);

    Console.Write("Value to convert: ");
    input = Console.ReadLine();
    double value = Double.Parse(input);

    double result;
    switch (opt)
    {
      case 1:
        result= TempConverter.CelsiusToFahr(value);
        break;
      case 2:
        result= TempConverter.FahrToCelsius(value);
        break;
      case 3:
        result= DistanceConverter.MileToKm(value);
        break;
      case 4:
        result= DistanceConverter.KmToMile(value);
        break;
      default:
        Console.WriteLine("Invalid option");
        return;
    }

    Console.WriteLine("Result: {0}", Math.Round(result, 2));
  }
}
```

This is how we compile this source file:

```
C:> csc /addmodule:CSMod.netmodule /addmodule:VBMod.netmodule
       MainMod.cs
```

This command compiles `MainMod.cs` into `MainMod.exe`. `MainMod.exe` is the main module in the assembly. The `/addmodule` compiler switch adds entries to the assembly's manifest, to indicate `CSMod.netmodule` and `VBMod.netmodule` are part of this assembly.

> *If we forget the `/addmodule` switch, we'll get a compiler error every time we try to access a type defined in one of the other (unspecified) modules. This is because the compiler doesn't know it's meant to look in these other modules to resolve the type definitions.*

Open `MainMod.exe` in the MSIL Disassembler, using the `/adv` (or `/advanced`) option, and view the manifest information in the assembly by double-clicking on the manifest icon. Here are the important parts of the manifest information:

```
.module extern VBMod.netmodule
.module extern CSMod.netmodule
...
.assembly MainMod
{
  .hash algorithm 0x00008004
  .ver 0:0:0:0
}
.file CSMod.netmodule
   .hash = (6C CB 79 30 7E D2 C0 E8 F2 57 4A 3F 0F 84 EC FC
       75 7D A9 B0 )
.file VBMod.netmodule
   .hash = (B3 F0 2D E0 C0 34 AC 48 50 76 CA 72 FC 9C 59 85
       16 C1 2A D7 )
.class extern public DistanceConverter
{
  .file CSMod.netmodule
  .class 0x02000002
}
.class extern public TempConverter
{
  .file VBMod.netmodule
  .class 0x02000002
}
.module MainMod.exe
// MVID: {43979DDE-E7E8-41C0-BD07-3718B82ECC9A}
.imagebase 0x00400000
.subsystem 0x00000003
.file alignment 512
.corflags 0x00000001
// Image base: 0x03090000
```

Notice the following points in this manifest:

❑ The manifest references the other modules in the assembly (`VBMod.netmodule` and `CSMod.netmodule`).

❑ The manifest also lists the public types defined in these modules. This information tells the Common Language Runtime which module to load when a user of the assembly uses one of our classes.

When we create a multi-file assembly, we must remember to deploy all the modules in the assembly. In the example we've just considered, we must deploy `VBMod.netmodule` and `CSMod.netmodule` along with the main module in the assembly, `MainMod.exe`.

Deploying Applications as Assemblies

In the previous section, we discussed how to create an assembly that consists of one or more modules. If we create a multi-file assembly, the main module in the assembly contains manifest information that identifies all the other modules in the assembly.

In this section, we're going to broaden our outlook and consider the physical organization of an entire application. Our discussions will lead us to consider three possible deployment scenarios for our application:

❑ For simple applications, we can deploy our application as a single assembly.

❑ For larger applications, we can split some of the functionality into separate assemblies. We can group related functionality into the same assembly, so that the CLR can load all the information it needs from a single assembly. We can relegate seldom-used functionality to a separate assembly, so that it is only loaded when required. For example, if you examine the classes in the .NET framework itself, you will see that Microsoft has included parts of namespaces in core assemblies, while other parts are relegated to secondary assemblies. We can also put resources (such as bitmaps) into another assembly, to make internationalization easier to achieve.

It is generally good practice to emphasize the logical organization of our application, by organizing our assemblies along namespace boundaries and implementing each namespace as a separate assembly.

Typically, we deploy all the assemblies into the same folder on the target computer. It's also possible to provide a configuration file that specifies a different subfolder destination for our private assemblies.

❑ If we want to deploy several applications that share a lot of common code, we can create common assemblies that are shared by all the applications. We can install the common assemblies into the Global Assembly Cache (**GAC**) on the target computer, so that the assemblies are accessible by multiple applications. We'll discuss the GAC later in this section.

Deploying Single-Assembly Applications

This is the simplest of our three scenarios, where we want to deploy an application that comprises a single assembly. To deploy such an application, all we need to do is copy the assembly onto the target computer. This is commonly known as **XCopy deployment** after the DOS command XCOPY, which can be used to simply copy a complete folder structure from the distribution media onto the target computer. Of course, you'll probably use drag-and-drop or copy-and-paste to deploy the application in Explorer, but the principle is the same. There is no need to register anything in the system registry, which means there is no danger of breaking how existing applications work on the computer. This eliminates 'DLL hell', which can happen when traditional Windows applications are installed on a computer. Such applications nearly always update the registry in some way, which may prevent existing applications from functioning correctly.

Uninstalling simple .NET Framework applications is also straightforward. All we need to do is delete the files that were copied during installation, such as the .exe and .dll files for the assembly, plus any configuration files we installed (we'll discuss configuration files later in this chapter). Compare this situation with the way we uninstall traditional Windows applications; we need to ensure all the registry entries are cleaned up, without breaking how all the other applications work. Uninstalling traditional Windows applications always gives us that nasty suspicion that part of the application lingers on in the dark recesses of the hard disk.

There are still some situations where we might want to package our .NET applications ready for distribution. For example, if we want our application to be downloaded over the Internet, we will typically place our application into a .CAB file so that it can be downloaded more easily. Alternatively, we can package our application into an .MSI file so that Microsoft Windows Installer can install it. This will enable users to install the application using Microsoft Systems Management Server (SMS), for example.

Deploying Applications using Private Assemblies

In this section, we'll describe how to deploy an application that contains several assemblies. For now, we'll assume these assemblies are only needed by this application, so that all the assemblies can be installed in the same folder (or sub-folder) as the main application assembly. Because these assemblies are just used by our application, they are called **private assemblies**.

> *Later, we'll describe how to create **shared assemblies**, which can be deployed in the central Global Assembly Cache so that they can be used by all applications.*

Deploying Private Assemblies in the Same Folder

Imagine we have a large application that provides several distinct services. It makes sense to organize this application into separate assemblies, so that the Common Language Runtime can load just the assemblies that are actually required when the user runs the application. Typically, one of the assemblies will be an .exe file, and the others will be .dll files.

Example of Deploying Assemblies in the Same Folder

Let's consider a simple example, where we have a single .exe assembly file and a single .dll assembly file. The DLL file contains useful functions that are used by the .exe file. We'll perform the following tasks:

- ❑ Write the source code for the DLL.
- ❑ Compile this source code into a .dll assembly file.
- ❑ Write the source code for the executable. Use the functionality offered by the DLL, as required.
- ❑ Compile this source code into an .exe assembly file. Tell the compiler which other assemblies we reference, so that it can resolve references to these assemblies.
- ❑ Deploy the .exe file and .dll file. The easiest deployment scenario is to install the .exe file and .dll file in the same folder.

Here's the source code for our DLL file. The source file is named my_useful_library.cs:

```
using System;

public class MyUsefulClass
{
  public static void MyUsefulMethod()
  {
    Console.WriteLine("Hello world");
  }
}
```

To compile this source file into a .DLL assembly file, run the C# .NET compiler as follows from the command prompt:

```
C:\> csc /target:library my_useful_library.cs
```

The /target:library compiler switch instructs the compiler to create a library (.dll) file.

Now let's look at the source code for our executable file. The source code file is named hello_world.cs.

```
public class HelloWorld
{
  public static void Main()
  {
    MyUsefulClass.MyUsefulMethod();
  }
}
```

To compile this source file into an .exe assembly file, run the C# compiler as follows at the .NET Framework Command Prompt window:

```
C:\> csc /reference:my_useful_library.dll hello_world.cs
```

The manifest in the executable file will contain a reference to the my_useful_library.dll assembly file, because of the /reference compiler switch.

The /reference compiler switch can be abbreviated to /r.

When we deploy our application onto the target computer, the easiest way is to install hello_world.exe and my_useful_library.dll into the same folder. We say that my_useful_library.dll is a **private assembly** for our application.

When the user runs hello_world.exe, the CLR searches for an assembly in one of the following locations:

❑ my_useful_library.dll

❑ my_useful_library\my_useful_library.dll

If the CLR can't find an assembly with a .dll file extension, it repeats the search looking for an assembly with a .exe file extension:

❑ my_useful_library.exe

❑ my_useful_library\my_useful_library.exe

If the assembly can't be located, the CLR throws a
`System.IO.FileNotFoundException`.

Creating and Referencing Culture-Specific Assemblies

The .NET Framework allows us to create several different versions of an assembly, to cater for different locales. For example, we can create an English version of the assembly, a Spanish version, a French version, and so on. Microsoft uses the term **culture** to denote the locale of the assembly. Later in this chapter, we'll see how to use attributes to set the culture when we create an assembly.

Applications can specify to which culture of our assembly they want to bind. When the CLR probes for the specified assembly, it looks in a subdirectory with the same name as the culture. For example, if we request the `my_useful_library` assembly and specify the en culture (English), the runtime will probe the following locations for the assembly:

❑ `en\my_useful_library.dll`

❑ `en\my_useful_library\my_useful_library.dll`

❑ `en\my_useful_library.exe`

❑ `en\my_useful_library\my_useful_library.exe`

Deploying Private Assemblies in a Different Sub-Folder

Since applications can grow to be extremely large, placing all the assemblies in the same folder might not be the best option; for example, if we have dozens of different assemblies in our application, we might prefer to organize these assemblies into a directory structure that reflects the hierarchical namespace structure in our application.

If we want to deploy a private assembly in a differently named sub-folder, we can create an **application configuration file** to tell the CLR where to look. The configuration file is located in the same folder as the requesting assembly, and has a `.config` filename suffix. For example, the configuration file for `MyApp.exe` would be named `MyApp.exe.config`.

The application configuration file is an XML file that tells the CLR where it can find our private assemblies. We write the configuration file as part of our development activities, and deploy the configuration file along with our application.

> *The .NET Framework makes extensive use of XML as the standard way of expressing configuration information, and for a host of other purposes. For example, XML is used to represent data while an application is disconnected from a database (see the* `System.Data.DataSet` *class); to represent tags in ASP.NET; to pass information to and from a Web Service (see* `System.WebServices.WebService`*), and so on.*

Let's see an example of how to create and use an application configuration file. Imagine we have an application that has two assemblies, located in the following paths:

```
C:\MyAppFolder\MyApp.exe
C:\MyAppFolder\MySubFolder\MyUsefulLibrary.dll
```

Here is an example of a configuration file named `MyApp.exe.config`. This is the configuration file for our application `MyModule.exe`:

```
<configuration>
  <runtime>
  <assemblyBinding
      xmlns="urn:schemas-microsoft-com:asm.v1">
    <probing privatePath="MySubFolder"/>
  </assemblyBinding>
  </runtime>
</configuration>
```

Note the following points about this configuration file:

- ❑ The top-level element must be named `configuration`. The `configuration` element can have a variety of child elements, to configure different aspects of run-time execution.

- ❑ The `runtime` child element specifies how the Common Language Runtime handles assembly loading and garbage collection.

- ❑ The `assemblyBinding` child element contains information about assembly locations and versions. This element must be qualified with the XML namespace `"urn:schemas-microsoft-com:asm.v1"` for the CLR to identify it properly.

- ❑ The `assemblyBinding` element has a child element named `probing`.

- ❑ The `probing` element has a `privatePath` attribute, which specifies the name of the sub-folder where the CLR should search for private assemblies. To enable users to specify multiple folders (for different assemblies) within the same configuration file, multiple directories can be specified, separated by a semicolon.

- ❑ Note that you must specify sub-folders here; you cannot specify an absolute folder, or a relative folder such as `..\SomeOtherFolder`. This rule minimizes the chance of conflicts with assemblies installed elsewhere on the computer.

> Remember that XML is case-sensitive, so you must type in
> the element names and attribute names exactly as shown in
> the example above. There are various other pieces of
> information we can specify in a configuration file, including
> network settings, cryptography settings, ASP.NET settings,
> and so on. For more information, see the `<configuration>`
> element in Visual Studio .NET Help.

When the user runs `MyApp.exe`, the CLR now searches for the `MyUsefulLibrary`
assembly in the following locations (in the order shown):

- `MyUsefulLibrary.dll`
- `MyUsefulLibrary\MyUsefulLibrary.dll`
- `MySubFolder\MyUsefulLibrary.dll`
- `MySubFolder\MyUsefulLibrary\MyUsefulLibrary.dll`

If the CLR can't find an assembly with a `.dll` file extension, it repeats the search
looking for an assembly with an `.exe` file extension:

- `MyUsefulLibrary.exe`
- `MyUsefulLibrary\MyUsefulLibrary.exe`
- `MySubFolder\MyUsefulLibrary.exe`
- `MySubFolder\MyUsefulLibrary\MyUsefulLibrary.exe`

One final item to point out is that the application configuration file is just plain XML
text, and is deployed onto the user's computer along with the application. If the user
wants to organize the private assemblies into a different sub-folder hierarchy from that
first envisaged, the user can edit the configuration file at any time to indicate the new
location of the private assemblies. There's no need for the user to change any registry
settings, so there's less chance than with COM of the user getting it wrong.

Deploying Shared Assemblies

Our previous discussions have shown how to create a private assembly, and deploy it
in an application's sub-folder so that the application can access it. It's also possible to
create shared assemblies, and add them to the **Global Assembly Cache (GAC)**. The
GAC holds information about all the shared assemblies that are accessible by all
applications running on our computer. For example, the assemblies essential for the
.NET Framework class library reside in the GAC.

This may sound a little like COM. We can create COM components that contain reusable functionality, and install these components to make use of this functionality. However, COM components are registered in the system registry, and this can cause conflicts with other versions of the component in the registry. .NET assemblies are not registered in the system registry, so the possibility of registry conflicts doesn't arise.

You may still wonder if GAC conflicts occur if we install a later version of our .NET shared assembly; they don't. When we add an assembly to the GAC, we must give our assembly a **strong name**. A strongly named assembly has a name, version, public key, and, optionally, culture information; these pieces of information uniquely identify the assembly, and prevent conflicts with any other assemblies.

It is worth noting, however, that Microsoft advises against making your application dependent on installing assemblies into the GAC, and recommends instead that you use private assemblies. Disk space is not regarded as a precious commodity on most platforms, and applications in separate application domains will load code separately even if it is located in the GAC, so you won't end up saving memory. Generally, keeping all of your application's files together, and avoiding dependence on GAC registration simplifies everybody's life.

> One situation in which use of the GAC is unavoidable is when you are developing .NET classes that use COM+ services – also known as Serviced Components; the .NET Framework provides a means of declaring COM+ settings using attributes, which allows us to use functionalities like distributed transaction management and object pooling. Assemblies that use serviced components in COM+ Server applications should be placed in the GAC. This is because the assembly needs to be located by two host processes; the client process (to bind to the assembly's types), and the COM+ surrogate process – dllhost.exe (to load and execute the assembly). It is unlikely that both of these processes will reside in the same folder as the assembly, hence the need to install it in the GAC.

Applications can specify precisely the assembly they want to use by providing a specific assembly name, version, public key, and optionally culture information. There is no way the application can accidentally pick up another assembly that is similar, because that other assembly would have a different name, version, public key, or culture information. This is a major step forward in the world of application deployment and configuration. It signals a possible end to DLL hell, which will be a merciful release for us all.

Note that we can only insert strongly named assemblies into the GAC; assemblies that are not strongly named (that is, assemblies that do not have a public key) cannot be added to it, because they do not contain enough information to prevent possible conflicts.

Culture information enables us to create variations of our assembly for different locales. For example, we can create one assembly that contains English text, another assembly that contains French text, and a third assembly that contains Spanish text. Each assembly can have the same name, version, and public key, but a different culture flag.

Let's summarize what we have covered so far. If we want to create a shared assembly that can be accessed by several applications, then we must perform the following steps:

❑   Create the shared assembly as a strongly-named assembly

❑   Create an application that uses the shared assembly

❑   Install the shared assembly into the Global Assembly Cache

Creating a Shared Assembly as a Strongly Named Assembly

To create a strongly named assembly, we must first generate a **public-private key pair**. Public-private keys are used extensively in the IT industry for the following security purposes:

❑   A company uses its private key to sign its applications, and then distributes these applications to users.

❑   Users need to verify the application comes from this trusted company. They can do this by using the company's public key to check the digital signature on the application. The only way the signature will be recognized is if it was created with the trusted company's private key (of course, this mechanism relies on the fact the company's private key really is private).

Public-private key pairs enable us to create strong names for our assemblies. The compiler uses the private key during compilation, and writes the corresponding public key into the assembly manifest. For more information about the theory of public-private key pairs, see *Keys, cryptography* in Visual Studio .NET Help.

Unfortunately we can't use Visual Studio .NET to create a public-private key, we need to use the **Strong Name tool** in the .NET Framework SDK. Open a .NET Framework command prompt window, and type the following command:

```
C:\> sn /k C:\classdesign\chapter08\MyKey.snk
```

This creates a public-private key pair file named `MyKey.snk` in the folder `C:\MyKeyFolder`. We can use this public-private key pair file to create a strongly named assembly. We've provided a simple example in the download folder called `signed_assembly.cs`, which looks like this:

```
using System;

namespace MyGlobalAssembly
{
  public class SignedMethod
  {
    public static void MyMethod()
    {
      Console.WriteLine("Hi");
    }
  }
}
```

The file is part of a project, MyGlobalAssembly, which also contains a source file named AssemblyInfo.cs. This file defines a set of attributes that will be used by the compiler to generate additional metadata for our assembly, such as its version number and public key:

```
using System.Reflection;
using System.Runtime.CompilerServices;

// General Information about an assembly is controlled through the
// following set of attributes. Change these attribute values to
// modify the information associated with an assembly.
//
[assembly: AssemblyTitle("")]
[assembly: AssemblyDescription("")]
[assembly: AssemblyCompany("")]
[assembly: AssemblyProduct("")]
[assembly: AssemblyCopyright("")]
[assembly: AssemblyTrademark("")]

// Version information consists of the following four values:
//
//      Major Version
//      Minor Version
//      Build Number
//      Revision
//
// You can specify all the values or you can default the Revision
// and Build Numbers by using the '*'

[assembly: AssemblyVersion("1.0.0.0")]
[assembly: AssemblyDelaySign(false)]
[assembly: AssemblyKeyFile("C:/classdesign/chapter08/MyKey.snk")]
[assembly: AssemblyKeyName("")]
```

In this example, [assembly: AssemblyVersion(...)] tells the compiler the version number to write to the assembly. [assembly: AssemblyKeyFile(...)] tells the compiler which public-private key file to use. This enables the compiler to generate a strongly named assembly.

Build the project from the Visual Studio .NET menu. This will create an assembly as a DLL and you can view this in the MSIL Disassembler. In the MSIL Disassembler window, double-click the MANIFEST node to view the assembly's manifest.

Notice that the manifest now includes a `publickey` property, which means that this is a strongly named assembly. In addition, notice that the `ver` property contains the precise version information we specified in `AssemblyInfo.cs`:

```
.assembly MyGlobalAssembly
{
  ...
  .publickey = (00 24 00 00 04 ... AC D4 D2 40 C1 )
  .hash algorithm 0x00008004
  .ver 1:0:0:0
}
```

The `publickey` property is a very long number. For efficiency, the Strong Name tool also generates an abbreviated version of the public key called the **public key token**. To see the public key token, run the Strong Name tool as follows:

```
C:\> sn /t C:\classdesign\chapter08\MyKey.snk
```

The public key token is displayed as follows (clearly, the number for the public key token will be different if you try this yourself):

```
Microsoft (R) .NET Framework Strong Name Utility Version 1.0.3705.0
Copyright (C) Microsoft Corporation 1998-2001. All rights reserved.

Public key token is 070bcd7fade41693
```

Creating an Application that Uses the Shared Assembly

We've provided a simple application to use the strongly named assembly. We'll describe how to view and build this application using Visual Studio .NET first, then we'll see how to do the same from the command line. The sample Visual Studio project is called `MyApp.csproj` and is in the `MyApp` folder with the rest of the code for this chapter.

The application has a simple source file named `shared_assembly.cs`, which looks like this:

```
using MyGlobalAssembly;

namespace MyApp
{
  class SharedAssembly
  {
```

```
      static void Main()
      {
        SignedMethod.MyMethod();
      }
   }
}
```

Notice that `Main` calls `SignedMethod.MyMethod`. The class `SignedMethod` is defined in the `MyGlobalAssembly` namespace, so we've included a `using` statement to import this namespace.

However, that's only half of the story. The `MyGlobalAssembly` namespace is defined in a different assembly, so we also have to tell the compiler which assembly to use. In Visual Studio .NET, expand the References entry in Solution Explorer. You will see that the References list includes a reference to `MyGlobalAssembly`. Right-click this assembly name, and select Properties from the Shortcut menu. The Properties dialog box appears as follows:

This dialog box indicates the following information about the referenced assembly:

❑ The name of the assembly is `MyGlobalAssembly`.

❑ The `Copy Local` flag is `False`. This tells the compiler not to copy the specified assembly into our application's output folder. This will force the CLR to look in the GAC for the assembly when we run the application.

> **When you add an assembly reference, the `Copy Local` flag is set to `True` by default. This will cause the compiler to copy the specified assembly to the output directory for our application. When you run the application, the CLR will locate and load this copy of the assembly, rather than the one in the GAC. To avoid this behavior, remember to set `Copy Local` to `False` whenever you add an assembly reference to a project if you want to use the GAC version.**

❑ The `Path` property tells the compiler where the assembly is currently located, at development time. We set this location when we added this assembly reference to the project.

❑ The `Strong Name` property is `True`, because the assembly was created as a strongly named assembly

❑ The `Version` property indicates the version number of this strongly named assembly

If we build this application in Visual Studio .NET, the assembly reference we've just examined provides all the information required by the compiler to locate the other assembly. Alternatively, we can compile the application from the command line; in this case, we must specify an `/r` compiler switch at build time, to tell the compiler about the assembly:

```
C:\> csc /r:C:\classdesign\chapter08\MyGlobalAssembly.dll
     shared_assembly.cs
```

Everything seems to be going well, until we try to run the application. The CLR attempts to load the referenced assembly. The runtime looks in our application's folder, on the (incorrect) assumption that the assembly is a private assembly. However, the assembly isn't there, because it's a shared assembly. Therefore, the CLR throws a `System.IO.FileNotFoundException`, and terminates the application.

To resolve this problem, we must install the shared assembly into the Global Assembly Cache (GAC).

Installing Shared Assemblies into the Global Assembly Cache

The .NET Framework provides a runtime tool named `gacutil.exe`, which enables us to install to and remove assemblies from the GAC. Open a .NET Framework command-prompt window, and move to the folder where the .DLL file resides. Type the following command:

```
C:\> gacutil -i MyGlobalAssembly.dll
```

> **As a user, you must have Administrator privileges to install assemblies into the GAC.**

The GAC is implemented as a folder named `Assembly` in the Windows folder (for example, `C:\Windows\Assembly`), and when we install an assembly into the GAC, `gacutil` copies the assembly into a special sub-folder beneath the `Assembly` folder. The `gacutil` tool devises a special name for the assembly's sub-folder, based on the name, version, public key, and culture of the assembly. This eliminates any possibility of installing an assembly on top of an existing assembly that happens to have the same filename.

To check that our assembly has been added correctly to the GAC, we can use the **.NET Framework Configuration** tool. Open Control Panel, double-click Administrative Tools, and then double-click Microsoft .NET Framework Configuration. Click the Manage the Assembly Cache hyperlink. This takes us to the Assembly Cache window

Click the View List of Assemblies in the Assembly Cache hyperlink. This displays information about all the assemblies in the GAC. Scroll down the list to find the shared assembly we just inserted.

Once you've installed the shared assembly in the GAC, you can run the application. When the application refers to types and members defined in the shared assembly, the CLR inspects the application's metadata to discover which assembly it needs to load. The runtime looks for this assembly in the GAC, finds it, and loads it into memory.

Generating Documentation for an Assembly

Documentation is important, there's little doubt about that. Once all the developers who have worked on a project have moved on to something new, documentation is all you'll have left to help you make sense of the design decisions made at the code level, and how these fit with the business model you will have made during the early stages of the project.

Using C# and Visual Studio .NET, there are two features we can use to make this easier. The first allows us to insert some descriptive documentation into each compiled assembly that gets deployed with the final application. Here is a place we can put copyright notices, version information, trademarks, descriptions etc. that will all help to identify exactly what the assembly contains.

The second feature we can use concerns documentation of the code itself. This is much more valuable to other developers, especially if we have produced an assembly designed for reuse – for example, a class library. We'll look at these two features in turn.

Using Assembly-level Attributes

In the previous section, we described how to create a shared assembly and install it into the Global Assembly Cache. The GAC insists that the assembly is strongly named, which means the assembly must contain public key information. As we saw earlier, the way to provide this public key is through the [assembly: AssemblyKeyFile] attribute. For example:

```
[assembly: AssemblyKeyFile("C:/classdesign/chapter08/MyKey.snk")]
```

As well as specifying the name of the public-private key pair file, we can also specify additional information, such as the following:

- ❑   Free-format title of the assembly
- ❑   Description of the assembly
- ❑   Company name
- ❑   Product name information
- ❑   Copyright information
- ❑   A trademark

The following example shows how to define this information. The source code for this example is located in the Documentation download folder. The documentation information is defined in the file AssemblyInfo.cs:

```
using System.Reflection;
using System.Runtime.CompilerServices;

//
// General Information about an assembly is controlled through the
// following set of attributes. Change these attribute values to
// modify the information associated with an assembly.
//
[assembly: AssemblyTitle("My Assembly")]
[assembly: AssemblyDescription("My cool assembly")]
[assembly: AssemblyCompany("My Company Inc.")]
```

```
[assembly: AssemblyProduct("My Product")]
[assembly: AssemblyCopyright("(c) My Company, 2002")]
[assembly: AssemblyTrademark("TM My Company")]

//
// Version information for an assembly consists of four values:
//
//      Major Version
//      Minor Version
//      Build Number
//      Revision
//
// You can specify all the values or you can default the Revision
// and Build Numbers by using the '*' notation

[assembly: AssemblyVersion("1.0.*")]
```

We can build this application using the command-line compiler from the Documentation folder in the code downloads for this book. Enter the following command:

```
C:\Documentation>csc /out:Documentation.exe *.cs
```

We can view the properties for the compiled assembly in Windows Explorer: select the assembly file in Windows Explorer, and select Properties from the Shortcut menu. For example, in Windows 2000, the Properties window shows the following information:

When we click on the Version tab, we can see detailed information about the assembly. For example, the Comments field appears as follows:

XML Documentation

The Visual Studio .NET C# compiler provides a unique command-line switch, /doc, which produces an additional output file when it compiles your code. The output file is in XML format and contains selected comments collected from your source code. For it to do this, the comments must be written in a particular format. In C#, this is done using three consecutive "/" characters, together with an XML tag name. For example, we'll add a few such comments to the types we defined in the file books.cs earlier:

```
using System.Collections;

namespace Books
{
    /// <summary>
    /// Inventory is a singleton class. It maintains a list of
    /// Books, indexed by ISBN.
    /// </summary>
    /// <remarks>
    /// Use the static property Instance to obtain a reference to
    /// the singleton. Then use the factory method CreateBook
    /// to create and add individual Books.
    /// </remarks>
    public class Inventory
    {
        /// <summary>
        /// Private member field containing a reference to the
        /// singleton instance.
        /// </summary>
        private static Inventory mInstance;

        /// <summary>
        /// Hashtable containing a collection of Book objects.
        /// </summary>
        private Hashtable mLibraryBooks;

    // and so on...

}
```

Note the following in the above code:

- ❏ The /// comments are added immediately before the type or member to which they refer.

- ❏ If we type /// in Visual Studio .NET, the <summary></summary> tags are automatically added for us.

To see the XML documentation file generated by these comments, we can either compile the code using the C# command-line compiler with the /doc switch, or we can configure Visual Studio .NET to do this for us. The command-line compiler can be invoked like this:

```
C:\> csc /t:library /doc:documentation.xml books.cs
```

As books.cs contains just type definitions, we have compiled it as a library using the /t switch. The /doc switch requires a filename to be used for writing the generated XML. In the example above, we have specified the file documentation.xml.

Alternatively, from Visual Studio .NET, right-click on the project in the Solution Explorer and select Properties from the menu. Then select Configuration Properties and enter documentation.xml against the XML Documentation File option.

In either case, when the project is compiled, the following XML is generated in the file documentation.xml:

```xml
<?xml version="1.0"?>
<doc>
  <assembly>
    <name>DocExample</name>
  </assembly>
  <members>
    <member name="T:Books.Inventory">
      <summary>
      Inventory is a singleton class. It maintains a list of
      Books, indexed by ISBN.
      </summary>
      <remarks>
      Use the static property Instance to obtain a reference to
      the singleton. Then use the factory method CreateBook
      to create and add individual Books.
      </remarks>
    </member>
    <member name="F:Books.Inventory.mInstance">
      <summary>
      Private member field containing a reference to the
      singleton instance.
      </summary>
    </member>
```

```
    <member name="F:Books.Inventory.mLibraryBooks">
      <summary>
      Hashtable containing a collection of Book objects.
      </summary>
    </member>
    <!-- etc. -->
  </members>
</doc>
```

You can see that the `<summary>` and `<remarks>` tags we typed have been extracted and placed with the C# type to which they refer.

The documentation for Visual Studio .NET defines a number of XML tags that are understood by the IDE and assisted by IntelliSense prompting. Also, it's useful to know that the comments in the `<summary>` elements are actually used by IntelliSense to describe fields, properties, and methods from your own classes during development.

You are not limited to the tags documented by Visual Studio .NET, you can actually use any valid XML tags in the /// comments and these will be extracted correctly by the compiler. This allows you to produce any format of XML you like, which can be subsequently processed into readable documentation using a suitable XSLT stylesheet.

In fact, Visual Studio .NET can do this too, although, at the time of writing, only the `<summary>` and `<remarks>` tags are processed correctly by the IDE to generate HTML format documentation using the option Build Comment Web Pages from the Tools menu. Using this option with our commented source code, we can produce HTML documentation that looks similar to this:

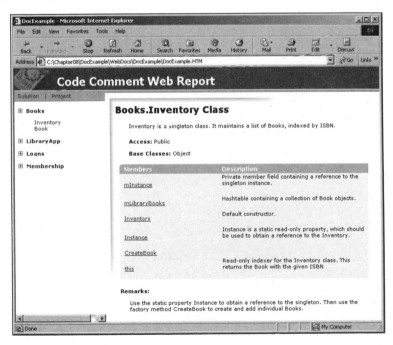

This is a great step forward from producing documentation manually and has the advantage that the feature is an integral part of the IDE.

It is a little frustrating that the current version of Visual Studio .NET does not support all of the XML tags documented. However, there are third-party tools that can process the generated XML and produce much more complete documentation. One such tool is called **NDoc**, which allows you to generate documentation based on the above mentioned XML. NDoc can be downloaded from http://ndoc.sourceforge.net. This software deserves a quick look for the following reasons:

❑ It's free

❑ As an open source product, it can be tailored for your own use

❑ It's written entirely in C# and documented using XML tags

❑ Documentation can be generated in compiled HTML format (CHM) and is visually styled like MSDN documentation.

One added benefit is that NDoc uses reflection to traverse the class hierarchy of the types defined in your assemblies and can produce documentation for inherited members too. The results can be quite satisfying. For example, we can load NDoc and select the Visual Studio .NET project – DocExample – used above. NDoc recognizes the assemblies produced by the solution and gives us some options to change the format of the generated documentation:

A simple mouse click then generates a documentation file for us in compiled HTML format. NDoc traverses the class hierarchy for all of the types defined in the assemblies we've specified, and builds the documentation in a similar format to that used for the .NET Framework documentation in MSDN:

346

Summary

In this final chapter, we've seen how to control the logical and physical organization of code in a Visual C# .NET application. In summary, we have covered:

❑ How to use namespaces to partition the application into logical groups of related types, and how these can relate to packages in a UML object model

❑ How to use assemblies and modules to break your applications into workable, reusable, and uniquely named sections, that could be written in multiple .NET languages

❑ How to compile and deploy your application as separate assemblies, including the use of DLLs, EXEs, and modules

❑ How to use the Global Assembly Cache to create a shared assembly that can easily be located by the CLR, and how the GAC should remove the DLL hell that happened with the Windows Registry

❑ How to build documentation into a compiled assembly

❑ How to use XML tags to produce and maintain professional-looking documentation with relatively little effort

C#

Class Design

Handbook

Appendix A

Support, Errata, and Code Download

We always value hearing from our readers, and we want to know what you think about this book and series: what you liked, what you didn't like, and what you think we can do better next time. You can send us your comments by e-mailing us at support@apress.com. Please be sure to mention the book title in your message.

How to Download the Sample Code for the Book

When you log on to the Apress site, http://www.apress.com/, simply go to the Downloads section of the site and find this book's page.

The files that are available for download from our site have been archived using WinZip. When you have saved the attachments to a folder on your hard-drive, you will need to extract the files using WinZip, or a compatible tool. Inside the Zip file will be a folder structure and an HTML file that explains the structure and gives you further information, including links to e-mail support, and suggested further reading.

Errata

We've made every effort to ensure that there are no errors in the text or in the code. However, no one is perfect and mistakes can occur. If you find an error in this book, like a spelling mistake or a faulty piece of code, we would be very grateful for feedback. By sending in errata, you may save another reader hours of frustration, and of course, you will be helping us to provide even higher quality information. Go to this book's page on apress.com to see any existing errata or submit your own.

forums.apress.com

For author and peer discussion, join the Apress discussion groups. If you post a query to our forums, you can be confident that many Apress authors, editors and industry experts are examining it. At forums.apress.com, you will find a number of different lists that will help you, not only while you read this book, but also as you develop your own applications.

To sign up for the Apress forums, go to `forums.apress.com` and select the New User link.

C#

Class Design

Handbook

Index

Index

A Guide to the Index

The index is arranged hierarchically, in alphabetical order, with symbols preceding the letter A. Most second-level entries and many third-level entries also occur as first-level entries. This is to ensure that users will find the information they require however they choose to search for it.